The First and Second
Sikh Wars

An Official British Army History

Reginald George Burton

Introduction and further reading by

Jon Coulston

WESTHOLME
Yardley

Originally published in 1911 by the Government Central Branch Press, India.

In order to retain authenticity, this text reproduces the original edition. Imperfections in type, print quality, line spacing, and text box alignment are as they were in the original. Where possible, smeared type, dirt specks, and other blemishes have been cleaned.

Westholme Publishing, LLC
904 Edgewood Road
Yardley, Pennsylvania 19067
Visit our Web site at www.westholmepublishing.com

ISBN: 978-1-59416-057-8 (paperback)
ISBN: 978-1-59416-565-8 (eBook)

Produced in the United States of America.

The First and Second
SIKH WARS

TABLE OF CONTENTS.

CHAPTER V.

THE PUNJAB AFTER THE WAR.

CHAPTER VI.

HERBERT EDWARDES' ADVANCE TO MULTAN.

CHAPTER VII.

THE FIRST SIEGE OF MULTAN.

CHAPTER VIII.

THE SIKH RISING.

CHAPTER IX.

THE SECOND SIKH WAR. THE PASSAGE OF THE CHENAB.

CHAPTER X.

CHILIANWALA.

CHAPTER XI.

THE SECOND SIEGE OF MULTAN.

CHAPTER XII.

OPERATIONS IN THE JULLUNDUR DOAB.

CHAPTER XIII.

GUJERAT.—THE END OF THE WAR.

MAPS AND PLANS.

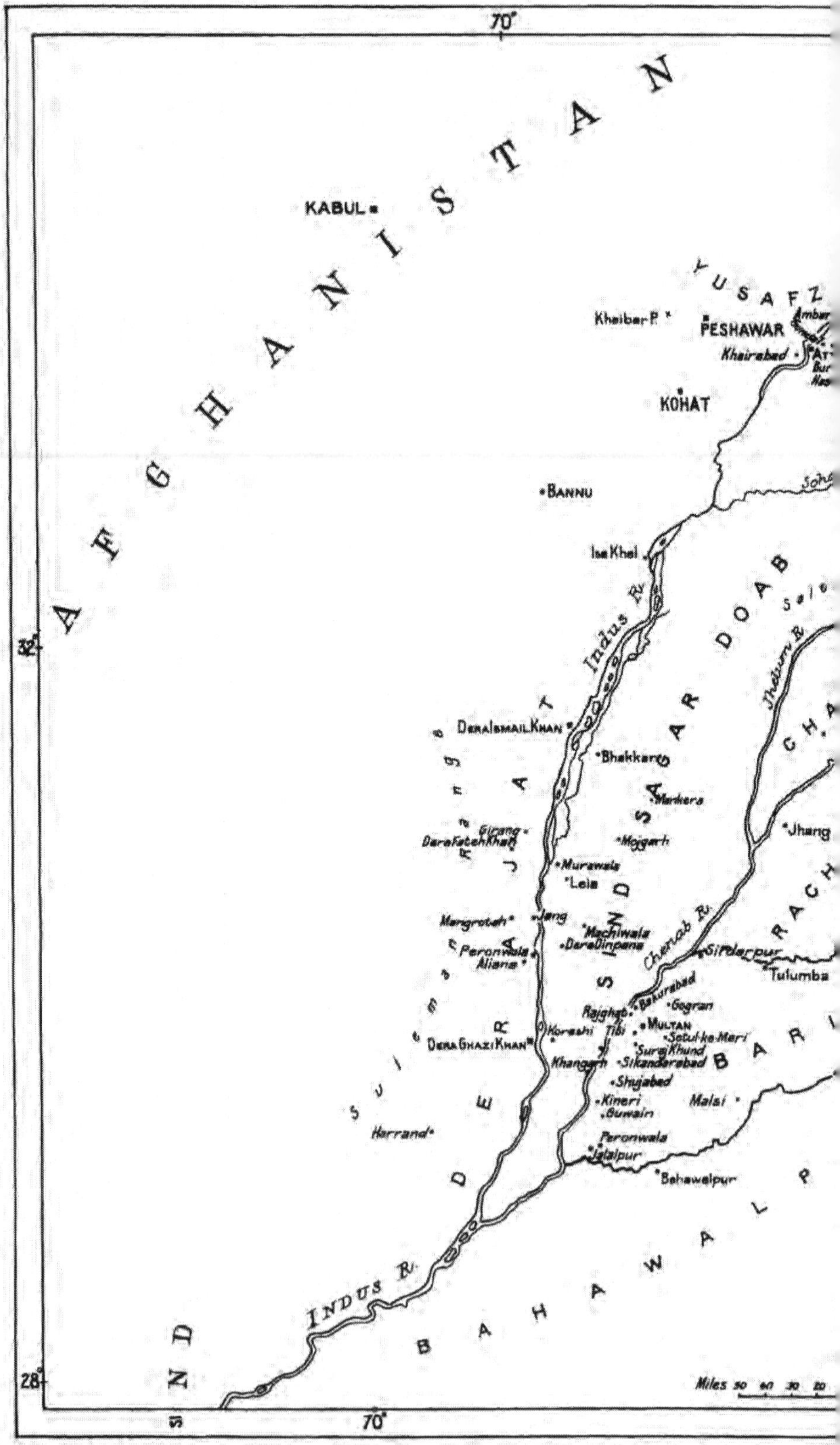
70°
AFGHANISTAN
KABUL
YUSAFZ
Kheiber P.
PESHAWAR
Khairabad
KOHAT
BANNU
Isa Khel
Indus R.
SAGAR DOAB
Jhelum R.
DERA ISMAIL KHAN
Bhakkar
Mankera
Jhang
Girang
Dera Fateh Khan
Mojgarh
Murawala
Leia
Mangrotah
Jang
Machiwala
Dera Dinpana
Peronwala
Aliana
Chenab R.
Sirdarpur
Tulumba
Bakurabad
Gogran
Rajghat
Tibi
MULTAN
Koreshi
Sotul-ka-Mari
Suraj Khund
DERA GHAZI KHAN
Khangarh
Sikandarabad
Shujabad
Kineri
Buwain
Malsi
Harrand
Peronwala
Jalalpur
Bahawalpur
DERAJAT
INDUS R.
BAHAWALP
Miles 50 40 30 20
32°
28°
70°

MAP No. 1

MAP OF THE PUNJAB

INTRODUCTION

The Sikh state based around the city of Lahore that was annexed by the British in 1849 was a relatively recent creation, but was singular for being the last major independent Indian polity and for its European-trained army. It is not easy to define this kingdom because "neither the geographical term 'the Punjab,' nor the religious one 'the Sikhs' are accurate synonyms for this state, as not all its dominions lay within the Punjab—The Five Rivers Land—nor did all the Punjab come under its sway. Likewise, not all its subjects were Sikhs, nor did it rule over all Sikhs, nor even over all territories under Sikh princes."[1] However, it was a militarised state to the extent that its army had become the dominant force in internal politics and external relations.

The Sikh army, known as the *Khalsa* ("the pure" or "the follower") had been developed from the elite warrior caste. Building upon the ethos of Sikh warrior culture, Maharaja Ranjit Singh (1780–1839) developed an army of 29,000 regular infantry, an artillery park of 192 guns, supported by traditional armoured and lance-armed cavalry. European instructors drilled the infantry regiments and imported technicians advised on the manufacture of muskets and cannon at Lahore. For the period of three decades up to Ranjit's death in 1839 the Sikh army dominated the region, defeating Afghan, Kashmiri and other neighbours. In 1802 it took Amritsar, in 1818 Multan fell, in 1819 Kashmir was annexed, and in 1833 and 1834 Ladakh and Peshawar were captured respectively. If the Punjabi state were to further expand territorially and dominate a larger sphere, then crossing the River Sutlej to the south-east would be inevitable, as would a clash with the British. The *Khalsa* represented the most formidable native army on the sub-

1. T.A. Heathcote, *The Military in British India: The Development of British Land Forces in South Asia, 1600-1947*, Manchester University Press, Manchester, 1995, 83.

continent (growing to 150,000 strong in 1845, including all arms), but it also sowed the seeds of its own destruction by its arrogant dominance of its own society.

This was an example of a polity overshadowed by a military caste and of the nominal rulers eventually seeking to throw off military domination. Such a situation might be likened to other historical contexts where the sword of state, perhaps originally fashioned as much to protect the rulers from their own wider society as to be instrumental in martial expansion, turned itself back on those rulers. The Roman Empire, with emperors bullied and occasionally replaced by their Praetorian Guard, is a case in point. Closer to the *Khalsa* as a military caste were the *mamluk* slave troops and their officers who came to dominate the Abbasid Caliphate in Baghdad in the ninth century AD and the rulers of Egypt from Cairo in the fourteenth century. The last centuries of the Ottoman Turkish Empire were similarly marked by the interests and revolutions of the Janissary slave regiments. However, in the Roman and Punjabi cases, unlike in the Abbasid, Mamluk Egyptian, and Ottoman Turkish states, the military cast was native to the parent society.

As control of government over the *Khalsa* slackened, so the latter marauded in the countryside and assassinated a series of leading officials, unpopular officers and, in 1843, even the Maharajah Shere Singh. In 1845 they murdered the Wazir Jawahir Singh. The Wazir's sister, the Maharani Jindan, courted the *Khalsa* leaders after his death and acted as regent for her son the (last) Maharajah, Duleep Singh, whilst secretly swearing vengeance and to bring about the destruction of the *Khalsa*. Her influence was such that two of the senior Sikh commanders in the First Sikh War, Tej Singh and Lal Singh, were actively working for her interests and moved their armies with treacherous hesitation. Jindan was supposed to have used her sexual wiles to further her plans, and she was one of those female "native" figures about whom the Victorians fantasised with particularly salacious pleasure (along, later, with the Rani of Jhansi during the Indian Mutiny).

At almost every stage of British expansion in India from the mid eighteenth century onwards a case could be made for wars being essentially defensive and reactive in nature, although India played its part as a field of conflict during the first two "world wars," the Seven Years War and the Revolutionary/Napoleonic Wars. This "empire by accident rather than design" stance was of course partly the ready self-justification of imperialists through history. A threat to already-established territories, or a need to intervene in the affairs of fractious or corruptly governed neighbours, could always be played up for political expediency. Indeed, at every stage, there were voices raised both for opportunist expansionism (often on the ground), and in favour of caution and non-involvement (often back home at the centre of empire). This was not necessarily the whole picture. Threats did exist (perceived or real), but the very presence in a region of an expansionist power could breed instability through fear of future conquest. Worst still, a vacillating policy might give off the most disquieting signals, combining supposed non-intervention and the rhetoric of peaceful intentions with a concern not to allow national reputation and honour to be impugned.

In northern India the British fought a series of short wars against different polities, first in the north-east in Bengal, then progressively through Bihar, Oudh, Rohlkand, and the North-West Provinces. They were drawn not only to the Sutlej frontier of the Punjab but also deep into Afghanistan. Meanwhile the Pindari and Mahratta War had secured vast territories for the British in central India (1817–19) with smaller states being gobbled up though the 1830s and early 1840s. The First Afghan War (1838–42) took British forces on their furthest excursion to date but, despite the final result being the successful installation of a British candidate as Afghan ruler, it had also resulted in the complete annihilation of a whole British expeditionary force made up of both British and Indian sepoy regiments (1841–42). This disaster had seriously damaged British prestige and the unprovoked annexation of Sind in 1843 did nothing to allay the fears of the remaining independent principalities in the region. Also in 1843 the Gwalior War was fought to suppress the local Maratta revolt, two sharp contests being fought on the same day.

The following list of dates summarises the chronology of the period:

1837–42: First Afghan War. 1837 Persian invasion of Afghanistan; 1841-42 disastrous British occupation and retreat from Kabul. 1842 restoration of British candidate in Kabul.

1843: Sind Campaign. Battles at Miani (February 17), Hyderabad (March 24). Unprovoked annexation of Sind by Sir Charles Napier.

1843: Gwalior Campaign. Battles at Maharajpur and Panniar (December 29). Mahratta revolt defeated.

1844: Southern Mahratta Campaign.

1845: Sind Frontier Hill Tribes Campaign.

1845–46: First Sikh War. Battles at Mudki (December 18, 1845), Ferozeshah (February 21–22, 1845), Baddowal (January, 21, 1846), Aliwal (January 28, 1846), Sobraon (February 10, 1846).

1848–49: Second Sikh War. Battles at Ramnuggar (November 21, 1848), Chillianwalla (January 13, 1849), Gujerat (February 21, 1849). Punjab annexed.

The developing mixture of British defeat, vacillation and aggression was specifically used by the Maharani Jindan and other Sikh leaders to whip up the *Khalsa*. Thus the First Sikh War arose partly from the Maharani's encouragement of the *Khalsa* to seek plunder in the direction of British territory, and despite plenty of prior intelligence from highly placed enemies of the Punjabi army, the Governor-General Sir Henry Hardinge (in office 1844-48) was sceptical of a threat, and when conflict came the British were initially unprepared. Thus the First Sikh War saw the Sikh armies cross the Sutlej and the British scramble to meet them. The Second Sikh War involved British invasion of the Punjab in order to bring to battle and destroy the Sikh armies which had formed to challenge British domination. The main actions of the two wars may now be briefly summarised.

On December 18, 1845, the British Commander-in-Chief, Sir Hugh Gough (in office 1843-49) force-marched The Army of the Sutlej (11,000 men and 42 guns) to meet Lal Singh's force of 8,000 cavalry, 2,000 infantry and 22 guns at Mudki. The Sikhs advanced and an initial artillery dual was followed by the British 3rd Light Dragoons and 4th Bengal Light Cavalry charging the Sikh horse to prevent them encircling Gough's force. The British infantry advance became confused as darkness fell but eventually pushed the Sikh troops off the field despite determined resistance.

More British troops joined Gough and he followed up the Sikhs to their fortified position around Ferozeshah. He was forced to delay to await another British column which brought his army up to 18,000 men and 65 guns facing Lal Singh with 17,000 troops and 120 guns. Attacking from the west around 3:30 p.m. on December 21, Gough's troops were at first repulsed from the defences. The Sikh counter-attack was thwarted at great cost by the 3rd Light Dragoons' charge, then further assaults broke into the Sikh camp. Withdrawing for the night, the renewed British attack on the 22nd broke in again more easily and the ensuing fight through the confused ground of the Sikh army's encampment saw the Sikhs ejected and 72 guns taken. A crisis now loomed as a second Sikh army of 30,000 troops and 70 guns under Tej Singh marched down from the north. The British cavalry were initially successful in holding off their opposite numbers but then confused orders sent them off the field leaving the infantry to form squares and face the enemy artillery and cavalry whilst the *Khalsa* infantry regiments closed. Then Tej Singh, claiming that the British cavalry withdrawal was a ruse, used this pretext to withdraw his own army from the field. This treachery perhaps saved Gough's exhausted force and the field was left to him. British casualties at 2,415 were heavy, especially amongst the European regiments, and despite a victory of sorts, Gough's unsubtly direct tactics were criticised. The Sikhs withdrew across the Sutlej, but this was only the first round of the war.

The next Sikh move was to fortify a base at Sobraon on the south bank of the Sutlej, linked to the Sikh bank by a pontoon bridge, occupied by 30,000 troops and 76 guns, again under Tej Singh. The plan was to launch small plundering expeditions into British territory and one such under Runjur Singh crossed over to besiege the base at Ludhiana. Facing them was a British force under Sir Harry Smith. After a skirmish at Baddowal on January 21, his 12,000 men and 28 guns faced Runjur Singh whose army now numbered 20,000 troops at Aliwal on the 28th. Smith's dispositions worked well, his infantry first assaulted Aliwal and then in the general engagement they advanced but periodically dropped to the ground to lessen the effect of enemy fire. The 16th Lancers made a famous charge against Sikh guns and the infantry beyond, losing a third of their number in a savage mauling. The Sikh army broke and fled across the river behind their position leaving 2,000 dead, and abandoning 60 guns and all their stores. This was a set-piece victory, elegantly won, and the first clear-cut, toe-to-toe defeat of the Sikhs in the war.

Smith marched to join Gough and on February 10 the British army of 15,000 troops and 78 guns assaulted Tej Singh's strongly fortified base at Sobraon. A heavy artillery bombardment was followed by escalades at three points along the defences. Each attack was repulsed and renewed repeatedly amid some confusion and poor co-ordination, until they eventually broke in. The 3rd Light Dragoons also moved through the entrenchments and overwhelmed artillery positions beyond. A stubborn fight through the base ensued until the Sikhs finally broke. The Sutlej was in spate and the (deliberately?) weakened pontoon bridge was swept away so that a large proportion of the 10,000 Sikh casualties were drownings during the rout. Gough sustained 2,300 casualties, winning a victory which effectively ended the war.

The Second Sikh War was occasioned by the Sikh military caste's non-acceptance of defeat in the First War and by feelings of betrayal by their nominal political masters. The British saw this "revolt" as treachery and determined early on to annexe the Punjab to solve the Sikh problem permanently. Two theatres of operations developed. The southern Punjabi province of Multan revolted and its governor, Mulraj Singh, turned against the Lahore government. The British moved fast and gathered a large enough army under Major-General William Whish to besiege the well fortified and wealthy city. In seven days of assaults, repulses, sallies, and counter-attacks the walls of the city were taken and the population slaughtered, but Mulraj held out heroically for a further twenty days in the citadel before surrendering unconditionally.

Elsewhere, in the second theatre along the River Chenab 250 miles to the north-east of Multan, Gough was operating against the Sikh commander Shere Singh. A drawn out and confused action on the banks of the Chenab at Ramnuggar (October 22 to December 1, 1848) saw the Sikhs punish Gough with skilfully deployed artillery and tactics which lured the British cavalry (14th Dragoons and 5th Bengal Light Cavalry) into disaster. Gough eventually crossed the river but failed to entrap the enemy who withdrew ahead of his forces.

Gough, at the head of the Army of the Punjab, pursued the Sikh army west from the Chenab to the River Jhelum and was determined to fight a decisive battle, aware of the diminished confidence of his superiors. The resulting bloody Battle of Chillianwalla (January 13, 1849) was not Gough's finest hour and was as close to a disaster as the British would come in India. Having decided to camp and await the next day for a set-piece fight, Gough prevaricated and was drawn into an encounter battle on unfavourable terrain. Command and control of his army was woefully inadequate and everything that could go wrong did. Like Balaklava five years later, it was marked by confused orders and a long, heroic advance across open ground against prepared artillery. This time it was a battalion of British infantry (24th Regiment) flanked by two sepoy battalions, rather than a brigade of light cavalry, but the blunder, actual achievement, and losses were comparable. The infantry reached their objective, spiking Sikh guns, having been ordered not to fire their muskets but rely solely on bayonets. Completely unsupported, they were then enfiladed by other guns and musketry, and forced to retire with fearful losses (515 casualties out of 1,096 who advanced). Isolated infantry actions were fought between the armies, but singular incompetence was displayed by the cavalry brigade made up of the 9th Lancers, the 14th Light Dragoons and two native regiments under Brigadier Pope. The latter, old, infirm, and with impaired eyesight was the worst kind of cavalry officer, an anathema to those, like the cavalryman and technical author Edward Nolan, who insisted on energy, split-second decision-making and ability to offensively exploit battlefield developments. Pope handled his troops hesitatingly and incompetently in the face of Sikh cavalry, causing them to withdraw rather than to charge the enemy, and their course took them through a British artillery line leaving it disrupted and prey in turn to the Sikh cavalry who fell upon the gunners mercilessly. Rather more effective actions were taken elsewhere on the field, notably with the 61st Regiment's capture of enemy guns, and a dashing charge by the King's Own Light Dragoons. The fighting continued until dark and the Sikh army withdrew taking most of its cannon. Gough claimed the victory of holding the field but had sustained 2,512 dead, wounded and missing. He immediately faced a backlash of hostile opinion at home which led to his replacement in command by Sir Charles Napier who had conquered Sind in 1843. However, the slow communications of news, decision-making, and the time taken for his successor to come out from Britain saved the old commander.

Gough, joined by Whish from Multan, then pursued the army of Shere Singh eastward to Gujerat where the latter had taken up a strongly entrenched position. The combined British army numbered 24,000 men and 96 guns, whilst the Sikhs, reinforced by Afghan cavalry, were some 60,000 strong with 59 guns. On February 21, Gough attacked in the full knowledge that the following battle would finally damn him or rescue his reputation. This time the British infantry were well and closely supported by artillery. They advanced into heavy fire, lying down at intervals to lessen losses, assaulted two heavily defended villages, and swept the Sikh centre away. The Sikh guns were suppressed by superior British weight of metal, and the Sikh cavalry wings were repulsed and pursued by the British cavalry accompanied by horse artillery. Gough's force sustained 800 casualties and captured all the enemy guns, and having broken the Sikh army had reversed the criticism and restored the commander's reputation.

THE SIKH ARMY WAS AN INTERESTING combination of traditional and modern elements. It was made up of a regular army (*Fauj-i-Ain*) of cavalry, infantry and artillery; irregular units; and the feudal levy (*Jagdir-i-Fauj*). The regulars were grouped in twelve brigades, or "camps" (*derahs*), each of three or four infantry battalions, a cavalry regiment, and one or two batteries. In 1845 the 150,000 strong *Khalsa* included 54,000 regular infantry, 6,000 regular cavalry, and 11,000 artillerymen. The irregular cavalry arm (the *Goorchurras*) had been particularly favoured by Ranjit Singh and they were made up of the Sikh social elite and their retainers. The *Goorchurras* fought wearing degrees of armour coverage dependent on their personal wealth and status. Some were armed with lances and all were remarked upon for their sharp swords and the danger they posed in close combat. The British observed them with interest, both for their archaising equipment and for their riding skills. They were said to have ridden with shorter stirrup leathers and tighter reins than their opponents, allowing them greater control and manoeuvrability.

The line infantry of the Sikh army were uniformed regiments of drilled, flintlock musket-armed troops. Predictably many of the muskets had been supplied by the British or copied from British models in the Lahore workshops. This incidental arming of future enemies was not a phenomenon confined to the later twentieth century, and many national armies across the globe were equipped with British "Tower" muskets. For example, Mexican infantry regiments marched into the Mexican-American War of 1846–47 bearing thousands of sub-standard and faulty weapons imported from Britain. Training for the Sikh cavalry, infantry, and artillery was supplied by European and American instructors of many nationalities, with French military culture and organization dominant. The over-arching question about the *Khalsa* formations was would they stand against British infantry and trade musket-volleys? In the event, they fought doggedly but were usually strongly positioned behind fortifications or other obstacles. In the Second Sikh War the ranks of the regular infantry had approximately 30 percent new recruits which must have affected performance. Their uniform consisted of British style blue trousers and red jacket, black cross-belts, and white turban. There were also large numbers of irregular infantry armed with swords, shields and matchlock muskets, including religious fanatics (*Akalis*), plus mercenary infantry and cavalry, including Afghans and Gurkhas. Many Honourable East India Comapany sepoys were seduced by the higher pay available in Sikh service.

The Sikh artillery was especially prominent within the *Khalsa*. Much care and resources had been lavished on it by Ranjit Singh and initially gunners had been recruited from the Muslim and Hindu communities. This was a security measure, balancing the non-Sikh element against the rest of the army. A clear parallel may be found in the playing off by Roman emperors of citizen praetorian infantry, recruited in Italy, against non-citizen Guard Cavalry drawn from the frontier auxiliaries. Similarly the Abbasid Caliphs balanced their Turkish mamluks with slave-troops from other regions, especially East Africans and Slavs. The Sikh artillery subsequently also recruited Sikhs, but it remained a dedicated arm of the *Khalsa* and the one element which inflicted a considerable number of casualties on the British who repeatedly remarked upon the tallness, ferocity and dedication of the gunners. Their cannon, which included a great range of calibres, from 3-pounders to 36-pounders, and some massive mortars, were considerably heavier than the British guns (some 24-, 32-, and 36-pounders at Ferozeshah, compared with British 6-, 9-, and 12-pounders), frequently outshooting them in counter-battery work, and often forcing the more vulnerable horse-artillery to withdraw. Sikh batteries were often said to have been cunningly masked. It is clear that they were well handled and skilfully directed. Traction of artillery using oxen, camels, and elephants was slow but heavier calibres of weapons could be employed in the field than was common in Europe. Similarly the American army during the Mexican-American War found that the use of oxen was very advantageous in this respect. The gunners were distinctly uniformed, again in British style, with blue trousers and jackets, one white cross-belt, and a black bear-skin with red cording.

The Sikh high command was politically compromised, particularly in the First Sikh War, so it is difficult to evaluate their qualities. However, they did make serious errors, deliberate or otherwise, notably standing at Aliwal and Sobraon with the army's back to the Sutlej, a fatal position in the event of withdrawal. On other occasions Sikh forces were able to retire with their guns and outdistance British pursuit. The defence of Multan was determined and heroic, and Sikh soldiers, both regular and irregular, fought with tenacity, sometimes fanaticism. However, there is evidence that they became increasingly intimidated by the British European infantry.

The British army which conquered the Punjab in 1849 was that part of the army of the Honourable East India Company under the Bengal Presidency, based at Delhi. Overall the Bengal forces consisted of seventeen regiments of cavalry (Bengal Light and Bengal Irregular), two regiments of European infantry, 68 native infantry regiments, three artillery battalions of six companies each, and a combined corps of sappers, miners and pioneers. It was supplemented by a varying number of Her Majesty's Crown regiments of European cavalry and infantry (Queen Victoria, reigned 1837–1901).

The infantry were using the 1833 *Field Exercise* system for manoeuvres in the field, and this was criticised by some contemporaries for its inflexibility and for the need for unorthodox solutions to emergencies. For example, when a battalion in line was required to reverse its face the front rank had to pass back through the line to become the front rank facing rearwards. At

Chillianwalla the 61st Foot was threatened from the rear and the unorthodox solution was for the rear rank simply to be ordered to turn round, thus saving precious time in an emergency. However, there was a gradual evolution which increased emphasis on extended, light infantry formations. The latter had a pedigree of periodic "rediscovery" through the American wars of the eighteenth century and the Napoleonic Wars, to be rediscovered yet again to accommodate the often broken terrain of colonial conflicts. Traditionally, either whole regiments were designated Light Infantry and trained accordingly, or, in a regiment of ten companies, one acted as light infantry. Thus it was notable during the Sikh Wars that three of the 32nd Foot's companies were in light formation at Multan, and two companies of the 24th Foot acted in this manner at Gujerat. By the 1830s regiments were under some pressure to train as light infantry so that they could multi-task, the number of specialist regiments of Light Infantry being small and their services usually unavailable in distant theatres.

Another evolving area concerning equipment and formation was the improvement of infantry firearms. A huge amount of research went into either refurbishing old stock to improve firing-rates, or to design new arms. Percussion-caps replaced the old flint-lock from the 1830s, thus reducing the number of misfires. Rifling of gun-barrels could potentially improve range and accuracy drastically but the Enfield rifled musket was only in production from 1853 and re-equipping of regiments with the latest designs was a slow process continuing through The Crimean War, so that the rear formations in the British army at the Battle of the Alma (1854) still carried smoothbores. Thus the British infantry during the Sikh Wars were firing more reliably than their predecessors in the Napoleonic Wars, but at the same maximum range of 150–200 yards. With musketry still so limited, there was a controversy over the effectiveness of the bayonet. Quite apart from the impediment it presented when fixed for muzzle-loading muskets, the proponents of "cold steel" (of whom there was a succession up to the First World War) opined that the halting of advancing formations to give fire could critically slow momentum in the attack. Thus the 24th Foot at Chillianwalla were reportedly ordered not to load their muskets. Those officers obsessed with the bayonet were able to continue their advocacy in part because colonial conflicts up to the 1890s had the potential for close combat with enemies bearing traditional, bladed weaponry (Kaffirs, Chinese, Zulus, Afghans, Mahdists, etc.).

In all the Indian wars of the eighteenth and nineteenth centuries the British infantry and cavalry formations were made up of a very small number of European regiments. At Mudki, Gough's forces consisted of 13 infantry battalions, 4 of which were European. At Ferozeshah it was 6 out of 21; at Aliwal 3 out of 11; at Sobraon 9 out of 21. In the Second Sikh War at Chillianwalla 4 out of 14 were European, whilst at Gujerat the numbers were 7 and 25. Ideally one European battalion would be brigaded with two native battalions, but sometimes brigades had to be made up wholly of native units. European regiments were always considered to have been more "steady" than native, and were often used to lead attacks, as at Chillianwalla. This presumably reflected a combination of institutional superiority-complex, prejudice, and self-regard, plus greater commitment, but not necessarily superior professionalism. In some battles observers noted examples of lapses in fire discipline by native regiments (Mudki) and a reluctance to closely support European battalions they were brigaded with (Ferozeshah). At the sack of Multan British officers were critical of the behaviour of individual European soldiers, but regarded the native forces as collectively more destructive. Again contemporary prejudices played their part. However, it seems that the sepoys were initially intimidated by the reputation of the *Khalsa*, but that their confidence grew with British victories. Most of the native regiments were styled Bengal Native Infantry and were made up of Indian sepoys with European officers. There were also two Gurkha battalions. Attitudes towards sepoys and their reliability of course changed radically with the great Indian Mutiny of 1857. Sepoys had often previously mutinied over pay, conditions, and terms of service, and been bloodily suppressed (1806, 1824), but in the Bengal Presidency to which the Mutiny was largely confined, the ideal ratio of Indian to European regiments of 2:1 had risen to 5 1/2:1. The Mutiny and its crushing involved levels of racial hatred and psychopathic violence on all sides, the shock of which poisoned Anglo-Indian relations for the next ninety years. One consequence was that the authorities limited native artillery and kept the more advanced firearms out of the hands of sepoys until the early twentieth century. Nevertheless, annexation of the Punjab gave the British a new source of manpower, drawn from one of the subcontinent's "martial peoples," which was largely loyal during the Mutiny.

There was little concession, by way of dress modification, to the Indian climate. Red woollen coats and blue woollen trousers were standard except for the green of the 60th Rifles at Gujerat. The tall, bell-shako of the First Afghan War period had been superseded for other ranks by a round, soft, peaked cap with a white, sometimes quilted cover, with or without a flap at the back to shade the neck. Some regiments wore the peaked "Albert" stovepipe shako, again with a cover. Officers were allowed greater latitude of dress, sometimes wearing quilted jackets. Sepoys were uniformed in the characteristic red coats and white cross-belts of British forces with either trousers or native *dhoti*. On their heads they wore a soft, peakless woollen cap, or a peakless bell shako. The Gurkhas wore "rifle" green. This was in some contrast to the much more relaxed dress of the Indian Mutiny period when lighter textiles, smocks, and *khaki* came into use, few battalions wearing their full scarlet regimentals in the field.

In India the British cavalry was also a mix of European Crown regiments and native Company regiments. The latter were either Bengal Light Cavalry or Bengal Irregular Cavalry. The numbers of European, native light, and native irregular formations at Mudki were, respectively, 1, 3, 1; at Ferozeshah 1, 3, 3; at Aliwal 1, 3, 2; at Chillianwalla 3, 4, 0; and at Gujerat 1, 5, 4.

All the European regiments were light cavalry, the 3rd Light Dragoons being present at Mudki, Ferozeshah, Sobraon, Chillianwalla, and Gujerat; the 16th Light Dragoons (Lancers) at Aliwal and Sobraon; the 9th Light Dragoons (Lancers) at Sobraon, Chillianwalla, and Gujerat; and the 14th Light Dragoons at Chillianwalla and Gujerat. They were armed with short, smoothbore carbines and the 1821 pattern light cavalry sword. From 1816 four regiments in Britain were designated Lancers with each rider equipped with a seven-foot long lance, sword, and one pistol, although in the Sikh Wars some men in the 16th continued to carry carbines. In 1840 all light regiments changed from red to dark blue jackets, except for the 16th Lancers who retained their red jackets. The traditional distinction between charging lines of heavy cavalry and the support roles (scouting, skirmishing, screening, picketing) of light cavalry became largely meaningless during the nineteenth century, especially in theatres where European cavalry were thin on the ground, heavy dragoons were generally absent, terrain was broken, and where native enemies employed light tactics.

Many of the controversies which surfaced in the full glare of public scrutiny during the Crimean War were already being discussed during the Sikh Wars. In particular, British swords were found to be poorly made and easily blunted, especially by their steel scabbards. Just as in the Charge of the Heavy Brigade at Balaklava, troopers found difficulty in penetrating opponents' thick clothing with their blades. This was in contrast to the razor-sharp swords of the enemy, and there was plenty of anecdotal evidence of the severing of heads and limbs. It is clear that although British cavalry retained the tactical initiative in the main battles, there were occasions when they were very badly mauled by Sikhs exhibiting superior horsemanship and fencing skills. British leather cavalry headgear was not deemed sufficiently protective. Light dragoons wore a stovepipe shako or a soft, round, peaked cap like the infantry; lancers wore the Polish-style, square-topped *csapska*. They resorted to tying a textile *pugri* around their heads for extra defence, with lengths hanging down the back to protect their vulnerable neck, in the native manner. Partly on the strength of Sikh War experiences, Nolan advocated the use of a metal helmet and even of a metal gauntlet for the left hand and forearm, reverting to seventeenth century practice. The lance was a controversial weapon, some observers like Nolan seeing it as an ineffective impediment in close combat and in irregular warfare, whilst the breaking of three Sikh infantry squares at Aliwal by the 16th Lancers was held up by its champions as a great achievement. Lancers continued to be used until beyond the First World War, charging with mixed fortunes at Balaklava (1854), Ulundi (1879) and Omdurman (1898).

The Bengal Light Cavalry regiments were equipped and trained in European fashion whereas the Bengal Irregular Cavalry employed native equitation, dress, and equipment. Much about native horsemanship and equipment was admired by British observers, such as rein-chains to protect the reins from being severed in combat, and short-legged riding-stance. One cultural transfer was the adoption of ring-mail epaulettes on jackets to protect the shoulders from sword-cuts. Not the least of these admirers was Nolan who had not only served in India (1843–51) but also toured the cavalry manoeuvres of Europe. He could compare the methods of Sikh and other native Indian traditions with those of the Cossacks in Russian employ, both in peace and in (Crimean) war. Nolan was especially scathing about the Indian regular cavalry, praising the irregulars and relating anecdotes of superior skills displayed at Chillianwalla.[2] Without the irregulars in British service, he opined, there would not have been the heroic figures of British light cavalry commanders who came to prominence in these wars, on the frontiers, and later during the Indian Mutiny. The practice of attaching these leaders' names to regiments (Christie's, Chamberlain's, Gardner's, Hodson's, Jacob's, Skinner's Horse, etc.) can best be paralleled by the Roman usage of naming newly raised Gallic cavalry regiments in the first century AD after their first commanders (*ala Frontoniana*, *Petriana*, *Siliana*, etc.). In both cases native equestrian cultures were being harnessed for imperial service and irregular formations eventually became permanent, regular regiments. The

2. L.E. Nolan, *Cavalry: Its History and Tactics*, Westholme, Yardley, 2007, 53, 62-8.

ala Petriana existed for four hundred years and disappeared with the fall of the Roman Empire in the west; Skinner's Horse survived the British Empire and celebrated its bicentenary in 2003.

The British cavalry was generally well handled in the Sikh Wars and made some celebrated formal charges, foreshadowing actions seen later in the Crimea. Generally the cavalry was used offensively, retained the initiative, and dominated superior numbers of enemy horse, just as at Balaklava. Initiative was seized and opportunities exploited. However, there were some serious lapses, as with the poor scouting at Mudki and the disastrous manoeuvring over treacherous ground at Ramnuggar. The worst instance of cavalry mismanagement was the confused order to retire at the Battle of Chillianwalla, on which Strachan simply comments that "the Chillianwalla débâcle, [was] a far greater stain on the British cavalry than the charge of the Light Brigade."[3]

Artillery made up the most highly regarded element of the Bengal army, and lessons learnt from the Sikh Wars about speed of draught teams and flexible deployment of guns added to contemporary design controversies. Indeed, gun, projectile, and carriage design had developed since the Napoleonic Wars, partly in the quest for horse artillery that could properly support cavalry. Faced with the heavy guns of the Sikhs, often placed in fortified positions, it was felt that the lightest guns (6-pounder horse artillery) were ineffective and both larger numbers of guns and increasingly heavy guns were brought into use, 9-pounders superseded by 12-, 18-, and 24-pounders. Shrapnel was increasingly favoured in colonial contexts where native formations might be open and occupying difficult ground. Heavy prior bombardment at Sobraon was crucial, and the 100-gun park employed in the Second Sikh War, hitherto unparalleled in British armies, was decisive in the victory at Gujerat.

Certainly the British army was not slow or hidebound when it came to the development of new weaponry, the adoption of modified tactical doctrine, and the employment of native skills and resources. However, warfare in India made its own special demands of topography and climate, and had its own martial traditions. Armies moved with much larger numbers of supernumeries and animals than in Europe, trailing great tails of servants, women, drovers, elephants, and camels, amongst which attrition was very high on campaign. How well British officers adapted to these conditions is ultimately evidenced by the string of battlefield victories won over native

3. H. Strachan, *From Waterloo to Balaklava. Tactics, Technology, and the British Army, 1815-1854*, Cambridge University Press, Cambridge and New York, 1985, 68.

armies that were very often superior in numbers. Campaigning was hard but the endurance of officers and men was extraordinary. A price for forced marches and bloody battles had to be paid in roadside casualties, exhaustion, sunstroke, desertion, alcoholism, tropical and venereal diseases, and floggings. The latter was much restricted during the course of the nineteenth century, to a maximum of 50 lashes in 1846, but only finally abolished in 1871. On a more positive note, quinine was becoming more available for combating malaria, and Chillianwalla was apparently the first battle in which British surgeons used anaesthetics.

Little attention has been paid so far to the officers in the British armies. Unsurprisingly many of the ranking officers throughout the Indian wars were Napoleonic wars veterans and/or long-serving India hands. This continued to be the case in the British army until these old warhorses—frighteningly vigorous by modern standards though many were—became just too superannuated. Sir Charles Napier, the "Conqueror of Sind" who died aged 71, served in Denmark, the Peninsular, Bermuda, and America during the Napoleonic Wars and the War of 1812, and latterly in the First Afghan War. Gough was a veteran of Talavera, Barossa, and Nivelle, and had distinguished himself in China. He died aged 90, a Viscount and Field Martial. Sir Harry Smith experienced the battles of Buenos Aires, La Coruña, Almeida, Sabugal, Vittoria, Toulouse, Washington, New Orleans, and Waterloo in the Napoleonic and American conflicts, and latterly served in the Gwalior War. He died a lieutenant general, aged 70. Sir Colin Campbell served in the Peninsular, on the Walcheren Expedition, and at New Orleans, in the First China War, and in the Second Sikh War (divisional commander at Chillianwalla and Gujerat). He went on to command the Punjab frontier forces on numerous expeditions in the early 1850s, returned to Britain, and was given the Highland Brigade in the Crimean War, distinguishing himself at the Alma and Balaklava. In 1857 he was made Commander-in-Chief, India, successfully suppressed the Indian Mutiny, returned to Britain and died, aged 71, a peer and a Field Martial in 1863.

Promotion through longevity was not an ideal system and was one which public opinion at home later blamed in part for some of the less decisive actions of the Crimean War (1854–56). It was also held responsible for contributing to the causes of the Indian Mutiny as well as to the initially sluggish British response to that crisis (1857–59). The system of purchasing commissions was also considered by its opponents to stultify promotion and to stifle young, imaginative officers, and this system continued until it was abolished by *The Regulation of the Forces Act* of 1871.

Fortunes could still be made by enterprising officers in India. Unfortunately, in this period Indian service did not have the cachet it gained later in the century when, after the Indian Mutiny, the Company Army was absorbed into the Crown forces, and the social nature of life in India also changed. Wealthy officers could exchange out of their regiments if their Crown formation was posted to India, whilst relatively poor officers could take advantage of the enhanced social status and the lower cost of living in the subcontinent. A kind of inverted snobbery was directed at "Indians" at home and this was particularly unfortunate because, for the period between the Napoleonic and Crimean Wars, much the best practical experience of warfare was to be gained in India. Nevertheless, some excellent officers were able to move between the spheres of home and India and their developed skills were of great service to the army. One such was William Morris, "the pocket Hercules," who was wounded charging as a lieutenant in the 16th Lancers at Aliwal, wounded again charging the guns at Balaklava as a Captain in the 17th Lancers in 1854, and died at Poona of dysentery in 1857 (aged 37). Another was Louis Edward Nolan, despite the fact that this officer actually saw very little combat until he was killed (aged 36) by the first Russian shell ahead of the Light Brigade at Balaklava. Instead he was a passionate observer of cavalry the world over, travelling extensively in Europe, the Levant, and India. He served in the 15th King's Hussars in India (Madras Presidency) from 1843 to 1851, and from 1844 was that regiment's riding master. He thus had the opportunity to study the native equestrian cultures at first hand and to discuss the recent wars with participants. He had the temerity to publish his thoughts on the supply of remounts (not only an "Indian," but a "writer"—most unsound!), and in his most influential work, *Cavalry: Its History and Tactics*, his approval of Sikh riding and combat techniques comes through very clearly.

The picture of the nineteenth century British army as one of aristocratic dandies, resistant to reform and military change, leading the flogged sweepings of the gutters of British society into battle, is no longer a sustainable parody. However, generalship at the top could at times be feeble, as was the case with Elphinstone in the First Afghan War and Raglan in the Crimea. Gough's conduct of battles in both Sikh Wars was certainly controversial and his retention of command after Chillianwalla was down to the length of communication time between India and Britain. These were the last wars in which commanders on the ground were almost free of political supervision from home. Before telegraph links it could take up to a year for the round trip. The French generals in the Crimea, linked to Paris by telegraph, were the first to have their political master dictating almost daily actions. Was Gough a simple Napoleonic general who threw infantry at the problem with little subtlety and high casualties sustained? To answer this question it is helpful to ask what alternative tactics might have been adopted, and to envisage these it is instructive to look back at the earlier Sind and Gwalior campaigns.

Sir Charles Napier's conquest of Sind was significant for a number of reasons, apart from its affects on the attitudes of neighbours to British expansion. The two battles fought at Miani and Hyderabad were won with a very small European element to the British forces. The native and irregular cavalry formations were well led and despite serious terrain obstacles were tactically dominant and decisive on the flanks. Napier's infantry at Miani (February 17, 1843) was deployed *en echelon* with his best troops, and one European regiment, Her Majesty's 22nd Foot, leading on the right so as to lessen the effect of fire coming from the village of Katri on the left. The bulk of the enemy infantry was concealed across the front in the dry bed of the River Fuleli so that when the 22nd advanced up to them it was in danger of being overwhelmed when ordered to attack. Instead the men refused, halted, and delivered multiple volleys into the mass before closing with the bayonet. Superior firepower was decisive, although the melee across the riverbed still lasted for an hour. The battle is marked as the first in which in despatches a British commander commended other ranks, not just officers. At Hyderabad on March 24 the British force of 5,000 troops attacked 16,000 Baluchis behind steep banks and an irrigation canal, again using the 22nd Foot to lead the five Bengal Native Infantry battalions present in the assault. Meanwhile officers at regimental level in the cavalry brigade on the right flank persuaded a vacillating brigadier that independent action should be taken against the positions to their front which they correctly suspected to be unmanned. They crossed over and overran the Baluchi left, then, keeping their men under tight control, they rallied, and swept away the vastly superior enemy cavalry reserve. While his infantry continued the assault on the enemy right and centre, Napier led the cavalry on his left flank round the Baluchi position completing a double-envelopment. Thus initiative and the ability to seize developing opportunities in the heat of battle were amply displayed by both the overall commander and by cavalry officers lower down the chain. British casualties were light at 270 and the enemy lost 2,000, presumably the majority in the ensuing cavalry pursuit.

By contrast, the two battles of the Gwalior War were slogging matches against determinedly defended Maratha positions. At Maharajpur on

December 29, 1843, Sir Hugh Gough's 4,800 infantry assaulted three enemy centres in succession, supported by 1,340 cavalry made up of the 16th Lancers and Light and Irregular regiments of Bengal cavalry. The 59 enemy guns were bravely served until overrun and the British sustained 797 casualties. It might be said that this was a taste of things to come under Gough's command in the Sikh Wars.

Gough certainly made mistakes when fighting the Sikhs. Sometimes reconnaissance was poor. Before Chillianwalla he vacillated and engaged in battle as a reversal of prior plans, but it could be argued that he could not have drawn back once so close to the superior Sikh army. What did improve was the co-ordination of artillery bombardments and infantry attacks, and the number and weight of guns deployed. Given that the Sikhs more often than not elected to fight defensively, entrenched positions had to be taken with the bayonet. Sending in infantry assaults without proper artillery support would have been positively Wellingtonian but there are signs that Gough did evolve his tactics. Losses were both inevitable and highest amongst the European infantry spearheading assaults. Such losses did not play well in the cold print of newspapers on breakfast tables back in Britain, but time, distance, and a continued record of winning battles eventually attained hero status for Sir Hugh "Tipperary Joe" Gough.

The following account of the First and Second Sikh Wars by Lieutenant-Colonel R.D. Burton is a straightforward narrative which draws heavily on official papers and personal memoirs, particularly the account published by Thackwell who was present at Ramnagar and Chillianwalla (see *Further Reading*, below). Nolan also quoted extensively from Thackwell on cavalry equipment and performance.

Burton's regiment was the 94th Russell's Infantry which bore this title in the period 1903–22. Thereafter it was redesignated the 1st Battalion of the 19th Hyderabad Regiment. In 1945 it was renamed The Kumaon Regiment and went into the Indian Army at Partition. Burton's work was compiled for the General Staff, India, and the individual copy of *The First and Second Sikh Wars* used for this reprint bears cancelled stamps from the Department of Defence and Headquarters Libraries. It was printed in 1911 by the Government Central Office Press at Simla (Shimla), the summer capital of the British Raj. This town was a combination of government centre, British cultural centre, and summer hill station enjoyed as an escape from the heat of the plain below. Only five years before the book was printed Simla was linked to the wider world by the engineering triumph that was the

Kalka–Simla Railway. The year of publication is significant because the book should be seen against the backdrop of the reform programme instituted from 1902 by Kitchener for the Indian Army. He unified the army so that it was no longer divided up between Madras, Bengal, and Bombay, as it continued to be after the Indian Mutiny despite the passing of the Honourable East India Company's Raj. There were some measures specifically designed to improve officer-training, partly in the light of shortcomings revealed by recent wars in Africa, and a new college was established at Deolali near Bombay (Mumbai). Thus Burton made his contribution to the education of officers with his clear and lucid account of the conquest of the Punjab.

Jon Coulston
St Andrews, November 2007

Further Reading

The Sikh Wars are a well-studied period of Indian history, not least because of the continuing proud self-identity of the Sikhs whose lands lie divided between India and Pakistan since Partition. In military history terms they are of interest because the tactics, technology, and even individual personnel feed into both the Crimean War and the Indian Mutiny, as the foregoing Introduction has attempted to make clear. This section on Further Reading roughly follows the structure of the Introduction.

For Sikh history and the *Khalsa*, useful accounts may be found in J.D. Cunningham, *The History of the Sikhs from the Origin of the Nation to the Battles of the Sutlej*, John Murray, London, 1849 (H.L.O. Garrett (ed.); reprint edition S. Chand, New Delhi, 1994); D. Featherstone, *Victoria's Enemies. An A-Z of British Colonial Warfare*, Blandford, London, 1989; J.S. Grewal, *The Sikhs of the Punjab*, The New Cambridge History of India II.3, Cambridge University Press, Cambridge, 1990; I. Heath, *The Sikh Army, 1799-1849*, Osprey, Oxford, 2005; I. Knight, *Queen Victoria's Enemies* 3, *India*, Osprey, Oxford, 1990.

The historical context of developing British rule in nineteenth century India is accessible in L. James, *Raj. The Making and Unmaking of British India*, Abacus, London, 1997. V. Kumar, *India Under Lord Hardinge*, Rajesh Publications, New Delhi and Allahabad, 1978, and P. Woodruff, *The Men Who Ruled India* 1, *The Founders*, Cape, London, 1953, cover more administrative detail.

On the Sikh Wars see H.C.B. Cook, *The Sikh Wars: the British Army in the Punjab, 1845-6, 1848-9*, Leo Cooper, London, 1975; S. David, *Victoria's Wars. The Rise of Empire*, Viking/Penguin, London and New York, 2006; D. Featherstone, *Victorian Colonial Warfare. India from the Conquest of Sind to the Indian Mutiny*, Cassell, London, 1992; D. Featherstone, *All for a Shilling a Day. The Story of H.M. 16th The Queen's Lancers During the First Sikh War, 1845-1846*, Leonaur Ltd, 2007; D. Featherstone, *At Them with the Bayonet. The First Sikh War, 1845-1846*, Leonaur Ltd, 2007; J. French, *Armies of the Nineteenth Century: The British in India 1825-59*, Foundry Books, Nottingham, 2006; G. Gough and A. Innes, *The Sikhs and Sikh Wars: the Rise, Conquest, and*

Annexation of the Punjab State, A.D. Innes & Co., London, 1897 (reprint Chadwyck-Healey Ltd, Cambridge, 2002); P.J. Haythornthwaite, *The Colonial Wars Source Book*, Caxton, London, 2000;

There are a number of valuable personal accounts relating to the Sind, Gwalior, and Sikh Wars which are full of incidental detail of interest to military and social historians alike: C. Allen (ed.), *A Soldier of the Company. Life of an Indian Ensign 1833-43*, Penguin, London, 1988; J. Anderson, *Sound Advance! Experiences of an Officer of HM 50th Regiment in Australia, Burma and During the Gwalior War, in India*, Leonaur Ltd, 2007; J.W. Baldwin, *A Norfolk Soldier in the First Sikh War. Experiences of a Private of H.M. 9th Regiment of Foot in the Battles for the Punjab, India 1845-6, Including a History of the Sutlej Campaign, December 1845-March 1846 by Gough and Innes*, Leonaur Ltd, 2005; J. Humphries (ed.), *The Hero of Aliwal. The Campaigns of Sir Harry Smith in India, 1843-1846, during The Gwalior War and The First Sikh War, with a short history of the Gwalior War and First Sikh War by Hugh Murray*, Leonaur Ltd, 2007; D.A. Sandford, *A Journal of the Second Sikh War. The Experiences of an Ensign of the 2nd Bengal European Regiment During the Campaign in the Punjab, India, 1848-49*, Leonaur Ltd, 2007; E.J. Thackwell, *Narrative of the Second Sikh War in 1848-49*, London, 1851 (reprint Elibron Classics, Adamant Media Corporation, Boston, 2002); R.N.W. Thomas (ed.), 'Daniel George Robinson. Letters from India 1845-49', in A.J. Guy, R.N.W. Thomas and G.J. DeGroot (ed.), *Military Miscellany* I. *Manuscripts from the Seven Years War, the First and Second Sikh Wars, and the First World War*, Publications of the Army Records Society 12, Sutton, Stroud, 1997.

Literature concerning the British Victorian Army and the British forces in India is predictably extensive. A selection of general works for the period includes C. Allen, *Soldier Sahibs. The Men Who Made the North-West Frontier*, Abacus, London, 2001; I.F.W. Beckett, *The Victorians at War*, Hambledon and London, London and New York, 2003; T.A. Heathcote, *The Indian Army. The Garrison of British Imperial India, 1822-1922*, David and Charles, Newton Abbot, 1974; T.A. Heathcote, *The Military in British India. The Development of British Land Forces in South Asia, 1600-1947*, Manchester University Press, Manchester, 1995 (includes Kitchener's reforms); R. Holmes, *Sahib. The British Soldier in India*, Harper Collins, London, 2005; W.H.G. Kingston, *Blow the Bugle, Draw the Sword. The Wars, Campaigns, Regiments and Soldiers of the British and Indian Armies During the Victorian Era, 1839-1898*, Leonaur Ltd, 2007; B. Mollo, *The Indian Army*, Blandford, Poole, 1981; H.E. Raugh, *The Victorians at War, 1815-1914. An Encyclopedia of British Military History*, ABC-CLIO Inc., Santa Barbara, 2004.

The organisation, formations, uniforms, equipment, tactics, and officers of the British forces may be further explored through M. Barthorp, *The British Army on Campaign* 1, *1816-1853*, Osprey, Oxford, 1987; W.Y. Carman (introduction), *Dress Regulations 1846. The Uniform of the British Army at the beginning of the Crimean War*, Arms and Armour Press, London, 1971; D. Featherstone, *Weapons and Equipment of the Victorian Soldier*, Arms and Armour Press, London, 1996; D.R. Headrick, *The Tools of Empire. Technology and European Imperialism in the Nineteenth Century*, Oxford University Press, Oxford, 1981; B.P. Hughes, *Firepower. Weapons Effectiveness on the Battlefield, 1630-1850*, Spellmount, Staplehurst, 1997; B. Robson, *Swords of the British Army. Regulation Patterns, 1788-1914*, National Army Museum, London, 1996; H. Strachan, *From Waterloo to Balaklava. Tactics, Technology, and the British Army, 1815-1854*, Cambridge University Press, Cambridge and New York, 1985.

For matters pertaining to nineteenth century cavalry in general, and cavalry in India in particular, the key work is The Marquis of Anglesey's *A History of the British Cavalry 1816-1919, Volume 1, 1816-1850*, Leo Cooper, London, 1973. For William Morris see M.J. Trow, *The Pocket Hercules. Captain Morris and the Charge of the Light Brigade*, Pen and Sword, Barnsley, 2006. Nolan's writings and their ramifications for contemporary cavalry controversies are discussed by J. Coulston, 'Introduction' to L.E. Nolan, *Cavalry. Its History and Tactics*, Westholme, Yardley, 2007, xi-xxxiv. Nolan's world is fully explored in H. Moyse-Bartlett, *Nolan of Balaklava and his Influence on the British Cavalry*, Leo Cooper, London, 1971. The heroic British commanders of irregular horse can be followed up in L.J. Trotter, *A Leader of Light Horse. The Life of Hodson of Hodson's Horse*, E.P. Dutton & Co., New York, 1901; A.M. Daniels, *Skinner's Horse. The History of the 1st Duke of York's Own Lancers*, Naval and Military Press Ltd, London, 2005; J. Skinner, *The Recollections of Skinner of Skinner's Horse*, Leonaur Ltd, 2006.

THE FIRST AND SECOND SIKH WARS.

CHAPTER I.

THE COUNTRY AND PEOPLE.

The Punjab.

As a geographical expression the Punjab, the country of the Sikhs, comprises the region between the five rivers from which it takes its name—the Sutlej, Beas, Ravi, Chenab, and Jhelum. But the modern political boundaries of the province have extended far beyond these limits, so as to include the cis-Sutlej districts, between that river and the Jumna, and the regions which lie beyond the Indus, known as the Derajat, reaching as far as the Suleman mountains. While the main portion of the Punjab consists of a level or undulating plain, desert in some parts and elsewhere highly cultivated tracts on the banks of the rivers, it comprises also a considerable mountainous region where the province extends into the Himalayas to the borders of Kashmir, and the lower Siwalik hills. In the south-eastern corner some offshoots of the Aravallis extend to Delhi and Gurgaon, while the Salt Range cuts off the north-western corner from the extensive plains of the south and east.

In this history we are in no way concerned with the hilly regions of the Punjab, for these were at no time embraced within the theatre of war during hostilities with the Sikhs, except for some desultory operations in the Jullundur Doab and neighbourhood. As the scene of operations was confined to the plains, the great rivers, obstacles which always play such an important part in war, were the most outstanding features of the topography of the country. The five rivers from which the Punjab takes its name, rising amid or beyond the slopes of the Himalayas, and fed in summer by the melting snows of the most lofty regions of the world, pour their waters into the Indus, which runs due south along the whole western frontier of the Province. Having steep banks and a wide alluvial bed, in which the streams frequently change their course, these rivers offer formidable obstacles to the passage of an army, particularly in June, July and August, when the water is at its greatest volume owing to the melting snow.

The whole of the vast plains of the Punjab are of alluvial formation, the soil being generally loam, from which in windy weather great quantities of sand and dust are carried in suspension by the air. In parts the rainfall is scanty and precarious, but the most populous towns and the most highly cultivated tracts lie in the eastern portion of the province about Amritsar and Lahore. Under British administration the aspect of the country has in the last sixty years undergone great changes, large tracts of what was formerly desert having been transformed by irrigation into regions of great fertility.

Climate.

The climate of the plains is one of great variations, of extreme heat and of bitter cold. From April to June the heat is as great as that of any part of India; from July to September, although the temperature is still high, it is modified by moisture, during the rainy season; after which it gradually grows colder until there are sharp frosts in December and January. In the latter month also the winter rains may be expected.

Origin of the Sikhs.

In order to comprehend fully the character of the Sikhs, the causes which led to our struggle with this great military community, and the determined opposition they were enabled to offer to our arms, it is necessary to explain their origin and progress; to give some account of the tenets of their faith; and to relate in outline their history from the earliest times until they first opposed us on the banks of the Sutlej.

The first Gurus.

In the early part of the sixteenth century Baba Nanak, a peasant of a village near Lahore, founded the religious sect which was to play such an important part in the history of India. The religion he preached was pure monotheism, and was in its original form in no way militant. At first it made little progress, and numbered few adherents during the teaching of the first two Gurus—Baba Nanak and Angad. Gradually, however, the new faith, founded on the Unity of God and the religious equality of man, made great headway, the philanthropy and tolerance of its tenets appealing to the hearts of men. Nanak claimed no miraculous power; his followers were not subjects, but "Sikhs" or disciples, and it was not until long after his death that he was invested with mystical attributes. Angad, who died in 1552, was succeeded by Amar Das, a Kshatriya, who was active in his teaching, and it is related that he was even listened to by the Emperor Akbar. After him came Ram Das, who obtained from Akbar a grant of the land now occupied by the Golden Temple at Amritsar, the holy of holies of the Sikhs.

Here he dug a tank, and began the building of the temple. His son and successor Arjan Mal completed the temple, and lived in great wealth and magnificence, widely increasing the numbers of the sect, and thus exciting the jealousy of the Mughal Government, whose dominion extended to the Indus. Although by this time a portion of the teachings of the faith had been committed to writing, it was Arjan who arranged the writings of his predecessors and compiled the *Granth*, or sacred book, whilst he inculcated in his followers fixed rules of religious and moral conduct. Sikhs were now to be found in every city and province of the Punjab; Arjan reduced their offerings to a fixed tax, and by this means and the employment of agents for collection, a kind of regular government was established, and the sect began to assume a political significance.

Foundation of Amritsar.

It was now that the new faith became subjected to that persecution which was alone necessary to transform it into a militant political force. Arjan was thrown into prison, where he died in 1606. The instigator of this persecution was Chandu Shah, the Mughal Governor of Lahore. At this time Har Govind, son of Arjan, was only eleven years of age, but he succeeded to the office of his father, whose death he was moved to avenge, and he is said either to have slain Chandu Shah himself, or to have procured his removal by the Delhi Emperor. In a short time Har Govind became a military as well as a spiritual leader.

Rise of Sikh power.

To this course of action he was probably in part influenced by the persecution of his father; and perhaps also by the teachings of the disciple Gur Das, whose writings are still extant, who declaimed against the bigotry of the Muhammadans and the asceticism of the Hindus, and who advocated the fusion of these creeds into the new religion, although he exhorted all to live peacefully and virtuously. He it was who invested the simple Nanak with the character of a mysterious prophet and of a direct instrument of the Almighty for the regeneration of the world.

Har Govind under these influences unsheathed the sword, and led his followers in the ranks of the Empire and against provincial governors and personal enemies. While his predecessors had abstained from animal food, he became a hunter and eater of flesh, in which his disciples imitated him, and, being a born leader of men, he soon organized a considerable military following. Eventually he became embroiled with the Imperial Government, and, after

Har Govind, first military leader.

For an account and translation of the *Granth* the reader is referred to "the Sikh Religion", 6 Volumes, by M. Macauliffe. 1909.

undergoing many vicissitudes, died in 1645, leaving the Sikhs a military and militant power. Thirty years later Guru Govind introduced the *Pahul*, the ceremony of initiation necessary to the attainment of Sikhism. He abolished social distinctions among his followers, in the persons in the first instance of a Brahmin, a Kshatriya, and three Sudras, whom he declared to be the *Khalsa*—the saved or liberated—investing them with the title of Singh, meaning lion, and metaphorically warrior, by which all Sikhs have since been known. Sikhs were to bathe from time to time in the sacred pool at Amritsar, and their locks were to be unshorn. Their energies were to be given to the profession of arms, and merit was to be gained in war alone. Govind thus united religious fervour with warlike temper, and entertained the design of founding a new empire on the ruins of declining Mughal power. Coming into conflict with the Imperial Government, he was driven from the Punjab early in the eighteenth century, but, on the death of Aurangzeb, he was summoned to camp by Bahadur Shah, and entered the imperial service. Eventually he proceeded south to Nander on the Godavery, where he was killed in 1708 by the sons of a Pathan whom he had slain. Govind was the greatest of the successors of Nanak, and to this day the Sikhs perform pilgrimages to Nander, where there is a colony of the Khalsa, and where they have erected a temple second only in sanctity to the Golden Temple of Amritsar.

Govind Singh.

Govind Singh nominated Banda, a native of Southern India, as his successor, to whose standard the Sikhs flocked when he reached the north. At Sirhind he defeated and slew the Musalman Governor, and then established a stronghold below Sirmur between the Sutlej and the Jumna, and harried the Saharanpur District. The Emperor Bahadur Shah marched against him, but Banda had already been defeated, and withdrew into the hills near Jammu. In 1713 the Mughal Viceroy marched against Banda, but was defeated by the Sikhs near Gurdaspur, where they had built a stronghold. Finally, however, the Sikhs, assailed by fresh forces, were vanquished, and Banda surrendered at Gurdaspur, and was taken to Delhi, where he and many of his followers were put to death. Subsequently the sect was vigorously persecuted, and the Sikhs were suppressed for a generation. In his *History of the Sikhs*, Cunningham thus recapitulates the story of their vicissitudes up to this point :

Vicissitudes of Sikhs.

> Thus, at the end of two centuries, had the Sikh faith become established as a prevailing sentiment and guiding principle to work its way in the world. Nanak disengaged his little society of worshippers from Hindu idolatry and Muhammadan superstition,

Two centuries of progress.

and placed them free on a broad basis of religious and moral purity; Amar Das preserved the infant community from declining into a sect of quietists or ascetics; Arjan gave his increasing followers a written rule of conduct and a civil organization; Har Govind added the use of arms and a military system and Govind Singh bestowed upon them a distinct political existence, and inspired them with the desire of being socially free and naturally independent. No further legislation was required; a firm persuasion had been elaborated, and a vague feeling had acquired consistence as an active principle. Sikhism arose where fallen and corrupt Brahminical doctrines were most strongly acted on by the vital and spreading Muhammadan belief."

It may be added that, as in the case of other sects whose vicissitudes are recorded in the history of the world, religious persecution gave to Sikhism that vivifying influence which was the necessary stimulus to permanence and progress. The weakness of the declining Mughal Empire after the death of Aurangzeb afforded a favourable opportunity for the rise of other nationalities in India during the eighteenth century. The Mahrattas established their power in Southern India, raided as far as Delhi, and watered their horses on the banks of the Sutlej. The Persian Nadir Shah marched to the Mughal capital; and his invasion was followed by the incursions of Ahmad Shah Abdali. Both these conquerors were harassed on the line of march by the Sikhs, who established themselves on the Ravi, and raised the fort of Ram Raoni near Amritsar, where the able leader Jassa Singh proclaimed the birth of a new power, the army of the Khalsa.

Jassa Singh, leader of the Khalsa.

In 1756, however, Taimur, son of the Durani Governor of Lahore, attacked the Sikhs, levelled their fort, and filled the sacred tanks with the ruins of their buildings. The Sikhs under Jassa Singh fled to the hills and when the Afghans retired, arose in great numbers, seized Lahore, and coined money there with the inscription "Coined by the Grace of the Khalsa in the country of Ahmad, conquered by Jassa." After capturing Delhi the Mahrattas drove the Sikhs from Lahore, but being defeated at Panipat in 1760, by the combined Afghan and Delhi forces, the Mahratta tide was stemmed for a time. The Afghan Ahmad Shah now retired again to Kabul, leaving deputies at Lahore and Sirhind, but the Sikhs gained additional strength in the absence of regular Government, and erected forts; among others, Charat Singh, grandfather of Ranjit Singh, established a stronghold north of Lahore at Gujranwala. In 1761 they assembled in force at Amritsar, performed their ablutions in the restored sacred pool, and ravaged the country on either side of the Sutlej; but in the following year they were dispersed with great slaughter by Ahmad Shah in his sixth invasion; and their chief place of Amritsar was again polluted and destroyed.

Reverses appeared only to add fuel to the flames. With a great accession of numbers, inspired by the lust of revenge and the hope of ambition, the Sikhs again rose 40,000 strong, plundered Kasur and Maler Kotla, and marched on Sirhind, where they defeated the Afghan Governor, destroyed Sirhind, where the mother and children of Govind Singh had been murdered a hundred years before, and spread over the country from the Sutlej to the Jumna. During the succeeding year the Afghans retired from Lahore, where the Sikhs established themselves, obliging their Musalman prisoners in chains to wash the foundations of their demolished mosques with the blood of hogs. The whole country from the Jhelum to the Sutlej was added to the Sikh dominion, and partitioned among the chiefs and their followers, who then assembled at Amritsar, and proclaimed their rule. During the next two years the political system of the Sikh Commonwealth was established, resolving itself into a confederate feudalism in which every Sikh was free, their moving principle being warlike sway and their instrument the sword—the steel of Govind. Each year they assembled at Amritsar.

Sikhs established at Lahore.

With varying fortunes the power of the Sikh confederacies was consolidated, and in 1785 we find them predominant from the frontiers of Oudh to the Indus. Their prestige is illustrated in the story of the traveller Foster who describes the alarm caused to a petty chief and his people by the appearance of two Sikh horsemen under the walls of their fort, and the assiduous services and respectful attention which the same number of troopers met with from the local authorities of Garhwal, and from the assembled wayfarers at a place of public reception.

The invasion of the Punjab in 1798 by Shah Zeman brought into eminence the youthful chief, Ranjit Singh, who was invested by the Afghan with royal power at Lahore. Henceforth the history of Ranjit Singh is the history of the Sikhs until they came into conflict with the British.

Ranjit Singh.

In 1788 the Sikhs asked the aid of the English against the Mahrattas, who were encroaching on their dominions ; but in 1803 we find 5,000 of this warlike people opposing, in the ranks of the Mahrattas, the arms of Lake at Aligarh. They afterwards submitted to Lake, and assisted him in the operations of the following year ; while these friendly relations culminated in an amicable engagement with Ranjit Singh in 1808. That great chief moulded the congeries of confederacies into a nation, established his ascendancy throughout the Punjab, and in 1809 concluded a treaty with Sir David Ochterlony, handing over the Sikhs between the Sutlej and the Jumna to British protection, and confining his own dominion to the country north and west of the former river. Under Ranjit Singh the Empire spread to the Derajat on the west, to Kashmir on the north, and to Multan on the south. The warlike character of this great people was maintained in their struggles with the Afghans, and their chief had sufficient acumen to avoid conflict with his powerful English neighbours.

Like the Mahrattas and other native powers of India, the Sikhs took into their employ European military adventurers. In 1822 the French Generals Ventura and Allard reached Lahore, and were given employment. "It has been usual" says Cunningham "to attribute the superiority of the Sikh Army to the labours of these two officers, and of their subsequent coadjutors Generals Court and Avitabile; but in truth the Sikh owes his excellence as a soldier to his own hardihood of character, to that spirit of adaptation which distinguishes every new people, and to the feeling of a common interest and destiny implanted in him by his great teachers." They were moreover brought up in the great school of war and in that struggle for existence which by the law of nature involves the survival of the fittest.

The Sikh regular army.

The early forces of the Sikhs were composed of horsemen, but they soon adopted the matchlock in place of the bow and spear. After his visit to Lord Lake's Army in 1805, Ranjit Singh began to form battalions of regular infantry, giving them good pay and directing personal attention to their dress and equipment; and by degrees the infantry came to be regarded as the principal arm. The European officers thus found excellent material into which to introduce western methods of discipline and training. The general constitution of a Sikh regiment was a commandant and adjutant, with subordinate officers to each company. The men were paid by deputies of the paymaster, the rolls being checked by clerks who daily noted down whether the men were present or absent. Each regiment had a Granthi, and the *granth* was deposited near the regimental colour. Light tents and pack animals were allowed for each battalion, and two cooks for each company. The men lived generally in barracks.

The Sikhs and the British.

The advance of British power and the extension of British dominions naturally alarmed the Sikhs. On the east the British border was advanced to the Sutlej, on the south Sind was annexed after Sir Charles Napier's campaign, and British armies occupied Afghanistan, thus hemming in the Punjab on the west also. But although Ranjit Singh viewed the rise of British Empire with alarm, he was sufficiently wise to realize the futility of armed opposition, and during his lifetime he repressed the warlike aspirations of those Sikhs who wished to oppose the British, who, the great chief foresaw, would soon colour the whole map of India red. In June 1839, Ranjit Singh died. He had consolidated a kingdom, and wrested the Province of Peshawar from the Afghans; he had armed and disciplined a hundred thousand men, and had raised a numerous artillery; and in his wisdom he had known how to keep peace with the English. But his death was the signal for internal dissensions, and a mutinous spirit arose in the army which in course of time rendered the troops the principal political power in the state. A condition of military anarchy supervened; the Khalsa were impatient at seeing the red line enclosing their territory on every side, and although they aided to some extent the avenging army in the march to Afghanistan after the Kabul disaster of 1841, a conflict became inevitable, in view of the overbearing character of the Sikh soldiery, and the geographical and political necessity for British expansion.

Anarchy after Ranjit Singh's death.

After several changes in the succession following on the death of Ranjit Singh his reputed son Dhalip Singh eventually succeeded, but being an infant, power was vested in the Maharani aided by a minister. One minister after another succeeed to power, and the court became a centre of intrigue and debauchery in which good government was impossible. In the middle of 1845, when the Sikh anarchy became acute owing to these causes and the increasing power of the army, Sirdar Jowahir Singh was Minister. He appears to have been a drunken debauchee, and in September he was put to death by the troops, who thus confirmed the ascendancy they had long in reality held. They dictated terms to the Sikh Government, and while they declared that they desired peace, there was a strong party clamorous for war, and they said that if the English troops marched to Ludhiana and Ferozepore, they would march too. The Sikh Army had, in fact, now entirely usurped the functions of Government; and the Lahore Durbar eventually agreed with the war party, in the fulfilment of whose views they foresaw the destruction of Sikh military power, and hoped thus to maintain their own position on the discomfiture of the vanquished.

CHAPTER II.

THE CAUSES OF WAR.

British prestige.

It is perhaps unnecessary to relate at length the immediate causes which led up to the conflict with the Sikhs, to detail the intrigues of the various leaders, and the circumstances of the state of anarchy, characterised by savage and bloody crimes, which ensued when the strong hand of Ranjit Singh was removed by death. The soldiery of the Punjab had witnessed from afar the disaster of the retreat from Kabul. It is true that they had seen also the advance of the victorious army, and the triumph of its return, which was celebrated with barbaric pageantry at Peshawar; but the British army had lost the prestige of invincibility which it gained during a hundred years of victory throughout peninsular India. The Sikhs not unnaturally feared the aggression of their powerful neighbour, and viewed with apprehension the British advance to the Sutlej. This advance had been carried out contrary to the policy of 1809, when the Jumna had formed the north-western boundary of British India, and the province of Sirhind became a buffer and neutral state separating it from the trans-Sutlej Punjab. Ludhiana had, indeed, long been occupied by a British detachment, but this, and the Subathu garrison, was the sole outpost of the advancing empire in that direction up to the period of the Afghan war in 1838. In that year 12,000 men assembled at Ferozepore, which had passed under British protection three years before, for the advance into Khorasan; and a division of troops was left there during the campaign. To support these two posts of Ludhiana and Ferozepore, a reserve was posted at Ambala in 1842. The occupation of Sind in the meantime threatened Sikh territory at Multan, and a bridge-of-boats was thrown across the Sutlej near Ferozepore, while small steamers plied on the river. The Sikhs then had come to think their independence menaced and war inevitable, while on their side the English expected to be forced into a collision with the overbearing soldiery of the Khalsa. The situation was naturally viewed from a different aspect from the two banks of the Sutlej; the Sikhs feared, and all India expected, that the power which, like Aaron's rod, had swallowed up all the other States of India, would now direct attention to further conquests; the British saw that in the predominance of the Sikh army the

The British advance.

machinery of regular Government would be broken up, and that bands of marauders would infest the country and endanger the peace. They naturally took measures for the protection of their frontier, which were misconstrued by the Sikhs into a menace to their liberty. It appeared only natural to orientals that the power which dominated the whole of peninsular India and Hindustan should desire to extend its territory to the geographical and historic boundary of India which was marked by the Hindu Kush.

British troops on the frontier.

Up to 1838 the troops on the frontier were—one regiment at Subathu and two at Ludhiana. Lord Ellenborough formed new stations at Ambala, Kasauli and Simla, and placed in all some 14,000 men and 48 field guns on the border. The next Governor-General, Sir Henry Hardinge, increased the force to 32,000 men, with 68 field guns, in support of which 10,000 men with artillery were at Meerut.

The Sikh Chiefs.

Meanwhile the chiefs of the Punjab, jealous of one another and fearing the power of the army, urged hostilities with the British in hopes of bringing about the fall of the martial power of the Khalsa, and the consequent, or at least subsequent, establishment oftheir own position and authority. The chiefs Lal Singh and Tej Singh urged them to war, and the men would assemble in groups in their camps and cantonments, and meet round the tomb of Ranjit Singh to talk of the battle in prospect and to swear fidelity to the Khalsa. In November 1845 it might have been perceived that war was inevitable. During that month the Sikh troops began to move in detachments from Lahore, and on the 11th December their army under Tej Singh and Lal Singh crossed the Sutlej between Hariki and Kasur.

Sikh military power.

From the short history which has been given of the rise and progress of the Sikhs, the motives by which this great people were inspired, and the prestige they had acquired under the rule of Ranjit Singh and in their struggles with the Afghans, it will be understood what a formidable power was arrayed against the British, who had hitherto found the peoples of India a comparatively easy conquest. Yet the mistake so frequently made by British authorities was made in this instance also. The British Government and army despised their enemies, and anticipated a victory no less easy than those gained in Southern India and in Hindustan. They appreciated neither the martial and religious spirit, the unity of feeling in the army, nor the strength of the training and organization they had undergone under Ranjit Singh, the Lion of the Punjab. The information as to the composition of the army of the Khalsa is not very complete. A detail of Ranjit Singh's infantry in 1835 was published in the *Delhi Gazette.* It shows 34 battalions, including some composed of Purbiahs and Gurkhas, and it mentions that 12 more battalions were in process of formation. A traveller in the Punjab the following year numbered the Sikh infantry at 40 battalions, each with 1,000 rank and file. He wrote :—" The privates are tall, thin men with good features; they are capable of enduring the fatigue of long marches for several days in succession; so that it has become a byword that the Punjabis have iron legs....the dress of the Sikh infantry consists of a blue turban with one end loose and spread to cover the head, back of the neck, and shoulders, and regulation coat in imitation of the French ; trousers of blue linen, tight at the ankles, musket, pouch, etc., with black leather cross belt." Their muskets were stated to be " of very inferior stamp, incapable of throwing a ball to any distance, and on quick and repeated discharges liable to burst; their firing is bad, as their sole object appears to be to aim at a regular and simultaneous volley, punishment awaiting any, the report of whose piece is a second too late. The consequence is, in their hurry to deliver their fire as one report, they never bring their muskets to the proper level, and their cartridges are all thrown upwards at an angle of about 30 degrees. On parade they give utterance to abusive expressions, striking freely any of a rank inferior to their own. The commandant canes the adjutant, who in turn strikes the officers at the head of companies, who again vent their ill-humour on the non-commissioned and privates......On their marches they encamp very regularly; and I saw 30,000 men, the Army of Peshawar, moved with as much facility as a single regiment on this (the British) side of the Sutlej. No wheeled carriage is allowed, and their own bazaars contain all they require. The Sikh Cavalry amounts to about 40,000, all irregular with the exception of three regiments under the command of Monsieur Allard."

Ranjit Singh's Army in 1836.

The cavalry appear to have been very inferior to the infantry, and were badly mounted and equipped. The Maharaja had some very good field guns, but his battering train was of no value. The guns were badly horsed, the animals being undersized, and the harness was of an inferior description. Ranjit Singh died in 1839, and it is not probable that the army improved after his death. Another statement says there were 15,000 regular cavalry, the famous " Ghorcharas." And besides the regular troops that have been detailed, there were the levies of various Sirdars, amounting perhaps to some 80,000 men.

Policy of the Governor-General.

Sir Henry Hardinge, the Governor General, was himself a soldier holding the rank of Lieutenant-General, and had served under Wellington in the Peninsular War. The state of affairs in the Punjab caused him to move from Calcutta to the Upper Provinces in the autumn of 1845, a step he had already decided on in June, when he wrote in a Minute to his Council:—

> To carry the pacific policy of the Government of India into effect, we have been content to suffer great inconvenience, considerable expense, and some risk, necessarily caused by the presence of a large disorganised Sikh force on the frontier, requiring, on our part, an army to be assembled for the protection of our frontier, and in close contact with that of the Sikhs. We have never relinquished the hope that some amelioration may eventually take place, affording the prospect of a re-establishment of a Sikh Government, able to carry on its ordinary functions. We have never abandoned the expectation that, after anarchy and military violence have long prevailed, these disorders, having reached their maturity, might subside, worn out and exhausted by their own violence; or that some man of superior capacity and master mind might appear amongst them, able to control this mutinous army, and to reconstruct a strong Sikh Government.

The correspondence of Major Broadfoot[1], Agent to the Governor-General on the North-West Frontier, depicted the state of anarchy, riot, and debauchery prevalent at this time in the Lahore Durbar. Writing to the Secret Committee, on the river Ganges off Monghyr on the 30th September 1845, Sir H. Hardinge said:—

> The forbearance of the Government of India has been carried to an extent beyond that which has been customary. Every military precaution has, however, been taken; advice and warnings have been repeatedly conveyed to the Lahore Government in the plainest language; even the risk of giving offence by such language has been incurred, rather than fail in the essential point of clearly defining the nature of our policy, and of having that policy well understood. I am convinced that our desire to see the Maharaja's Government re-established on a basis of independence and strength is well known to the most influential and leading chiefs. Their personal interests endangered by the democratic revolution so successfully accomplished by the Sikh Army, may induce those chiefs to exert all their efforts to compel the British Government to interfere; but these attempts and any danger resulting from them will be attributable, not to our forbearance but to their personal fears for life and property. You may be assured that whilst I shall omit no precautions and be prepared for any event, I shall persevere in the direct course I have hitherto pursued, of endeavouring by moderation, good faith, and friendly advice to avert the necessity of British interference by force of arms in the affairs of the Punjab.

Anarchy at Lahore.

On the 21st September the Sikh Minister, Jowahir Singh, was put to death by the soldiery at Lahore; the Rani was declared Regent, and, as the Governor-General wrote from Agra on the 23rd October,

[1]Appointed in November 1844.

the government if such it could be called was carried on at the dictation of the *Punchayats* of the Army. The Army at the same time announced, in forbidding the Diwan to communicate direct with the British Agent, that in future no letter to the English was to be written until the army had deliberated on its contents. They declared, however, that they desired peace, but that if troops marched from our stations to Ludhiana and Ferozepore, they would march too; if not, that each power should keep its own territory in peace.[1]

British military movements.

It has been asserted that the outbreak of hostilities with the Sikhs was in great measure due to their alarm at the attitude of the British Government, and the movement of British troops, which were considered a menace to their independence. With regard to this the Governor-General wrote from Ambala on the 2nd December 1845, that in consideration of the improbability of the Sikh Army crossing the Sutlej, he had determined that no movement should be made towards the river by the forces from Ambala and Meerut, and that he had postponed any change in the present distribution of troops. He had on the 26th November met Sir Hugh Gough, the Commander-in-Chief and Major Broadfoot at Karnal, and in pursuance of this policy he had ordered the countermarch of the 9th Lancers, which the former had directed to proceed from Meerut to Ambala. He had, however, made certain preparations, news of which, probably in an exaggerated form, no doubt reached the Lahore Durbar. Writing to the Commander-in-Chief on the 24th October, the Governor-General said:—"On or before the 12th November arrangements will have been made by which the Commissariat Department will be prepared to equip nearly two-thirds of the force at, and in advance of Meerut, with the necessary means of marching at the shortest notice. In the present state of our relations with the Lahore Government, I do not anticipate the probability of any emergencies arising which can require the army to take the field this autumn. Nevertheless, having to deal with a mutinous Sikh army, which has usurped the functions of the government, and whose caprice may at any time force on a rupture with our forces on the frontier, I have deemed it advisable to be prepared with the means of movement to the extent noted in the margin, and as it is desirable that the arrangement should be made on the most economical scale, the whole will be hired at the halting rates."

7 Troops Horse Artillery.
6 Companies Foot Artillery.
4 Light Field Batteries.
2 Regiments Dragoons.
3 Regiments Light Cavalry.
5 Regiments European Infantry.
13 Regiments Native Infantry.
6,100 Sappers and Miners.
2 Regiments Irregular Cavalry.

[1] Major Broadfoot to the Secretary to the Government of India, 26th September 1845.

In his letter of the 2nd December already alluded to, the Governor-General states that he has made all preparations for the eventuality of war, including the intention of bringing up, from stations in rear of Meerut, the troops noted in the margin which, with the exception of the artillery, would be cantoned at or near Kimra, 28 miles from Ludhiana, and 10 miles in advance of Sirhind. At the same time he wrote :—

Preparations for war.

4 Companies European Artillery from Cawnpore.
1 Troop Horse Artillery.
4 Regiments Native Cavalry.
5 Regiments Native Infantry.

I shall not consider the march of the Sikh troops in hostile array towards the banks of the Sutlej as a cause justifying hostilities, if no actual violation of our frontier should occur. The same privilege which we take to adopt precautionary measures on our side must be conceded to them. Every forbearance shall be shown to a weak Government struggling for existence against its own soldiers in a state of successful mutiny.

The Sikhs had in the meantime been endeavouring to tamper with the British native army on an extensive scale, appealing to their religious prejudices and making lavish promises of promotion and reward. But the native army remained loyal to the British Government.

From a letter written by Major Broadfoot to the Commander-in-Chief on the 20th November, it would appear that hostilities were imminent, although both the Agent and the Governor-General seem to have considered up to the last moment that the Sikhs would not cross the Sutlej. On that date the Agent wrote :—" During the night of 17th the chiefs had agreed on and the Durbar had ordered in writing the following plan of operations :—The Army was to be divided into seven divisions, one to remain at Lahore, and the rest to proceed against Rupar, Ludhiana, Hariki, Ferozepore, and Sind, while one was to proceed to Peshawar ; and a force under Raja Gulab Singh was to be sent to Attock. Each division was to be of 8,000 to 12,000 men : against Ferozepore under Sham Singh Atariwala ; against Hariki, Raja Lal Singh ; against Ludhiana, Sirdar Tej Singh, the new Commander-in-Chief, and against Rupar, a brother of Sena Singh Mujitia. The force under Sham Singh was to be 4,000 horse, and two brigades of infantry, with guns ; under Raja Lal Singh, 4,500 horse and two infantry brigades; under Sirdar Tej Singh, four brigades of infantry (one of them irregulars and one new levies) and 1,000 horse.

Sikh movements.

In spite of this virtual declaration of war, the Governor-General retained his optimistic opinions, and on December 4th wrote from Ambala to the Secret Committee:—

The Governor-General reviews the situation.

The Rani and Sirdars[1] are becoming more and more urgent that the Army should advance to the frontier, believing that in the present posture of affairs the only hope of saving their lives and prolonging their power is to be found in bringing about a collision with the British forces. The Sikh Army moves with evident reluctance. My own impression remains unaltered. I do not expect that the troops will come as far as the banks of the Sutlej, or that any positive acts of aggression will be committed; but it is evident that the Rani and the Chiefs are, for their own preservation, endeavouring to raise a storm, which, when raised, they will be powerless either to direct or allay. I shall await the reply[2] from Lahore to Major Broadfoot's last communication to the Vakil. If the reply from the ostensible Government, acting under the control and at the dictation of the Army, is hostile, I shall at once order up troops from Meerut and other stations to the support of our advanced army, persevering up to the last moment in the sincere desire to avoid hostilities.

It may be said that the Governor-General's view of the situation was neither justified by the march of events at Lahore, nor by considerations of military exigency. In his anxiety to avoid war he imperilled the military situation, exposed himself to the chance of defeat in detail, and the small garrisons of Ferozepore and Ludhiana to the risk of a disaster which was only averted by the enemy's lack of enterprise. Even policy itself was not served by an exhibition of military weakness on the frontier where a display of armed force might have reduced the Khalsa to submission, and thus averted hostilities. The situation immediately prior to the war may perhaps be compared with that in South Africa before the outbreak of hostilities in 1899. Sir H. Hardinge considered, rightly or wrongly, that military preparations would evoke hostile action; and as a statesman he was obliged to utilise all peaceful means before the resort to arms; the event proved hostilities to be inevitable, where a show of strength at the outset might have averted them.

In connection with these remarks, the following extract from a letter written by Sir H. Hardinge to Major Broadfoot in June 1845 is interesting:—

Every despatch from England inculcates a pacific policy; and we must show that military men in the conduct of affairs usually transacted by civil officers, on which peace or war hangs by a slender thread, can be trusted for their prudence as safely as those who, in the event of war would have no military reputation to gratify

[1] Tej Singh and Lal Singh.

[2] No reply appears to have been received.

A strong Sikh Government as our advanced guard, occupying the five rivers between the Indus and the Sutlej, is a sound military and political arrangement. The advantage is evident, and British India, already overgrown, requires no addition by the appropriation of territory so long possessed by an ally whose interests have always been opposed to those of the British Government's enemies."

Disposition of the British forces.

On the outbreak of war the British forces were disposed as follows: At Ferozepore, an exposed and unfortified cantonment, under Major General Sir John Littler :—

2 Troops Horse Artillery,
2 Light Field Batteries,
62nd Foot,
8th Native Light Cavalry,
3rd Irregular Cavalry,
12th, 14th, 27th, 33rd, 54th and 63rd Bengal Native Infantry,

altogether some 7,000 fighting men.

At Ludhiana, higher up the Sutlej, and about 80 miles distant, was a small fort with a garrison under Brigadier H. M. Wheeler, C. B.—

2 Troops Horse Artillery.
50th Foot.
1 Regiment Native Cavalry.
11th, 26th, 42nd, 48th and 73rd Bengal Native Infantry.

About 5,000 fighting men.

At Ambala, 80 miles from Ludhiana, and 160 from Ferozepore, the garrison was under Major-General Sir W. R. Gilbert. :—

3rd Light Dragoons.
9th, 31st, and 80th Foot.
4th and 5th Light Cavalry.
Governor-General's Bodyguard.
16th, 24th, 41st, 45th, and 47th Bengal Native Infantry.

At Kasauli—the 29th Foot.

At Subathu—the 1st Bengal European Regiment.

Altogether 10,000 fighting men.

At Meerut there was a force of 9,000 men and 26 guns, including the 9th and 16th Lancers, 3rd Light Cavalry, and 10th Foot.

The Nasiri and Sirmur battalions of Gurkhas were near Simla and Dehra Dun respectively.

From the records of the time it would appear that the native regiments of the Bengal Army had for some time been undergoing that deterioration of discipline which culminated a dozen years later in the great mutiny. They were no longer the soldiers of Lake and Hastings, the heroes of Laswari, of Seringapatam, and of expeditions overseas. In the snows and deserts of Afghanistan and amid the bloody scenes of the Khurd Kabul Pass and Jagdalak they had lost much of their ardour and prestige, while they had seen the defeat and slaughter of their hitherto invincible European comrades. They fought well on occasion, when led by their British officers and stimulated by the presence and example of British regiments; but their training and their discipline left much to be desired; they feared the Sikhs, and their demeanour in action was uncertain. This was exemplified by their behaviour at Mudki and Ferozeshahr, where they shirked the fight; although they retrieved their reputation in subsequent actions.

The native troops.

The characteristics of the leaders of the opposing forces will manifest themselves as the drama is unfolded. On the Sikh side there were commanders undoubtedly brave, but possessing neither that moral courage which alone can command success, nor that confidence in the prospects of their cause which is so great an incentive to victory; while the honest purpose of some of them was at least open to imputation.

Leaders of the opposing forces.

The British had many leaders who had graduated in the great school of war, among them men with the experience of the Peninsula and Waterloo, and of the Gwalior campaign and Afghanistan. Sir Hugh Gough, the veteran officer in chief command, was a brave and daring soldier, a fine leader of men possessing the confidence of his troops. Like all great leaders, he knew that the only way to command success was to press the fight to a finish, and he had not that fear of a heavy casualty list which has possessed so many of his successors. He had, in fact, those great qualities of character which make for success, however dearly-bought it may be.

CHAPTER III.

THE FIRST SIKH WAR. MUDKI AND FEROZESHAHR.

(*Map 2.*)

The Sikhs cross the Sutlej.

On the 11th December 1845, the Sikh Army, nearly 50,000 strong, with 100 guns, under Sirdars Lal Singh and Tej Singh, crossed the Sutlej in the vicinity of Hariki, and took up an entrenched position at the village of Ferozeshahr, 10 miles east of Ferozepore, which place was threatened but not attacked. Sir John Littler had thrown up a line of entrenchments, and showed a bold front; but it is difficult to understand why the Sikhs did not overwhelm this isolated garrison. Cunningham states that Lal Singh and Tej Singh had for their object not the destruction of a British division, but to get their own forces dispersed. But this idea of the treachery of the Sikh leaders and their sinister designs towards the Khalsa appears to have been carried to an absurd extent. Having once taken the field, it is not probable that they were guided in their actions by any such ulterior and far-fetched motives.

Advance of the British.

The Governor-General had at length, on the 8th December, given directions for the Ambala force to move forward on the 11th for the relief of Ferozepore, he himself accompanying the Commander-in-Chief with the army, which he joined near Ludhiana. The garrison of the latter place, with the exception of a small force left to man the fort, also joined the advancing army, which arrived at Mudki on the 18th December 1845, after a harassing march of 150 miles. The troops from the different places in the Sirhind Division had been directed to move by forced marches on Bassian, where supplies had been collected, and on the 13th December the Governor-General issued a proclamation[1] amounting to a declaration of war. The marches to the point of concentration, and from thence to Mudki, were long and difficult, along roads of heavy sand, where water was scarce and the short halts scarcely admitted of either cooking or repose, while the air was so charged with dust that the troops suffered severely from this cause and the thirst it created.

[1]Appendix I.

After a rapid march of 150 miles in six days, the British troops detailed in the margin,[1] under General Sir Hugh Gough, G.C.B., Commander-in-Chief, arrived at Mudki, 20 miles from Ferozepore, on the 18th December, and soon after noon took up their encamping-ground in front of the village. On arriving at Wadni information had been received that the Sikhs had detached a portion of their army to oppose the British and their advanced parties retired in the morning before the cavalry piquets. The British troops were in a state of exhaustion after their long march when at about 3 P.M. it was reported that the Sikhs were advancing to the attack, to the number of 15,000 to 20,000 infantry, the same number of cavalry, and 40 guns. These numbers appear to have been over-estimated and they had probably only some 4.000 or 5,000 infantry, besides 10,000 horse and 22 guns. The British troops were hurried into action, the cavalry and horse artillery being pushed to the front while the infantry and field batteries followed in support.

Arrival at Mudki.

One division under Major-General Sir Harry Smith.
Brigade under Major-General Sir John M'Caskill.
Brigade under Major-General W. Gilbert.
5 Troops Horse Artillery.
2 Light field batteries.
1 Cavalry Division.

The country was flat, covered with low, and in some places thick jungle, but the first part of the action was fought on open ground with occasional large acacia trees, into which the enemy climbed, and inflicted heavy loss by their fire on the British troops. The mounted troops quickly checked the enemy's advance.

Battle of Mudki, 18th December, 1845.

While the 9th Irregular Cavalry and part of the 4th Light Cavalry under Brigadier Mactier threatened the enemy's right, the 3rd Light Dragoons, with the 2nd Brigade of cavalry, consisting of the Body-Guard and 5th Light Cavalry, with the remainder of the 4th Light Cavalry, swept round the left of the Sikh Army and along the whole rear of its infantry and guns, temporarily silencing the latter and putting the hostile cavalry to flight. During these operations the cavalry got into thick bush, and lost severely from the fire of the Sikh infantry, which, together with their artillery, was screened behind the jungle and the sandy hillocks which dotted the plain.

Cavalry action.

In the meantime the twelve British battalions formed from echelon of brigades into line and advanced to the attack, the horse artillery was in support, and moved close up to the jungle, where the enemy's foot assailed the advancing battalions. Night was now closing in, and the jungle was so thick and the dust that filled the

The infantry attack.

[1] For detail of the Army of the Sutlej see Appendix II.

air so darkening, that little could be seen. With their flanks protected by cavalry, however, the 50th Foot leading, the British infantry rushed upon the enemy, engaged them with the bayonet, drove them back with slaughter, and took 17 guns. The fight was maintained during an hour and a half of dim starlight, amid a cloud of dust which obscured the air, until the battle ceased with the retirement of the enemy upon their main body at Ferozeshahr. In this action the British casualties amounted to 872 killed and wounded. The enemy's loss was not ascertained.

Retirement of the Sikhs.

On the morning of the 19th December the British wounded and nineteen captured guns were brought in under cover of the cavalry outposts, which were pushed forward for this purpose. Information was received that the enemy was moving out to the attack, and the troops were marched out to a position in front of Mudki; but as the Sikhs did not appear, they turned in again at one o'clock, and the afternoon was undisturbed. At night the army was reinforced by the arrival of the 29th Foot, the 1st European Light Infantry, and a division of heavy guns; the 29th having marched from Kasauli and the 1st Europeans from Subathu, at the rate of from 20 to 30 miles daily. This brought the British to a strength of 16,700 men and 69 guns.

Advance on Ferozeshahr.

No movement took place on the 20th, but on the 21st the British Army under Sir Hugh Gough with Sir H. Hardinge (who had volunteered his services) as second-in-command, moved out in the direction of the Sikh position at Ferozeshahr, leaving the sick and wounded at Mudki. Instructions had been sent the previous evening to Sir John Littler, who commanded the troops at Ferozepore, to effect a junction with the Commander-in-Chief in the attack on the Sikh position, which was in an entrenched camp in the form of a deep horseshoe round the village of Ferozeshahr, equidistant from both Mudki and Ferozepore.

Cavalry and Artillery
as at Mudki.
Infantry.
First Division, Major-General Sir Harry Smith.
18th Brigade, Brigadier Hicks.
31st Foot.
2[illegible]th and [illegible]7th Native Infantry.
2nd Brigade, Brigadier Ryan
50th Foot.
42nd and 48th N. I.
Second Division, Major-General Sir Walter Raleigh Gilbert.

The British Army under Sir Hugh Gough, composed as detailed in the margin, struck camp at 3 A. M. on the 21st December 1845, and marched an hour later, moving in the direction of Ferozeshahr. Progress was slow, the army moving on a broad front and the morning being dark. It was not until they approached the Sikh position that news was received that Sir John Littler's

1st Brigade, Brigadier Taylor.
29th Foot.
80th Foot.
41st N. I.
2nd Brigade, Brigadier McLaren.
1st European Light Infantry.
16th and 45th N. I.
Third Division, Brigadier Wallace.
9th Foot.
2nd, 26th and 73rd N. I.

force had not marched until 8 A. M. Sir Hugh Gough, ever fiery and impetuous, wished to attack without waiting for this reinforcement; but Sir H. Hardinge exercising his authority as Governor-General, decided that there should be no attack until the junction was effected.

Major-General Sir John Littler.
2 troops Horse Artillery.
1½ Light Field Battery.
8th Light Cavalry.
3rd Irregular Cavalry.
1st Brigade, Brigadier Reed.
62nd Foot.
12th N. I.
14th N. I.
2nd Brigade.
Brigadier Ashburnham.
33rd N. I.
44th N. I.
54th N. I.
Det. Sappers.

The junction with Sir John Littler was effected at 1-30 P.M., when the Army was again placed at the disposal of the Commander-in-Chief by Sir Henry Hardinge, who resumed his post as second-in-command. While the troops halted for breakfast, Sir Hugh Gough rode forward to make a personal reconnaissance of the enemy's position.

The army was now drawn up in front of the southern and western faces of the Sikh position. The 2nd Division was on the right, its outer flank protected by a troop of horse artillery and the 3rd Light Dragoons and 4th Light Cavalry. The 3rd Division, separated from the 2nd by the massed guns under Brigadier Brooke (two troops horse artillery, two 9-pounder batteries, and a battery 8-inch howitzers) occupied the centre; Sir John Littler's Division from Ferozepore was on the left, having on its right flank two troops horse artillery, the Body Guard, and the 5th Light Cavalry; and on its left two 9-pounder batteries, the 3rd Irregular Cavalry, and the 8th Light Cavalry; Sir Harry Smith's Division formed a general reserve in rear of the centre. His two brigades were separated by nearly a mile of ground occupied by the mass of artillery, the 1st Brigade being on the right.

The right attack was led by Sir Hugh Gough; the left by Sir Henry Hardinge. Much valuable time was lost in making arrangements for the attack, and the forward movement did not take place until 4 P.M., a late hour to begin a battle, particularly on the shortest day in the year when only some two hours of daylight remained. Sir Harry Smith states[1] that none of the Generals of

[1] Autobiography of Sir Harry Smith. London, John Murray, 1903.

Division "were made the least aware of how or what or where they were to attack. The army was one unwieldy battalion under one commanding officer who had not been granted the power of ubiquity."

Battle of Ferozeshahr, 21st December 1845.

The action began with an artillery duel, while the British infantry lay down in order of battle; but as the Sikh guns proved superior both in numbers and weight of metal, the British artillery was moved to a second position nearer to the enemy's entrenchments, the infantry advancing at the same time. Littler's Division now advanced to attack the Sikh right, the approach to the enemy's works being made under a galling and destructive fire. The troops approached to within 150 yards of the Sikh battery, when the order was given to charge. But the enemy stood manfully to their guns, causing such havoc in the ranks of the 62nd Foot that the Brigadier directed them to retire, which they did in good order, having sustained a loss of 17 officers and 186 men. The native regiments at the same time gave away, and the Division, being thus repulsed, fell back upon the 9th Foot and 26th Native Infantry, of the 3rd Division.

Repulse of Littler's Division.

The Sikh greeted the repulse of Littler's Division with loud shouts of triumph, and the news of this reverse passed down the British line before the remainder of the force was led to the attack.

The right Brigade under Brigadier Taylor now moved to the attack supported by Brigadier McLaren's Brigade in echelon on the left. The 80th and 29th Foot rushed forward in the face of a murderous fire, crossed the Sikh entrenchments, captured the guns at that point, and penetrated the enemy's camp. Here the hostile infantry made a determined stand, and a fanatical charge was carried out by a body of Akalis [1] in chain armour, who inflicted considerable loss before they were bayoneted. These two brigades having destroyed the Sikh gunners, who fought to the last, found more infantry drawn up behind the guns, and only drove them to take cover among their tents after a desperate fight, during which the enemy's swordsmen charged again and again with great valour.

General attack.

The centre Division now joined in the attack, but were staggered for a time by the heavy fire of guns and musketry with which they were met. Their left was not only checked, but was actually falling back, when the 9th Foot were rallied by Captain Borton,[2] and Sir Harry Smith brought up Brigadier Ryan's Brigade from the reserve and re-established the battle in that part of the line. The 50th Foot at

[1] Fanatical ascetics. [2] Afterwards General Sir Arthur Borton, K.C.B.

this point bore the brunt of the attack of four of Avitabile's battalions, which, Sir Harry Smith relates, were "at this moment in their bearing noble and triumphant." But, led by the General, Colonel Petit, and Brigadier Ryan, the 50th charged into the enemy's trenches, drove them back after a hand-to-hand conflict, captured the guns, and put the Sikhs to flight. Pushing forward with the 50th in line, and joined by many stragglers from the right of his line, and by a detachment of the 1st Europeans under Captain Seaton, Sir Harry Smith attacked and captured the village of Ferozeshahr, where a scene of awful slaughter ensued, as the enemy would not lay down their arms. Here many horses and camels were captured.

When Sir Harry Smith's Division was brought up, the 3rd Dragoons carried out a fine charge right through the enemy's lines, and again proved the value of shock action.

Capture of the Sikh position.

In the meantime Gilbert's Division had wheeled to their left after carrying the entrenchment, and charged along the line, capturing and spiking many guns. They then made towards the village of Ferozeshahr, but on the way were scattered by the explosion of a powder magazine, which destroyed many, and broke up McLaren's Brigade, part of which retired to the entrenchments, while others joined Sir Harry Smith in Ferozeshahr, as already related.

As the darkness and confusion were increasing, the Commander-in-Chief now withdrew the scattered forces from the Sikh Camp, and formed a bivouac about 300 yards from the entrenchments.

Operations of Sir Harry Smith.

Meanwhile Sir Harry Smith had already pushed on beyond the village of Ferozeshahr and captured the enemy's camp half a mile farther on, where, being joined by more stragglers, his force amounted to some 3,000 men. He had seen during his advance that the victory appeared to be complete, but as night set in he found that the enemy was in force to his front and right, and that his position was critical. He therefore attempted to form up his miscellaneous collection of troops in a semicircle in front of the enemy's camp, his flank being well thrown back towards the village. Scarcely had he made these dispositions when the enemy drove back his right by a sharp attack; but the darkness prevented them from continuing their success. At length all the stragglers, with the assistance of Major Hall, 16th Grenadiers, who was mortally wounded, were collected upon the 50th which was well in hand. These consisted of some of the 9th Foot under Major Barwell and the 19th, 24th, 28th, and 23rd Native Infantry. The moon now rose, and the night being nearly as bright as day, the enemy discovered the isolation of the force and gradually closed in upon them, keeping up a destructive fire. The losses became momentarily heavier; the men were dead-tired, and many were killed in their sleep. The enemy got a gun to bear on their rear, and at 3 A.M. Sir Harry Smith saw that his position was no longer tenable. The Sikhs, shouting and cheering, were closing in on every side, calling out that the British were in their power. Sir Harry Smith[1] then made a feint to attack, opened fire and drew off under cover of the smoke, the 50th leading, so that they might head the charge through any opposition that was met with. Leaving Ferozeshahr on his left the British general continued his retreat, guided by the moon and the dead soldiers on the line of his advance. Several officers urged a retreat on Ferozepore, but Sir H. Smith refused to listen to their advice. Shortly afterwards the troops reached the village of Misriwala, where they found Sir John Littler's force which had halted there after being repulsed.

Here Sir Harry Smith met Captain Lumley, officiating Adjutant General, who gave him a direct order to collect every soldier and march direct to Ferozepore. Sir Harry Smith, however, refused to take such an order from any one but the Commander-in-Chief in person, and falling in his men he was guided by Captain Christie of the Irregular Horse to Sir Hugh Gough's camp.

The same spirit animated the other leaders, Sir Hugh Gough and Sir Henry Hardinge, and the courage of the British troops was unshaken, but the native regiments were much disheartened and unnerved.

The Sikhs had also suffered terrible losses, but during the night they reoccupied their entrenchments, and opened fire on the British bivouac. One gun in particular caused so much annoyance that a party of the 80th Foot under Colonel Bunbury, with the 1st Bengal Europeans under Major Birrell, was sent out against it, and after this gun had been captured and its detachment killed the weary troops passed the remainder of the night in comparative peace.

At dawn the British army was drawn up to renew the attack.

Renewal of the battle, 22nd December 1845.

The infantry was formed in line, supported on both flanks by the horse artillery, whilst fire was opened by the heavy guns in the centre, and by a flight of rockets. A Sikh masked battery returned this fire, dismounting some of the guns and blowing up a tumbril. The Commander-in-Chief now placed himself at the head of the right of

[1]For these details the author is indebted to the *Autobiography of Sir Harry Smith*, a most valuable work published by John Murray in 1903.

the line ; Sir H. Hardinge at the head of the left. The line advanced, and, unchecked by the enemy's fire, drove them rapidly out of the village of Ferozeshahr and their encampment ; then, changing front to the left, the force continued to sweep the camp, bearing down all opposition, and dislodged the enemy from their whole position. The line then halted as if on a day of manœuvre, receiving its two leaders with a cheer as they rode along the front, and displaying the captured standards of the Khalsa Army.

Defeat of the Sikhs.

While this battle was in progress, a Sikh army of some 30,000 men under Tej Singh had been watching Ferozepore, unaware that Sir John Littler's force had been withdrawn. On the 22nd this army advanced against the British left, and, having driven in the parties of British cavalry, came into action two hours after the Sikhs at Ferozeshahr had been finally driven from their position. Bringing up a numerous artillery, this fresh force made a demonstration against the captured village, opening a heavy cannonade on the troops in occupation of the camp and entrenchments. But the Commander-in-Chief directed his cavalry to threaten both flanks of the enemy, and prepared to attack with his infantry, when the Sikhs drew off and abandoned the field.

Casualties.

The total Sikh force at the battle of Ferozeshahr appears to have been about 47,000 men and 88 guns, including Tej Singh's force. The British army numbered some 11,000 and was weaker in artillery. The Sikhs killed were estimated at 2,000, and 75 guns were taken. On the British side the casualties were :—*Killed*. British officers, 37 ; native officers, 17 ; men, British 462, native 178 ; total 694. *Wounded*. British officers, 78 ; native officers, 18 ; men, British 1,054, native 571 ; total 1,721. The excess of casualties among the British troops, although these were so greatly in the minority, is notable. The native troops did not fight with their usual spirit, and the brunt of the battle fell upon the Europeans.

Comments on the operations.

The first phase of the operations, which closed with the battle of Ferozeshahr, is interesting and instructive, although it discloses more valour than science on either side both as regards its strategical and tactical features. The delay in moving troops to cope with the political situation, due to the Governor-General's belief in the prospect of the maintenance of peace and to his anxiety to avoid hostilities, has already been discussed. Had the Sikhs realized the value of a bold offensive, and had they concentrated their full strength against the decisive point—the British force at Mudki—and driven their attack well home, it is almost certain that they would have met with complete success. Fortunately for us, however, they were lacking in enterprise, and both at Mudki and Ferozeshahr (where Tej Singh arrived too late to affect the issue) they lost their opportunity by employing only a portion of their force.

The British attack at Ferozeshahr was made so late in the day that the arrival of darkness caused confusion, and might have led to disaster. The delay was primarily due to Littler's late start from Ferozepore, that officer not having marched till 8 A.M., or four hours after the force under Sir Hugh Gough had left camp; but it is also to be noted that after he arrived (1-30 P. M.), two-and-a-half hours of valuable daylight were lost before the attack began.

When delivered, the attack appears to have resolved itself into a series of disconnected assaults, with the inevitable result that there was no decisive issue. Had the enemy been held to their position all along the line while the main attack was pressed home against their right and right centre, it would seem that the operations would have been more successful. The enemy, if defeated, would have been driven off their line of retreat, and the British would have interposed between their forces and those of Tej Singh. In criticising this action, however, it must be remembered that the density of the bush made intercommunication between units difficult, and that gaps were caused in the British lines by the bad behaviour of the Bengal Native troops, who had no stomach for the fight and did not support their British comrades. Victory was due entirely to the fine spirit of the British troops and to the determination of the Commander-in-Chief to succeed at all costs.

In connection with the converging movement of the two British forces before Ferozeshahr, it is of interest to recall Napoleon's maxim:—'It should be laid down as a principle that the junction of armies should never take place near the enemy, because they lay themselves open to defeat in detail.' Risks may be taken against an Asiatic enemy known to be lacking in enterprise, which would be unjustifiable in a European war, but it may be said that if converging movements are to succeed it is essential that the clearest instructions should be issued to all concerned, that the problems of time and space should be accurately worked out, and that every effort should be made to maintain communication, so long as the forces are apart. These principles were not observed in this instance. The orders issued by the Commander-in-Chief to Sir John Littler are not extant, but it is plain that Sir Hugh Gough expected him to march at the same time as he did himself; yet Littler writes in his despatch:—'In pursuance of instructions received *from the Governor-General*, I moved out of Ferozepore

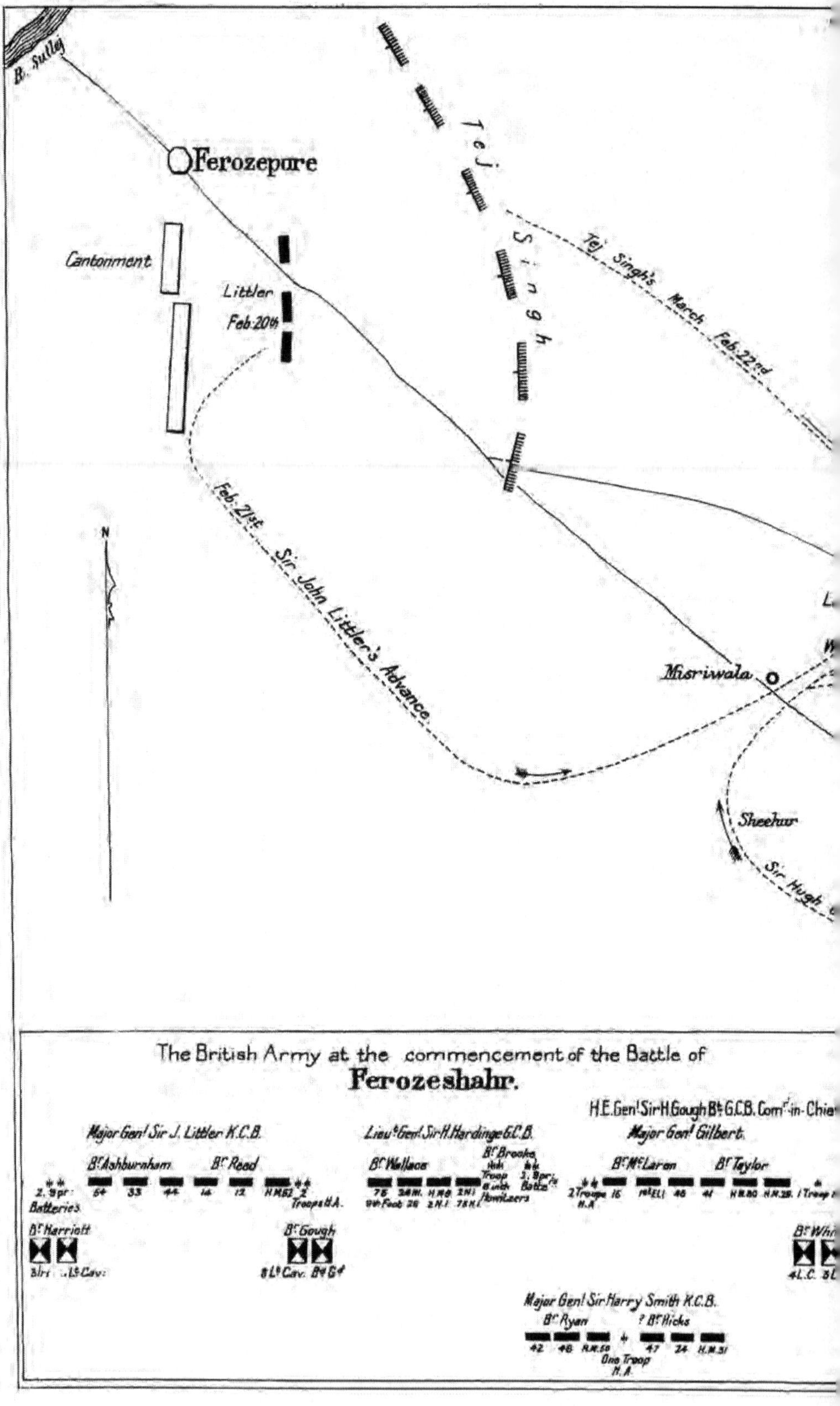
R. Sutlej
Ferozepore
Cantonment
Littler
Feb. 20th
Tej Singh
Tej Singh's March Feb. 22nd
Feb. 21st Sir John Littler's Advance
Misriwala
Sheehur
Sir Hugh
N
The British Army at the commencement of the Battle of
Ferozeshahr.
H.E. Genl. Sir H. Gough Bt. G.C.B. Comr.-in-Chie
Major Genl. Sir J. Littler K.C.B.
Br. Ashburnham
Br. Read
2. 9pr. Batteries
54
33
44
14
12
H.M.62
2 Troops H.A.
Br. Harriott
3 Irr. Lt. Cav.
Br. Gough
8 Lt. Cav.
Bd. Gd.
Lieut. Genl. Sir H. Hardinge G.C.B.
Br. Wallace
Br. Brooke
Troop 8 inch Howitzers
2. 9pr. Battns.
73
9th Foot
24 N.I.
26
H.M.9
2 N.I.
2 N.I.
73 N.I.
Major Genl. Gilbert
Br. McLaren
Br. Taylor
2 Troops H.A.
16
1st E.L.I.
45
41
H.M.80
H.M.29
1 Troop
Br. Whi
4 L.C.
Major Genl. Sir Harry Smith K.C.B.
Br. Ryan
? Br. Hicks
42
48
H.M.50
One Troop H.A.
47
24
H.M.31

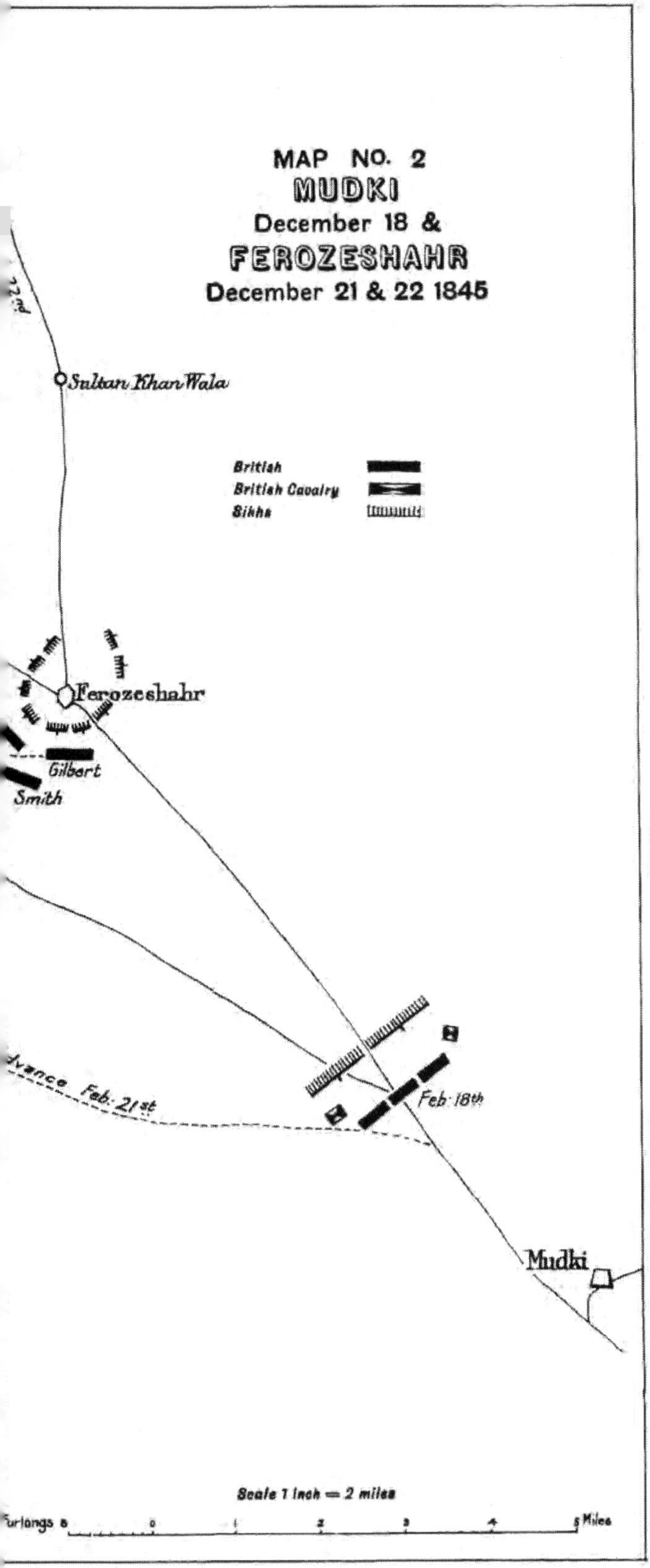

MAP NO. 2
MUDKI
December 18 &
FEROZESHAHR
December 21 & 22 1845
Sultan Khan Wala
British
British Cavalry
Sikhs
Ferozeshahr
Gilbert
Smith
Feb. 21st
Feb. 18th
Mudki
Scale 1 inch = 2 miles
Furlongs 8 0 1 2 3 4 5 Miles

at 8 A.M. As a result we see the British force incurring the very risk of defeat in detail to which Napoleon referred. But while discussing the subject of single versus multiple lines of operation in this campaign it must not be forgotten that in more recent times the increased holding powers of the rifle and the improvements in means of communication have greatly minimised the risks of the latter form. This was clearly recognized by Moltke, whose consequent predilection for multiple lines is well known, and who wrote in his '*Instructions to Superior Commanders*' in 1869:—"Incomparably more favourably will things shape themselves if, on the day of battle, all the forces can be concentrated from different points towards the field of battle itself; in other words, if the operations have been conducted in such a way that a final short march, from different points, leads all available forces simultaneously upon the front and flanks of the adversary. In that case strategy has done the best it can ever hope to attain, and great results must be the consequence."

CHAPTER IV.

ALIWAL AND SOBRAON.

(*Maps 3, 4 and 5.*)

Movements of the opposing forces.

After their defeat at Ferozeshahr the Sikhs retreated hastily across the Sutlej. Sir Hugh Gough encamped at Sultan Khan Wala, being in no position to assume the offensive until reinforced with fresh troops, guns, and ammunition. Practically all the ammunition had been expended, and the troops were exhausted. The Sikhs gathered fresh courage from the enforced inaction of the British army; they brought up reinforcements of guns and men from Lahore; and early in January showed signs of renewed aggression, making predatory incursions in the direction of Ludhiana, and thus threatening the British line of communications.

9th Lancers.
16th Lancers.
3rd Bengal Light Cavalry.
4th Irregular Cavalry.
Two Batteries Artillery.
10th Foot.
3 regiments N. I.
1 Company Sappers.

British troops were in the meantime hurrying towards the scene of action. On the 6th January Major-General Sir John Grey arrived with a force of 10,000 men, detailed in the margin, having left Meerut between the 10th and 16th December. Ludhiana was reinforced by the Sirmur and Nasiri battalions of Gurkhas, the 30th Native Infantry, and a regiment of cavalry, under Brigadier Godby.

The Sikhs at Sobraon.

The enemy meanwhile threw a bridge over the river at Sobraon where there was also a ford, constructed bridge-heads, and showed a disposition to cross. The British General thereupon moved up the left bank of the Sutlej on the 12th January, so that his centre was opposite Sobraon, while his left was watched and communication with Ferozepore kept up by the Division of Sir John Grey.

Sir Harry Smith's Division and Cureton's cavalry were posted on the right opposite the ford and ferry of Hariki. Gilbert's Division was in the centre, and Sir Robert Dick's on the left.[1] The enemy in the meantime was very active, constructed a bridge-

[1] The British Army was reorganized on 1st January 1846, as detailed in Appendix II.

of-boats, pushed over his whole army, and entrenched himself on the left bank of the river, " a movement " says Sir Harry Smith " unparalleled in the history of war from time immemorial." The British were unable to oppose the passage, which was unmolested, and the Sikh outposts were thrust forward, obliging the British protective troops to fall back, while the camp was fortified in front by heavy guns brought up from Ferozepore.

The reason of the failure to oppose this passage was that the right bank of the river was high, and commanded the British bank, while the bridge was thrown over at the bend of the river. Here the Sikhs established themselves in an entrenched position which they filled with heavy guns.

Operations about Ludhiana.

The predatory bands in the Ludhiana direction were becoming bolder; they entered the cantonment at that place, and burnt some of the officers' houses and barracks, but avoided the combat when interrupted by the Sirmur battalion and other troops. At this time the enemy had a small garrison of mercenary Rohillas, Yusafzais, and Afghans in the town and fort of Dharamkot, in the direction of Ludhiana, which were filled with guns. On the 17th January 1846, Sir Harry Smith was sent against this place with an infantry brigade and a light field battery. Starting two hours before daylight, he reached Dharamkot, 26 miles distant, at 2 o'clock in the afternoon, and investing it with his cavalry, summoned the enemy to surrender. His flag of truce was received, and the garrison were given 20 minutes, at the end of which time they hauled down the Sikh flag and hoisted a white one. They were allowed to march out and lay down their arms as prisoners of war.

March of Sir Harry Smith.

While Sir Harry Smith was on the march, the Commander-in-Chief received information that the Sirdar Ranjur Singh had crossed from Philour (a fortress on the right bank of the Sutlej) at the head of a numerous force of all arms, and established himself in a position at Baranhara, between the old and new courses of the Sutlej, not only threatening the city of Ludhiana, but indicating a determination to cut the line of communications, by which British reinforcements were marching, between Bassian and Rajkot. The safety of the rich and populous town of Ludhiana had been in some measure provided for by the presence of three battalions of Native infantry under Brigadier Godby, the gradual advance of reinforcements, including the 53rd foot, and the position of the Shekawati Brigade near Bassian.

On receipt of intelligence of the movements of Ranjur Singh, Sir Harry Smith with the brigade from Dharamkot and Brigadier

Cureton's cavalry was directed to advance by Jagraon towards Ludhiana; his second brigade under Brigadier Wheeler moving on to support him. On the 19th January Sir Harry Smith marched with the infantry to Kohari, half-way to Jagraon, leaving orders at Dharamkot for Brigadier Cureton to join at Jagraon on the 20th. At Jagraon he was joined by the 16th Lancers and guns, and by the 53rd foot,[1] which he had ordered in from Bassian. He had got into communication with Brigadier Godby, from whom he received urgent requisitions for relief; and he had information on the 20th that the enemy was still at Baranhara. The Sikhs had a small garrison and a few hundred horse, in the fort of Budowal while the strong fortress of Gangrana, 10 miles to the south of Budowal, was also occupied.

Action of Budowal, 21st January 1846.
16th Lancers.
18 guns.
31st Foot.
53rd Foot.
24th and 47th N. I.

Sir H. Smith now commanded the force detailed in the margin, the British Infantry including 250 convalescents, while the Native infantry was also very weak. He left two companies of native infantry and his wheeled transport in the fort at Jagraon, and marched half an hour after midnight, when the moon was up, by the direct road, intending to leave Budowal on his right. Every two hours he sent information of his intentions[2] to the officer commanding at Ludhiana, who had orders to meet him with his force within three miles of Budowal on a strong hill and position at Sonnact. His orders for the march were in writing. After marching sixteen or eighteen miles to within two miles of Budowal he received at dawn a message from Brigadier Godby to the effect that the enemy had moved from Baranhara and was encamped with his whole force at Budowal. He had two alternatives, either to force a passage by the direct road, or to make a flank march leaving Budowal on his left. He adopted the latter plan, marching over deep sand, while the enemy moved on a parallel line to cut him off, having good roads and cover from some villages. The British cavalry moved parallel with the enemy, protected from the fire of his guns by a low ridge of sandhills, the guns moving in rear of the cavalry with orders to open a heavy fire and check the Sikh advance when a favourable opportunity occurred. This fire produced some loss and confusion in the ranks of the Sikhs, who had been keeping up a furious fire with their guns on the British infantry. The baggage guard had been reinforced, and orders were sent for the baggage to close up and keep on the outer

[1] The officer commanding 53rd Foot, begged for a day's halt, as his transport was done, but he came on when ordered to "march if possible".

[2] They are not extant.

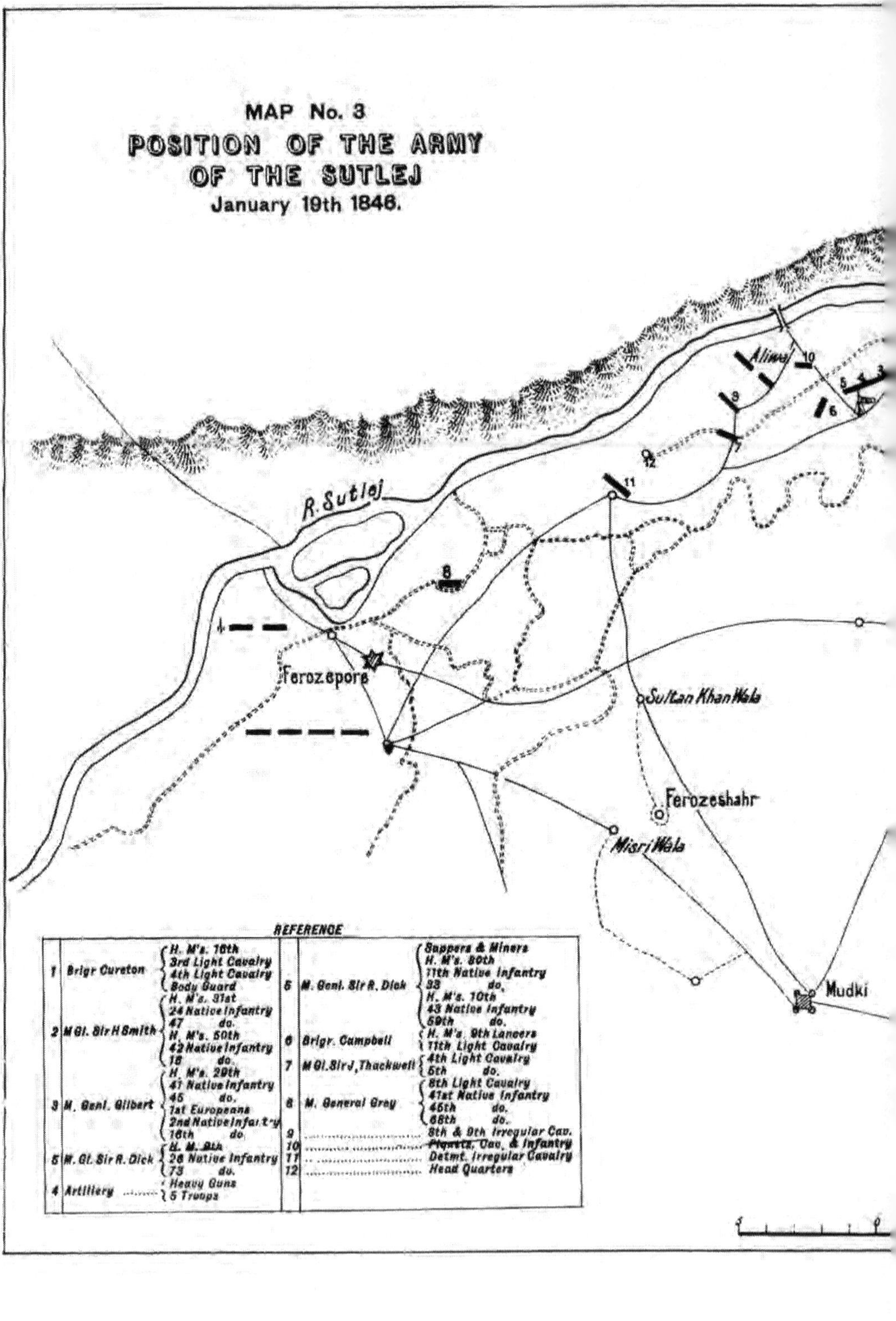
MAP No. 3
POSITION OF THE ARMY OF THE SUTLEJ
January 19th 1846.
R. Sutlej
Aliwal
Ferozepore
Sultan Khan Wala
Ferozeshahr
Misri Wala
Mudki
REFERENCE
1 Brigr Cureton: H. M's. 16th, 3rd Light Cavalry, 4th Light Cavalry, Body Guard
2 M Gl. Sir H Smith: H. M's. 31st, 24 Native Infantry, 47 do., H. M's. 50th, 42 Native Infantry, 16 do.
3 M. Genl. Gilbert: H. M's. 29th, 41 Native Infantry, 45 do., 1st Europeans, 2nd Native Infantry, 16th do.
5 M. Gl. Sir R. Dick: H. M. 9th, 26 Native Infantry, 73 do.
4 Artillery: Heavy Guns, 5 Troops
5 M. Genl. Sir R. Dick: Sappers & Miners, H. M's. 80th, 11th Native Infantry, 33 do., H. M's. 10th, 43 Native Infantry, 59th do.
6 Brigr. Campbell: H. M's. 9th Lancers, 11th Light Cavalry
7 M Gl. Sir J. Thackwell: 4th Light Cavalry, 5th do.
8 M. General Grey: 8th Light Cavalry, 41st Native Infantry, 45th do., 68th do.
9 8th & 9th Irregular Cav.
10 Piquets, Cav. & Infantry
11 Detmt. Irregular Cavalry
12 Head Quarters

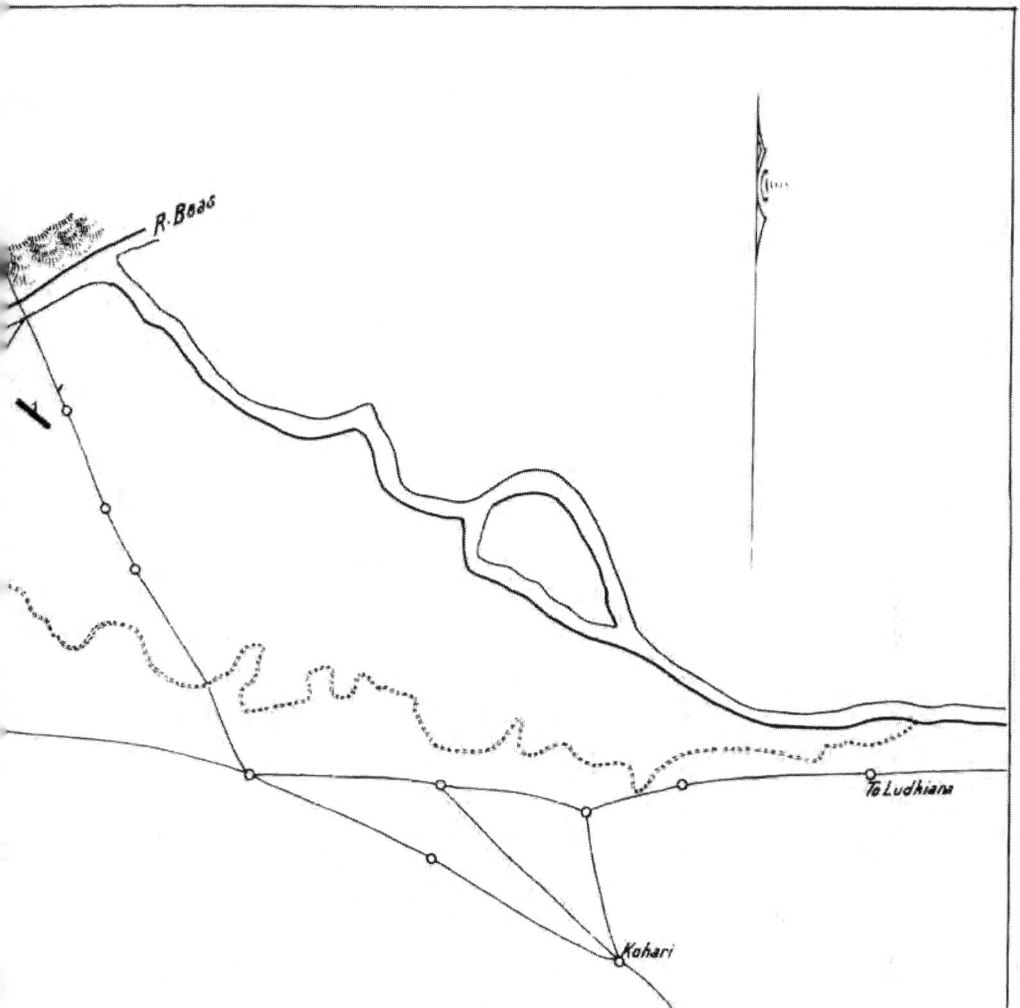
R. Beas
To Ludhiana
Kohari
Jagraon
Bassian
Scale 1 inch 5·18 miles
5
10
15
20
25

flank and as much ahead as possible. Many of the camel-drivers abandoned their animals and the baggage was plundered by the inhabitants of the hostile villages in the neighbourhood. As the column moved forward under the cannonade the enemy formed a line of battalions across the British rear, with guns in the intervals. But the British general kept on his way in echelon of battalions, the cavalry supporting in echelon of squadrons, with the guns in rear. The enemy, although in overwhelming numbers, did not attack, but clung to his stronghold of Budowal. Thus, with the loss of 69 killed, 68 wounded and 77 missing, as well as a considerable amount of baggage, the relief of Ludhiana was effected. Brigadier Godby had not received communication in time to co-operate. The Sikh cavalry cut off all the stragglers from the baggage, and the 53rd Foot, who furnished the baggage guard, suffered comparatively heavy losses, having 36 killed and two wounded. Sir Harry Smith encamped in front of Ludhiana, his outposts keeping a watch upon the enemy, to guard the line of communications *viâ* Bassian.

Relief of Ludhiana.

Meanwhile reinforcements were moving up, and threatening the Sikh position at Budowal; so Ranjur Singh fell back on the night of the 22nd and entrenched himself to cover the passage of the Sutlej at the Talwan ford near the village of Aliwal. Sir Harry Smith at once occupied the abandoned position at Budowal. On the 26th January the British general was reinforced by some cavalry and guns, and by the 2nd Brigade of his Division under Brigadier Wheeler. The enemy on the same day received an accession of strength of 12 guns and 4,000 regular infantry, known as Avitabile's battalions, which encamped on the right of the main army, and entrenched himself strongly in a semi-circle, his flanks resting on the river, his position covered by forty or fifty guns, howitzers and mortars.

Sir Harry Smith's force was organized as follows:—

Artillery—Major Lawrence.

22 Guns Horse Artillery,

6 Guns Field Artillery.

Cavalry—Brigadier Cureton.

1st Brigade—Brigadier McDowell.

16th Lancers, 3rd Light Cavalry, 4th Irregular Cavalry.

2nd Brigade—Brigadier Stedman.

Governor-General's Body Guard, 1st Light Cavalry, 5th Light Cavalry.

Shekhawati Cavalry Brigade.—Major Forster.

Infantry.

1st Brigade.—Brigadier Hicks

31st Foot, 24th N. I., 36th N. I.

2nd Brigade.—Brigadier Wheeler.

50th Foot, 48th N. I., Sirmoor Battalion.

3rd Brigade.—Brigadier Wilson.

53rd Foot, 30th N. I., Shekhawati Battalion.

4th Brigade.—Brigadier Godby.

47th N. I., Nasiri Battalion.

A total of 10,000 men.

Battle of Aliwal, 28th January 1846.

At daylight on the 28th the troops moved forward towards the enemy, the cavalry in front in contiguous columns of squadrons of regiments, two troops of horse artillery in the intervals of brigades; the infantry in contiguous columns of brigades at intervals of deploying distance: artillery in the intervals followed by two 8-inch howitzers on travelling carriages brought into the field from Ludhiana. Brigadier Godby's Brigade, which had marched out from Ludhiana the previous evening, was on the right; the Shekhawati Infantry on the left; the 4th Irregular Cavalry considerably to the right for the purpose of sweeping the banks of a wet nullah on that flank, and to prevent the enemy's horse from attempting an inroad towards Ludhiana, or any attack on the baggage collected round the fort of Budowal.

In this order the force moved towards the enemy, a distance of six miles, led by officers who had been employed with patrols in reconnoitring the Sikh position and the approaches to it. Previous to the march information had been received that the enemy would move at daylight either on Jagraon, Budowal or Ludhiana, and from the tops of the houses of the village of Purein Sir H. Smith had a distant view of them in motion and directly opposite his front on a ridge of which the village of Aliwal might be regarded as the centre. His left appeared still to occupy its ground in the circular entrenchment, his right was brought forward and occupied the ridge. The British general immediately deployed his cavalry into line, and moved on. As he neared the enemy, the ground became most favourable for manœuvre, being open and hard grass land. The cavalry was ordered to take ground right and left by brigades, thus displaying the heads of the infantry columns, which deployed into line on reaching the hard ground. Brigadier Godby's brigade was now in direct echelon to the rear of the right,

The account of the battle of Aliwal is taken *in extenso* from Sir Harry Smith's report.

the Shekhawati Infantry in like manner to the rear of the left; the cavalry in direct echelon and well to the rear of both flanks of the infantry; the artillery massed in the right, centre and left. After deployment it was found that the enemy's left outflanked the British, so the general broke into open column and took ground to his right. When he had gained sufficient ground, the troops wheeled into line. There was no dust and the sun shone brightly. The manœuvres were performed with the celerity and precision of the most correct field day, and the glistening of the bayonets and swords of this order of battle was most imposing as the line advanced. Scarcely had it moved 150 yards when at 10 o'clock the enemy opened a fierce cannonade from his whole line. At first the shot fell short, but quickly reached the British line. Sir Harry Smith, being thus close upon the enemy and able better to ascertain his position, was compelled to halt the line under fire for a few moments, until he found that by bringing up his right and carrying the village of Aliwal, he could with great effect precipitate himself upon the Sikh left and centre. He therefore quickly brought up Brigadier Godby's Brigade, and with it and the 1st Brigade under Brigadier Hicks made a rapid charge and carried the village and two large guns. He then ordered the line to advance and the battle became general. The enemy had a numerous body of cavalry on the heights to his left, but Brigadier Cureton with the right brigade of cavalry dashed in among them and drove them back upon their infantry. Meanwhile a second charge to the British right was made by the light cavalry and the Body Guard. The Shekhawati Brigade was moved well to the right in support of Brigadier Cureton, when the enemy's encampment was observed and seen to be full of infantry. Brigadier Godby's Brigade was immediately brought upon it by changing front and taking the enemy's infantry in reverse. They drove them before them and took some guns without a check.

While these operations were going on on the British right, and the enemy's flank was thus driven back, Sir Harry Smith observed Brigadier Wheeler's Brigade charging and carrying guns and everything before it in a manner which displayed the coolness of the Brigadier and the gallantry of his troops the 50th Foot, 48th Native Infantry and Sirmur Battalion. The 50th suffered severe loss. On the left Brigadier Wilson and the 53rd Foot and 30th Native Infantry were opposed to Avitabile's battalions and emulated their comrades on the right.

The enemy, driven back on his left and centre, endeavoured to cover the passage of the river with his right, strongly occupying the village of Bhundri, but Sir Harry Smith directed a squadron of the 16th Lancers under Major Smyth and Captain Pearson to charge a body to the right of the village, which they did in the most gallant and determined style, bearing everything before them with the lance as a squadron under Captain Bere had previously done. This charge was supported by the 3rd Light Cavalry under Major Angelo. The largest gun on the field and seven others were captured, while the 53rd Foot carried the village with the bayonet, and the 30th Native Infantry wheeled round to the rear of it. Lieutenant-Colonel Alexander's and Captain Turton's troops of horse artillery, under Major Lawrenson, dashed among the flying infantry, killing numbers, until about 800 or 1,000 men rallied under the high bank of a nullah, and opened a heavy but ineffectual fire from below the bank. The 30th Native Infantry were immediately directed to charge their left flank, while in a line in rear of the village. They rushed in among the Avitabile troops, driving them from under the bank and exposing them once more to a deadly fire of twelve guns within 300 yards.

The 53rd Foot moved forward in support of the 30th Native Infantry by the right of the village. The battle was now won, and the British troops were advancing in perfect order to the passage of the river. The enemy, completely hemmed in, were precipitating themselves in disordered masses into the ford and boats, in the utmost confusion. The 8-inch howitzers soon began to play upon the boats, when the *débris* of the Sikh army appeared on the opposite bank of the river, flying in every direction, although a sort of line was attempted to cover their retreat, until all the British guns began a furious cannonade, when they rapidly receded. Nine Sikh guns were on the river by the ford, to cover which they appear to have been unlimbered. Two others were sticking in the river, two were seen to sink in a quicksand, and two were dragged to the opposite bank and abandoned. These were spiked by Lieutenant Holmes, 11th Irregular Cavalry and Gunner Scott of the Horse Artillery, who rode into the stream and crossed, covered by the guns and light infantry. The enemy's guns, 67 in number, were all taken or destroyed, as well as 30 jingalls attached to Avitabile's battalions which aided in the defence of the village of Bhundri. The camp, baggage, and stores of ammunition and grain fell into the hands of the victors. The enemy fought with resolution, meeting the cavalry in hand-to-hand fight; in one charge of the 16th Lancers the Sikh infantry threw away their muskets and came on with sword and shield against the lance. It is noticeable that the native troops had recovered their spirit and fought well in this action, while "the intrepid little Gurkhas of the Nasiri and Sirmur Battalions in bravery and obedience were exceeded by none." The British loss amounted to 151 killed, 413 wounded, and 25 missing.

Defeat of the Sikhs.

After the battle the Sikhs evacuated Gungrana, and on the 29th Sir H. Smith blew up the fort of Budowal.

Results of the battle.

On his return march he observed that the Sikh peasantry appeared to be less friendly, but that the Musalmans rejoiced in being under the British Government. As a result of this victory the enemy abandoned all his posts south of the Sutlej from Hariki to Nunapur Makhowara, and country yielding a revenue of upwards of twenty-five lakhs of rupees submitted to British rule. The only post now held by the Sikhs south of the Sutlej was their position at Sobraon.

The operations which led up to the victory of Aliwal furnish in the first place an instructive example of that dangerous operation—a flank march, carried out in the presence of a superior force. The march was well executed and the retirement upon Ludhiana was covered with skill and steadiness. At the time there was much adverse comment on what was regarded by the ignorant as a set back to the British army at Budowal. But the British general was right in not engaging in battle with his small force, in keeping in view his main object, the relief of Ludhiana, and in neglecting minor issues and avoiding a doubtful action when so much depended on his concentration of the forces for the defence of the British line of communications. With more enterprise, the Sikhs might have forced a battle, but as usual they showed reluctance to assume a vigorous offensive. Of the battle of Aliwal there is little to say, except that the methodical and skilful conduct of the operations offer a contrast to the tactical methods which characterised the other battles of this campaign. The result of proper tactical arrangement, including a reconnaissance of the country and the enemy, was seen in the defeat of the Sikhs with comparatively small loss to the victors. The British force numbered some 10,000 men; there is no record of the numerical strength of the Sikhs; but Ranjur Singh's army was probably at least equal to that of his opponent. The Sikhs fought manfully and with desperation, having their backs to the river in a position where defeat entailed destruction. Yet the British loss was only 590 as compared with 872 at Mudki, where there were 10,000 British and some 15,000 Sikhs; and 2,415 at Ferozeshahr, where there were 16,000 British and 30,000 Sikhs. But in making comparisons it must be remembered that the ground at Aliwal was more favourable to the attackers; the native troops had recovered their courage, and behaved well; and that the Sikhs, although as usual they offered a stout resistance, had suffered severely at the previous battles, and lost much of the confidence with which they began hostilities.

The victory of Aliwal had an important effect from a political point of view. As Sir Harry Smith wrote:—" All India was at gaze and ready for anything. Our army—truth must out—most anxious, the enemy daringly and exultingly regarding himself invincible, as the bold and most able and energetic move of Ranjur Singh with his whole force in throwing himself between my advance from Jagraon *viâ* Budowal to Ludhiana most fully demonstrated. It is the most scientific move made during the war, whether made by accident or design, and had he known how to profit by the position he had so judiciously occupied, he would have obtained wonderful success. He should have attacked me with the vigour his French tutors would have displayed and destroyed me, for his force compared to mine was overwhelming; then turned about upon the troops at Ludhiana, beaten them, and sacked and burned the city—when the gaze I speak of in India would have been one general blaze of revolt."

Having provided for his sick and wounded and replenished his ammunition and stores, leaving Brigadier Wheeler to command the troops on the Upper Sutlej, Sir Harry Smith marched on the morning of the 3rd February on his way back to the Commander-in-Chief. He had with him the force detailed in the margin, the remainder being left with Brigadier Wheeler. He reached the right of the army five days later.

16th Lancers.
3rd and 5th Light Cavalry.
One regiment Irregular Horse.
3 troops Horse Artillery.
31st, 50th and 53rd Foot.
47th N. I.
Sirmur and Nasiri Battalions.

Junction of Sir Harry Smith with the main army.

On the 8th the Governor General arrived in camp from Ferozepore, where he had been since the battle of Ferozeshahr, and on the 9th all Generals of Divisions, Brigadiers, and Heads of Departments were summoned to the Commander-in-Chief's tent to hear the plan of operations. The enemy's works had been repeatedly reconnoitred, during the time the Head-Quarters were at Nihalki, by the Commander-in-Chief and his staff, and the engineer and artillery officers. The Sikh position was found to be covered by formidable entrenchments occupied by not less than 30,000 men, the best of the Khalsa troops, with 70 pieces of cannon, united by a good bridge to a reserve on the other bank, on which they had a considerable camp and some artillery, commanding and flanking his field works on the south bank.

Operations before Sobraon.

The period between the occupation of the position in front of Sobraon and the battle of the 10th February was not one of absolute quiescence.

On the 14th January the Sikhs came over in force, and the Commander-in-Chief ordered out two divisions of infantry and some cavalry, when an exchange of artillery fire took place. On the 13th

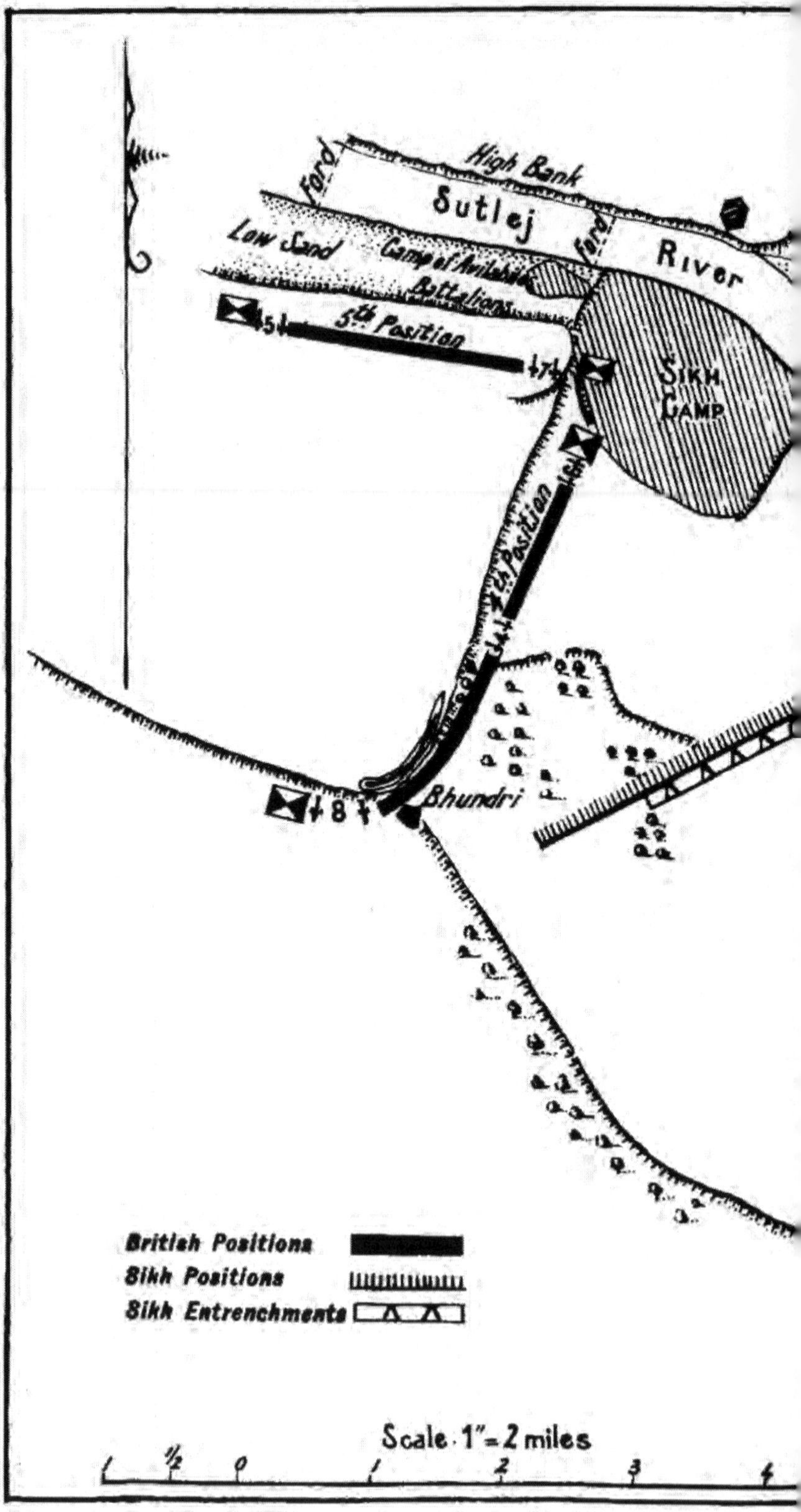

High Bank
ford
Sutlej
River
ford
Low Sand
Camp of Avitabile's Battalions
5th Position
Sikh Camp
Bhundri
British Positions
Sikh Positions
Sikh Entrenchments
Scale 1" = 2 miles
1 ½ 0 1 2 3 4

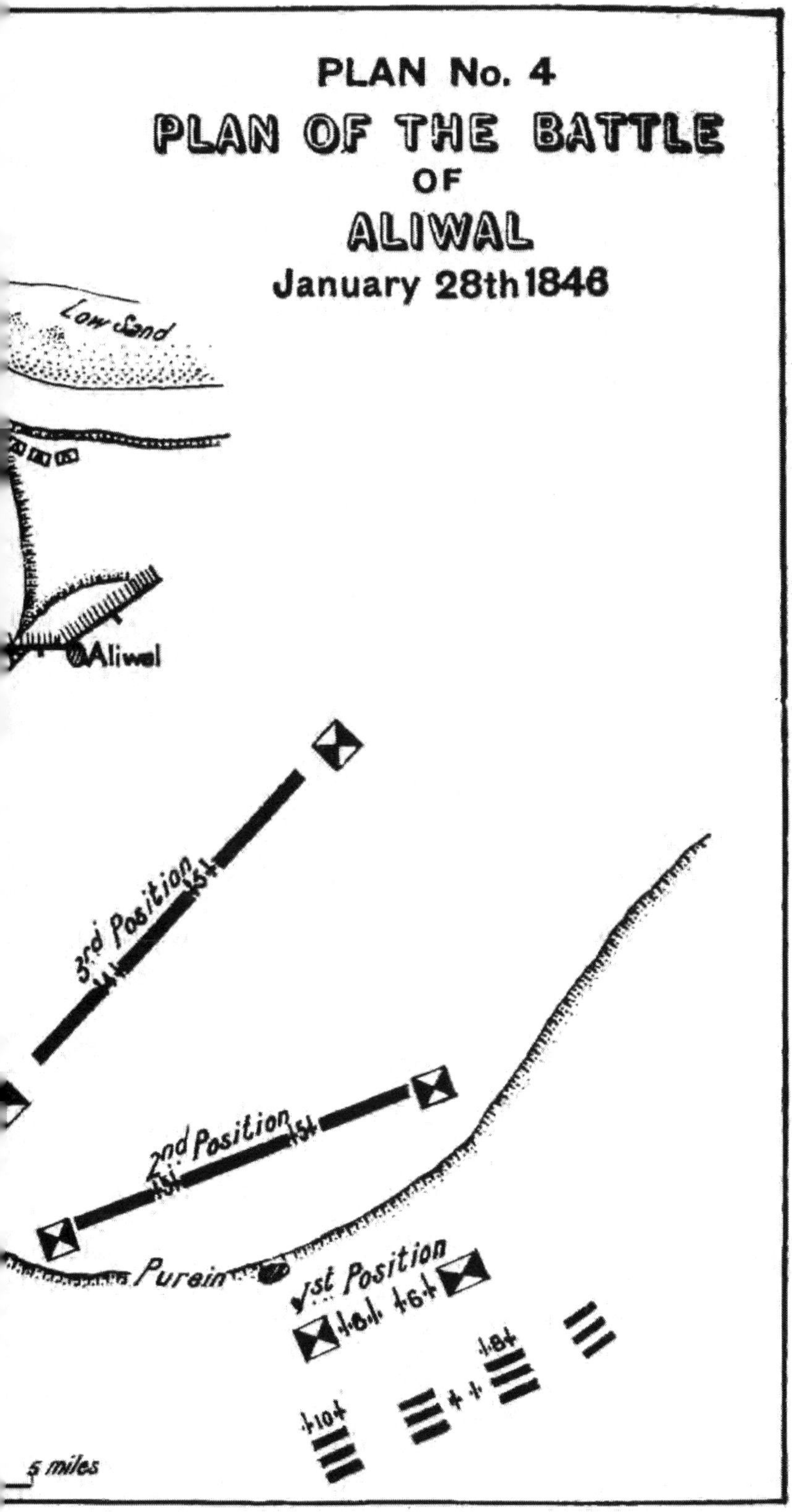
PLAN No. 4
PLAN OF THE BATTLE
OF
ALIWAL
January 28th 1846
Low Sand
Aliwal
3rd Position
2nd Position
Purein
1st Position
5 miles

there was a good deal of firing at the outposts, and next day some Sikh sowars made a rush at the piquets at Sobraon, but were driven back by the piquets of the 2nd Irregular Cavalry, and for some days there was a good deal of skirmishing. This long period of inactivity afforded great facilities for reconnaissance.

The Commander-in-Chief resolved to dispose the mortars and battering guns on the alluvial plain within range of the enemy's piquets at the post of observation in front of Kodiwala and at Little Sobraon. This was done and the two posts occupied near daybreak on the 10th February 1846, without opposition. The battering and field artillery was then put in position on an extended semi-circle, embracing within its fire the works of the Sikhs. These works were very strong, and were held by some 20,000 men. The enemy had gradually brought the greater part of their force into the entrenchment on the left bank of the Sutlej, and, as at Aliwal, the position formed a bridge-head with the flanks resting on the river, and occupying a perimeter of some 4,000 yards, the river line being about 2,750 yards in extent. They placed 65 guns in battery; here, as in other battles of the campaign, the soldiers did everything and the leaders nothing. Each inferior commander defended his front according to his skill and his means, and the centre and left, where the disciplined battalions were mainly stationed, had batteries and salient points as high as the stature of a man, and ditches which an armed soldier could only leap with difficulty. A considerable part of the line was defended only by slight entrenchments; at the right flank the looseness of the sand rendered it impossible to throw up parapets, and here irregular troops were posted and the position was guarded by a line of two hundred *zamburaks*, supported to some extent by a salient battery and by heavy guns on the opposite bank of the river. The Sikhs were depressed by the defeat at Aliwal, and by the sight of the dead bodies of those who had fallen in that battle floating down the river. Tej Singh commanded in the entrenchment while Lal Singh was with the cavalry higher up the river.

The Sikh position.

The spirits of the British had revived with the victory of Aliwal, and the arrival from Delhi of a formidable siege train and ample stores of ammunition added to their confidence. The troops were disposed as shown in the plan of the battle, Sir John Littler still holding Ferozepore and watching the ferry over the Sutlej. It had been intended to open the cannonade at day-break, but a heavy mist hung over the plain and river, necessitating a delay until the rays of the sun had penetrated it and cleared the atmosphere.

British dispositions.

The two brigades of Major-General Sir Robert Dick's division stood on the British left, ready to assault the extreme right of the Sikh position. The 7th Brigade, in which were the 10th and 53rd Foot under Brigadier Stacy, was to head the attack, supported at 200 yards' distance by the 6th Brigade under Brigadier Wilkinson. The 5th Brigade, under Brigadier the Hon'ble T. Ashburnham, was in reserve, and was to move forward from the entrenched village of Kodiwala, leaving, if necessary, a regiment for its defence. In the centre Major-General Gilbert's division was deployed for support or attack, its right resting in the village of Little Sobraon. Major-General Sir Harry Smith's division was formed near the village of Gatta with its right advanced towards the Sutlej. Brigadier Cureton's Cavalry threatened the ford at Hariki and Lal Singh's horse on the opposite bank. Brigadier Campbell, taking an intermediate position between Major-General Gilbert's right and Sir Harry Smith's left, protected both. Major-General Sir Joseph Thackwell, who was in command of the Cavalry Division, was in reserve on the left with the remainder of the cavalry, ready to act as circumstances might demand.

Artillery action.

The rising sun rapidly dispelled the mist, when a magnificent picture presented itself. The batteries of artillery were seen in position ready to open fire, and the plain covered with the British troops with the fortified village of Rodawala on the left rear strongly held by infantry. The enemy appeared suddenly to realise their danger; their bugles sounded the alarm and their drums beat to arms, and in a few minutes they manned their batteries and opened fire on their assailants. As soon as the mist cleared the British battery near Little Sobraon opened fire, but it was half-past-six before the whole of the artillery fire was developed. All the guns, mortars, and howitzers, aided by a rocket battery, were, however, unable to silence the Sikh guns, which were behind well constructed batteries of earth, planks, and fascines, or to dislodge troops covered either by redoubts or epaulments or within a treble line of trenches. The effects of the cannonade were severely felt by the enemy, but it became necessary to supplement it by musketry and the bayonet.

The British attack at Sobraon, 10th February 1846.

At nine o'clock Brigadier Stacy's Brigade, supported on either side by Captains Horsford and Fordyce's batteries, and Lieutenant-Colonel Lane's troop of horse artillery, moved to the attack in line. The guns, as the infantry moved forward and halted only to correct their movements when necessary, took up successive positions at the gallop, until at length they were within three hundred yards of the Sikh heavy batteries. The attack was supported by the 6th Brigade under Brigadier Wilkinson, but so hot was the fire of the cannon, musketry, and *zamburaks*, kept up by the Khalsa troops, that for some time it appeared impossible that the entrenchments could be won. At length the British soldiers drove the Sikhs before them within the area of their encampment, the 10th Foot not firing a shot until it was within the enemy's works.

The 5th Brigade was now directed to move on in support, and Major-General Gilbert's and Sir Harry Smith's Divisions to throw out their light troops to threaten the works, aided by artillery. When these attacks of the centre and right began, the fire of the heavy guns had to be first directed to the right, and gradually ceased owing to the ammunition running short, the officer commanding the artillery having brought into the field not half the amount that had been ordered. The two Brigades which had passed the entrenchments now held their own with difficulty, and were threatened by the weight of the whole force within the Sikh encampment, so the demonstrations with skirmishers on the centre and right had to be converted into close and serious attacks. Sir Harry Smith's first attack on the entrenchments was repulsed; the Sikh soldiers fought with desperation, and when their entrenchments were taken with the bayonet, strove to recover them by the fiercest conflict, sword in hand, so that for 25 minutes the fight raged at close quarters.

Cavalry charge.

On the British left the battle was still uncertain, when Sir Joseph Thackwell led two squadrons of the 3rd Light Dragoons, and the 4th and 5th Light Cavalry into the enemy's camp in single file through openings in the entrenchments made by the sappers. The Sirmur Battalion on the left of the Second Division was retiring, but when they saw the 3rd Dragoons ride to the trenches they rallied and passed between the horses into the entrenchments. When Sir Joseph Thackwell got to about 120 yards from the Sikh right, he rode forward and found a place where the cavalry could get into the entrenchments in single file, about sixty yards from the Sikh right, and as he brought the cavalry up the enemy began to give way gradually. Riding into the ditch and up the parapet, the squadrons were formed one after the other and led to the charge over broken ground to near the ford under a fire of grape from a battery only 150 yards off. The first squadron was obliged to give way before the mass of retreating Sikhs, but rallied, and cut down the defenders of the batteries and field works. This diversion by the cavalry enabled the first and second divisions to enter the line of entrenchments with little loss. The first squadron suffered some loss from the British artillery fire.

The Sikhs did not run, but fought to the last with their swords until, pressed by the victors on every side, slowly and with heavy loss they were driven back to the river, and precipitated in masses over the bank and over the bridge, where many were drowned in the waters of the Sutlej which a sudden rise of seven inches had rendered scarcely fordable. In their efforts to reach the other bank through the stream they suffered terribly from the fire of the horse artillery. Sir Hugh Gough wrote in his despatch :—" Hundreds fell under this cannonade; hundreds upon hundreds were drowned in attempting the perilous passage. The awful slaughter, confusion, and dismay were such as would have excited compassion in the hearts of their generous conqueror if the Khalsa troops had not, in the earlier part of the action, sullied their gallantry by slaughtering and barbarously mangling every wounded soldier whom, in the vicissitudes of attack, the fortune of war left at their mercy." He especially noticed the bravery of the Sirmur and Nasiri battalions of Gurkhas, who, " of small stature but indomitable spirit, vied in ardent courage in the charge with the grenadiers of our own nation, and, armed with the short weapon of their mountains, were the terror of the Sikhs throughout this great combat."

Defeat of the Sikhs.

Sixty-seven guns, over two hundred *zamburaks*, numerous standards, and vast munitions of war fell into the hands of the victors. The Sikhs' loss was estimated at some 10,000 men. On the British side there were 320 killed and 2,063 wounded. This decisive battle brought the campaign to a close. The British army stood triumphant on the south bank of the Sutlej, from which the last of their enemies had been expelled by sheer force of the bayonet. The army of the Khalsa, broken in organization and shattered out of all semblance of the proud host that had crossed the Sutlej two months before, fled towards Lahore. Some 20,000 men were assembled on the way, and marched to their sacred city of Amritsar.

Results of the battle.

The battle of Sobraon showed that the Sikhs had not profited by the lesson of Aliwal, which should have proved to them the danger of contending with a British army, with their backs to the river into which they must be driven in the event of defeat. It may be considered that the British general might have crossed the river elsewhere, and thus manœuvred the Sikhs out of their strongly-entrenched position, but this would have entailed a division of force, both to hold the enemy while the turning movement took place, and to guard an exposed line of communications, whilst it might have led to the prolongation of a war that was brought to a conclusion by a bold and

Comments.

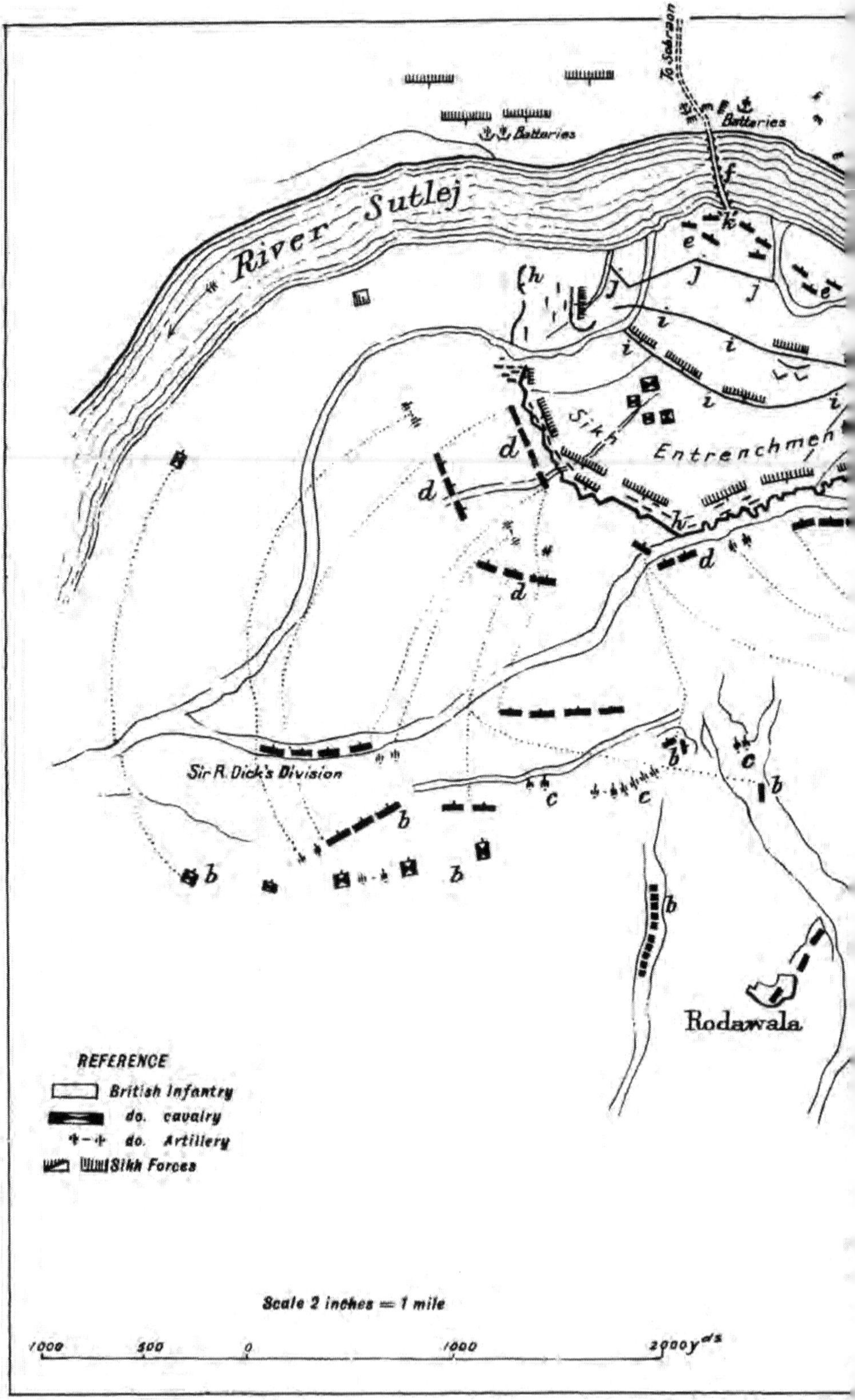

To Sobraon
Batteries
Batteries
River Sutlej
Sikh Entrenchment
Sir R. Dick's Division
Rodawala
REFERENCE
British Infantry
do. cavalry
do. Artillery
Sikh Forces
Scale 2 inches = 1 mile
1000
500
0
1000
2000 yds

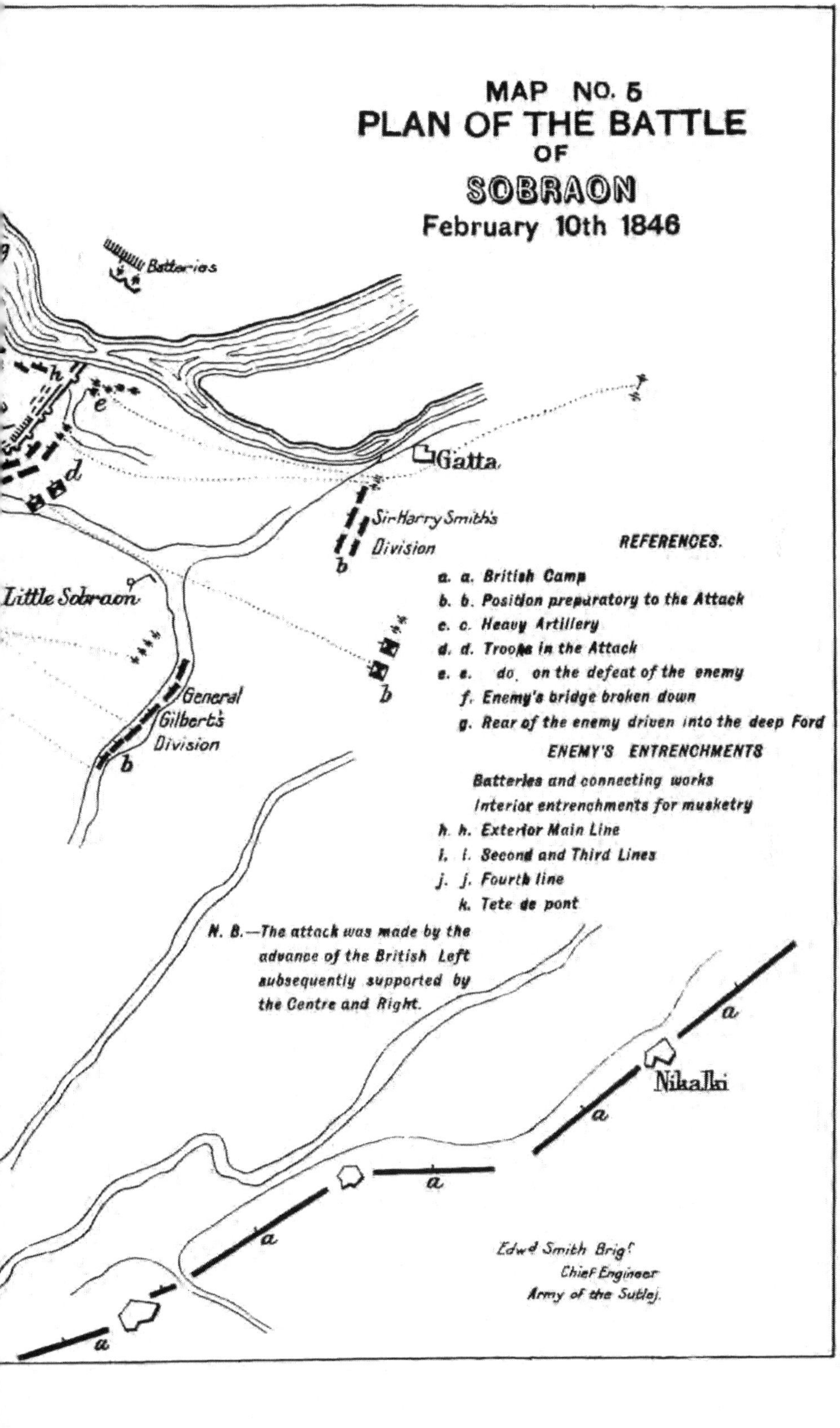
MAP NO. 5
PLAN OF THE BATTLE
OF
SOBRAON
February 10th 1846
Batteries
h
e
d
Gatta
Sir Harry Smith's
Division
b
Little Sobraon
b
General
Gilbert's
Division
b
REFERENCES.
a. a. British Camp
b. b. Position preparatory to the Attack
c. c. Heavy Artillery
d. d. Troops in the Attack
e. e. do. on the defeat of the enemy
f. Enemy's bridge broken down
g. Rear of the enemy driven into the deep Ford
ENEMY'S ENTRENCHMENTS
Batteries and connecting works
Interior entrenchments for musketry
h. h. Exterior Main Line
i. i. Second and Third Lines
j. j. Fourth line
k. Tete de pont
N. B.—The attack was made by the advance of the British Left subsequently supported by the Centre and Right.
a
Nikalki
a
a
a
a
Edwd Smith Brigr
Chief Engineer
Army of the Sutlej.

decisive stroke. It was no doubt best to attack the enemy where he stood, and, sure of the fighting power of his troops, and strong in the determination of his own character, the British general felt a just confidence of victory. But the tactics of the battlefield appear to have been somewhat faulty, the attack being first made in a desultory fashion, with two brigades launched against one point while the rest of the army remained stationary. The defenders were thus able to concentrate their entire strength against the point attacked, first on one flank, and then on the other. The principle of being in superior force at the decisive point was not observed. Had a simultaneous attack been made all along the line, and the troops for the decisive attack then pushed in at the selected point, it is probable that the victory would have been gained with smaller loss to the assailants. But almost the whole army was held in reserve just out of reach of the enemy's guns while the attack on the Sikh right was made by a comparatively small force.

The battle was over at 11 o'clock, when the Commander-in-Chief caused a portion of the bridge to be burnt and sunk, with what object is not apparent, as it might have been used for the passage of the army. The Governor-General returned to Ferozepore the same afternoon to superintend the passage of the troops, and during the night the advanced brigades of the British army crossed the Sutlej. Early on the 12th the bridge near Ferozepore was completed, and on the 13th the Commander-in-Chief, with the whole force excepting the heavy train and the division left to collect and bring in the wounded to Ferozepore with the captured guns, was encamped in the Punjab at Kasur, sixteen miles from the bank of the river opposite Ferozepore and thirty-two miles from Lahore. The Governor-General joined the Camp on the 14th.

Submission of the Sikhs.

Next day the Minister Raja Gulab Singh and other emissaries arrived at the British Camp with power to agree to such terms as the British might dictate. These terms included the surrender of the territory lying between the Sutlej and Beas river, and the payment of one and a half crores of rupees as indemnity for the expenses of the war; the disbandment of the Sikh army, and its reorganization on the system and under the regulations which obtained in the time of the Maharaja Ranjit Singh; the surrender of all the guns that had been brought against the British, and other arrangements with regard to boundaries of the Sikh State, and its administration, which would be determined at Lahore. The indemnity was subsequently settled to the extent of a crore of rupees by the cession to the British Government of the State of Kashmir, which was then handed over to Gulab Singh as an independent kingdom on payment of the specified sum.

On the 18th February the boy Maharaja Dhalip Singh made his submission at the British Camp at Laliana, from whence he accompanied the Governor-General to Lahore. The remainder of the Sikh army under Sirdar Tej Singh and Raja Lal Singh, on retiring from Sobraon, encamped at Raibam, about eighteen miles east of Lahore, to the number of some 20,000 men. They were gradually disbanded and the Sikh army was limited to 20,000 infantry and 12,000 cavalry. It was agreed that British troops should remain in occupation of Lahore until the end of the year, and a British Agent, Major Henry Lawrence, was appointed to exercise control over the Council of Regency.

CHAPTER V.

THE PUNJAB AFTER THE WAR.

Settlement of the Punjab.

Although the Sikh Army had been defeated and the Sikh nation subdued, the spirit of the Khalsa was by no means broken. The battles had taken place only on the bank of the Sutlej, on what was to all intents and purposes British territory; the capital of the Punjab had indeed been occupied, but not a British soldier had been seen beyond the Ravi, and large bodies of undefeated Sikh troops, which had not taken part in the campaign, were quartered in other parts of the Punjab—in Peshawar, in Derajat, and in Multan. British officers, many of whose names afterwards became famous, were deputed to various parts of the province for the settlement of the country. At Peshawar was Major George Lawrence; John Nicholson, Abbott, Edwardes, Reynell Taylor and Lake were among others employed on this service. There was some trouble in Kangra where the Governor refused to recognise the new régime but although the fort was strong, the garrison wisely surrendered when British troops arrived.

In April 1847 the Governor-General was able to write the Secret Committee, "Everything is perfectly quiet, and nothing has occurred worthy of remark." A few days earlier he had written, "The Sikh authorities composing the Durbar appear to be carrying on the Government of the country, under the British Resident, with a sincere desire to insure a successful result, while from Peshawar Major G. Lawrence wrote on April 19th: "The arrival of British functionaries in this remote and hitherto neglected portion of the Empire may be considered its salvation. To such a state had oppression driven the people that all were ready to rise against their rulers, which they most assuredly would have done had they not been deterred by the prompt suppression of the Kashmir insurrection."[1] Peshawar had been kept in order under the strong rule of General Avitabile, but he had left in 1843. The treasury was now empty, and the irregular troops were clamorous for pay. The regular Sikh army at Peshawar under General Gulab Singh, was 6,000 strong. Of the other British officers who have been named, Lieutenant John Nicholson was placed in charge of Hazara; General

[1] By 10,000 Sikhs under Sher Singh, accompanied by Lawrence as British Agent.

Cortlandt, of the Sikh service, had the strip of territory across the Indus, between Peshawar and Dera Ghazi Khan; Lieutenant Edwardes was at Bannu in the Derajat. One of Major Lawrence's assistants, Lieutenant Herbert, was afterwards the defender of Attock. The Governor of Hazara was Sirdar Chattar Singh, father of Sher Singh, both of whom played a leading part in the Sikh rising of 1848.

Sikh intrigues.

It was only to be expected that there would be constant intrigue at Lahore, particularly so long as the Maharaja Dhalip Singh was a minor, and his mother the Maharani a power in the palace. Already in February 1847, Prema, late a commandant in Maharaja Ghulab Singh's service, came to Lahore and began intriguing with several officers and men of Sikh corps with a view to creating a disturbance. There was a design to kill the Resident and several of the members of the Lahore Darbar who were obnoxious to the Maharani; but the plot was discovered, and the Maharani was removed to Sheikapur.

But although there were intrigues at Lahore, while the Khalsa nourished the hope of regaining their lost power, and retained their pride of race, the second Sikh war did not arise from any of these causes but from a disturbance at Multan originating with Diwan Mulraj, the Musalman Governor of that place.

Affairs at Multan.

Towards the end of 1847 Mulraj expressed a wish to resign his office, rendering an account to the Darbar for such taxes as he had collected and leaving the Government to realise the balance. Mulraj had accepted a lease of the Province for three years, and on the Resident's[1] remonstrance agreed to return to Multan and continue in office until 10th March 1848, when he would be relieved. Accordingly in April, Mr. Vans Agnew, with Lieutenant W. A. Anderson of the Bombay European Regiment as assistant, was directed to proceed to Multan as Political Agent, Sirdar Khan Singh Man being appointed to succeed Mulraj. As escort these officers took with them a Gurkha Regiment of the Sikh Army, together with some guns and cavalry.

On the 17th April Mr. Vans Agnew, Lieutenant Anderson, and Sirdar Khan Singh Man arrived at the Rajghat at Multan, where they encamped, proceeding next morning to the Idgah, where they intended to stay, and where they were visited by Diwan Mulraj, who requested Mr. Vans Agnew to inspect the fort, troops, and stores, which he agreed to do on the 19th April. In

[1] Sir Frederick Currie, acting for Major Henry Lawrence who was on leave in Europe.

the early morning the two British officers went to the fort, accompanied by Sirdar Khan Singh Man, and an escort of two companies of the Gurkha Regiment and twenty-five troopers. The Diwan came to the Kamar Kota Gate to meet them. When they arrived at the outer gate the grenadier stationed there asked the Diwan what were his orders as to allowing the British officers to enter the fort. The Diwan replied: "The Sahib is master." The Diwan then said that it would be inadvisable to allow the crowd in attendance to enter also. Mr. Vans Agnew accordingly took in with him only one company; and he directed the officer in command of it to place his guards in the positions previously held by the Diwan's soldiers. On leaving the fort Mr. Vans Agnew and Diwan Mulraj proceeded side by side on horseback, while Lieutenant Anderson and Sirdar Khan Singh Man followed. On arriving at the drawbridge a soldier thrust a spear at Mr. Vans Agnew and slightly wounded him. The sepoy then made a rush, and cut at him over the shoulder with his sword, upon which the British officer knocked him down with his stick, receiving another wound on the arm, while Lieutenant Anderson was attacked by other Musalman sepoys, sword in hand, and wounded in several places in the thigh, the shoulder, the back of the neck and the face. Mulraj had in the meantime ridden on to the Amkhas, and as they passed that place on the way to the Idgah, it was seen that his people were bringing out some guns, from which fire was opened on the wounded officers.

Outbreak at Multan.

From the Idgah Mr. Vans Agnew sent off letters, including one to the Nawab of Bahawalpur, and sent a message to the Diwan telling him that he did not consider him to blame. The Diwan said he was coming to pay him a visit, but procrastinated, and on the morning of the 20th April a gun was fired from the fort, the shot striking the mosque in which the officers were. The Sikh escort guns under Colonel Esra Singh engaged them, and fire was continued during the day; after dark the Diwan's troops attacked the Idgah on every side, the artillerymen with their commander went over to the enemy, Sirdar Khan Singh Man was seized, and the two officers, fighting to the last, were barbarously murdered. Their property was all pillaged and their heads were cut off and taken to the Diwan. The whole escort also went over to the Diwan.

When the news of this outrage reached Lahore, the Resident ordered off to Multan from Lahore the only disposable Sikh regiment, to be met on the road by a field battery from Ramnagar, and all the available irregulars under Sirdar Attar Singh, Kaliwala, the Commander of the irregular troops, accompanied by Diwan Dina Nath on the part of the Durbar. He also ordered General

Cortlandt to move down from Dera Ismail Khan with a battalion of Musalmans and another of Purbiahs, a regiment of cavalry and a troop of horse artillery. On the 22nd April he wrote to the Governor-General that he had "put in motion upon Multan from different points 7 battalions of infantry, 2 of regular cavalry 3 troops and batteries of artillery, and 1,200 irregular horse." He at the same time wrote "The fort of Multan is very strong, and full of heavy cannon of large calibre. This cannot be taken possession of by direct attack. Except the Multan garrison Mulraj has not many troops, and only five or six field guns. He is very unpopular both with the army and the people". Sir F. Currie also desired to send Lahore Column under Major-General Whish; but in view of the advanced season of the year the Commander-in-chief was opposed to the despatch of British troops, who must suffer severely from the climate. Multan was 220 miles from Lahore, and the same distance from Ferozepore. The strength of the fort rendered it certain that a prolonged siege would be necessary. It was also held that the rebellion of Mulraj was against the Durbar, and should be dealt with by Durbar troops. In the meantime Mulraj was strengthening his position at Multan, and while delay meant an accession of strength, both moral and material to the rebel, it also involved loss of prestige to the British and the growth and dissemination in the Army of the Khalsa of that spirit of disaffection which was only natural in a people inspired with the ideals of the Sikh religion.

CHAPTER VI.

HERBERT EDWARDES' ADVANCE TO MULTAN.

(*Map 6.*)

On the 22nd April Lieutenant H. B. Edwardes,[1] who was in camp at Dera Fateh Khan, occupied with settlement work in the Bannu district, received a letter from Mr. Vans Agnew written after the first attack. This letter was addressed to General Cortlandt, asking for assistance. Lieutenant Edwardes at once resolved to march on Multan with his force of 2 guns, 20 *zamburaks,* 12 companies of infantry, and 350 sowars. He wrote to Lieutenant Reynell Taylor in Bannu to put Subhan Khan's Musalman regiment and the four remaining guns of the Peshawar troop of horse artillery, to which his two guns belonged, into boats at Isakhel, and send them down the Indus to the Leia ferry, where they could disembark and push on to Multan. The Kardar of Leia had received instructions from Mulraj to seize the boats, raise 3,000 men, and hold the place, but he fled to Multan when Lieutenant Edwardes crossed to Leia on the 25th April, the instructions referred to not having reached him.

Situation in the Derajat.

Leia was an important city, the capital of the Doab between the Indus and the Chenab, and its possession alone struck a blow at the prestige of Mulraj, and prevented hundreds of mercenaries from flocking to his standard. The Doab swarmed with Baluchis and Pathans ripe for mischief. Edwardes began to entertain men in his army, both for the purpose of holding Leia and to prevent them from joining the rebels. His position was precarious. Reinforcements could not reach him from Bannu until the 7th or 8th May ; the rebel Sikhs in Multan were in treacherous correspondence with his troops ; and Mulraj might advance with a large force and destroy him while in this disadvantageous situation.

Lieutenant Edwardes at Leia.

He was encamped south-east of the city, covering it from Multan, and, expecting the advance of a British force from Lahore, he wrote—" My mind is made up. I shall throw up entrenchments here and stand. Great ends will be secured by my success;

[1] Afterwards Sir Herbert Edwardes.

immense confusion follow a retreat.'' He at the same time suggested to the Resident that Bahawal Khan, Nawab of Bhawalpur, might be called upon to cross the Sutlej at once and co-operate with a British force from Lahore and a Brigade from Sind. In the meantime Edwardes raised a force of some 3,000 Pathans and Baluchis, and he had with him a great support in Faujdar Khan, a clever Pathan of good family, related to many of Mulraj's chief officers, and acquainted with every mercenary on both banks of the Indus. On the evening of the 29th Edwardes received intelligence that Mulraj had sent a force of 4,000 men and eight heavy guns across the Chenab to oppose him; and that this force was expected to reach Leia on the 1st May at latest. Four courses were open to Edwardes:—

1. To entrench himself inside or outside the city of Leia.

2. To move north-east on Mankera, a fort of great strength, 50 miles from Leia.

3. To proceed three marches to Bakkar, opposite Dera Ismail Khan, where there was a small fort, and await the arrival of General Cortlandt with re-inforcements expected at Dera on May 2nd.

4. To recross the Indus and await General Cortlandt under the fort of Girang.

The first plan was hazardous in view of the weakness and doubtful loyalty of his force. The fort of Mankera was held by a Sikh garrison, while the third plan involved a dangerous march. Edwardes therefore decided to retire to the Indus and await General Cortlandt at the other bank, especially as the Killadar of that place was a Pathan of his appointment. He accordingly marched on the 30th April to the left bank of the Indus, at Murawala, opposite Dera Fateh Khan, having first sent a small party of newly-raised Pathans to seize the fort of Mojgarh, 24 miles north-east of Leia, where they were ordered to strengthen themselves by entertaining more men, and to lay in provisions. At Murawala he collected boats for embarkation, but resolved to await events for another day on the left bank of the Indus.

Advance of Mulraj's army.

On the morning of the 2nd May Mulraj's advanced guard suddenly appeared at Kofila, only eight miles from Leia. Still doubtful whether the enemy's guns had come or not, Edwardes advanced the whole of his cavalry to Leia under Sirdar Muhammad Alam Khan, Barakzai, and Faujdar Khan, Alizai, to reconnoitre and cover the retreat. On their way they heard that Mulraj's main body and guns had reached Machiwala, sixteen miles south of Leia, but they went to Leia, reconnoitred to Kofila, and withdrew at midnight.

At mid-day Lieutenant Edwardes had struck his camp, and by nightfall he crossed the whole of the baggage and cattle to the right bank of the Indus, keeping only his infantry and guns on the left bank. The men lay down in a crescent formation, fully accoutred, with the empty boats drawn up ready for embarkation in rear, awaiting the return of the cavalry. At dawn the cavalry and guns crossed in two detachments, and the infantry brought up the rear at eight o'clock, about the time that the enemy were marching into Leia, twelve miles distant.

Edwardes retreats.

This withdrawal of Edwardes before the advance of a superior force is a model which affords a most valuable example for all time.

Writing with regard to it to the Resident at Lahore on the 8th May, he said :—

You seem to have estimated most truly what would be the conduct of the Futteh Pultun; and most arduous and anxious was the task I had after the discovery of their correspondence with the rebels to manœuvre a retreat without showing distrust, and preserve discipline without bringing on resistance. A word, at any moment, would, I felt, involve us in a camp row. The Poorbeahs stuck to me like trumps; and, being more aware than I could be of how far things had gone among the Sikhs, they were so evidently on their guard, and showed such open expectation of a mutiny that I had the greatest difficulty in repressing their zeal, and preventing them from hurrying on the very catastrophe they dreaded. So ticklish was it at the last moment on the left bank of the Indus that the Poorbeahs refused to cross the river without me, and I could not trust the Sikhs to go over either first or last, least in one case they should keep the boats on the right bank, and in the other go over to the enemy on the left; so that I was at last obliged to march every company into a boat of its own, at one sound of the bugle and cross them all in a body, along with me."

Capture of Mangrota.

The next move in the game was the capture by Edwardes of the fort of Mangrota, between Dera Fateh Khan and Dera Ghazi Khan, important owing to its position on General Cortlandt's line of advance from the latter place. Edwardes now resolved to send General Cortlandt to Dera Ghazi Khan with the main force and to cross the Indus himself with six companies of Musalman regular infantry, two guns, 14 *zamburaks*, and his new levies of 1,000 Pathans, to collect revenue. General Cortlandt, who had joined him a week before, accordingly marched on the 12th May with 6 guns, 6 *zamburaks* one Sikh and one Musalman regiment, and about 200 troopers.

Lieutenant Edwardes had intended to move simultaneously, but he heard that Mulraj's force of 4,000 men and 10 guns, which had retreated from Leia on the 17th May, had halted on reaching the Chenab. They had retired on the information that Bahawal Khan of Bahawalpur was threatening an advance on Multan, but, finding that there was no fresh movement, they halted as stated. Edwardes now decided that, as no British force would move against Multan until the cold weather, the only thing to be done was to order Bahawal Khan to cross the Sutlej with his army, and encamp somewhere in the vicinity of Multan.

Action at Leia.

On the evening of the 15th May Lieutenant Edwardes' piquet at Leia heard that the rebels, 500 sowars, 2 guns, and some *zamburaks* had reached Gultan-ki-Kot, 20 miles from Leia. They had orders to retire before a superior force, but, afraid of their being pressed, Edwardes reinforced them during the night with 200 men. The piquet had already fallen back across a *nala*, a mile on the western or Indus side of Leia ; and, hearing of their retreat, the enemy hurried on to Leia with 300 or 400 horse and some *zamburaks*. At Leia they heard that the piquet had retired and, being weak, would fall an easy prey. They therefore pushed on to the *nala*, and were surprised to find a force nearly equal to their own. The rebels opened fire with their *zamburaks*, but the piquet boldly plunged into the *nala*, forded it, and attacked the enemy, whom they defeated after a short struggle, and drove some miles beyond Leia, killing 12 men and taking some prisoners and all the *zamburaks* with a loss to themselves of only two wounded.

Movements of the Bahawalpur Army.

On the evening of the 16th May information reached Edwardes that 6,000 to 7,000 horse and foot, with 15 guns, were marching on Leia, and he consequently withdrew all his men to the other bank of the Indus. Edwardes now assumed the responsibility of directing Bahawal Khan to cross the Sutlej and threaten Multan, as the only means of saving Dera Ghazi Khan and relieving the pressure on his own and Cortlandt's forces, which combined were not more than half the strength of the enemy, who could cross the Indus at any point. As Edwardes wrote to the Resident at Lahore—"If Bahawal Khan threatens Multan, he will confine Mulraj therein, prevent his undertaking expeditions to the provinces and collecting their revenue, and cut him off from getting more recruits. If General Cortlandt and I are driven into Akalgarh,[1] it will release the provinces from our control, stop the revenue, and send every recruit to Mulraj."

Junction of Edwardes and Cortlandt.

On the 18th May, General Cortlandt, who was encamped on the right bank of the Indus opposite Dera Din Pana, reported that the enemy had crossed at Peronwala ferry, below his position. This

[1] The fort of Dera Ismail Khan.

report proved unfounded; but the enemy had concentrated at that point, the move on Leia having evidently only been a feint. Edwardes therefore resolved to put his guns and infantry into boats, and join Cortlandt, his cavalry marching on the right bank of the river. Accordingly on the evening of the 18th he despatched the whole of his cavalry, magazine, spare store-carts, heavy baggage, and as many infantry as he had no boats for, by land, and as soon as the moon rose embarked his four guns and the majority of his infantry in 27 boats, and floated down the branch of the Indus which passes under Dera Fateh Khan. The river was high and rising daily, rendering navigation dangerous, and the Mullahs refused to proceed any farther when they reached the main stream, so they anchored until daylight, when they pushed off again. By 9 A. M., on the 19th they were abreast of General Cortlandt's camp at Jang, but were unable to approach owing to an island lying between and the shallowness of the inland stream. Edwardes therefore went on 14 miles farther south to Peronwala ferry, where the enemy had been threatening to cross for three days past. The cavalry reached General Cortlandt's camp, a distance of 50 miles, by noon, and many of them went on in the evening to Peronwala ghat, having accomplished 64 miles in the 24 hours, a considerable feat at that season.

The defeat of their advanced guard at Leia and the rapid removal of Edwardes' force and its appearance at Peronwala had a considerable moral effect on the enemy in the field and the people of the surrounding country. This was especially important at a time when at least one of the regiments with the British officer was contemplating treachery. And at Dera Ghazi Khan a victory gained over the rebels by loyal adherents still further contributed to the enemy's dismay.

Operations on the Indus.

On the morning of 22nd May General Cortlandt marched for Dera Ghazi Khan, which he was to reach in three stages; and on the 24th Edwardes moved to Aliana, 32 miles north of Dera Ghazi Khan. The enemy had marched also, and Edwardes found that they had moved to Koreshi, on the left bank of the Indus, opposite Dera Ghazi Khan, with the object of seizing a fleet of boats collected there by Longa Mal, the rebel leader who had been defeated at Dera Ghazi Khan. They were, however, forestalled by a party sent by Edwardes for the same purpose. On the evening of the 26th Edwardes and Van Cortlandt joined forces at Dera Ghazi Khan, the latter having embarked at daybreak in 33 boats at Aliana. In the canal Kasturi Wahu, which ran inland under the city, he found moored the 39 boats previously referred to, collected by Longa Mal for the passage of Mulraj's troops. He thus had sufficient boats to throw 6,000 men across the Indus at once, while the enemy had none. Edwardes was now free from anxiety. The only enemy left on his side of the Indus was Mokam Chand, Kardar of Harrand, 50 miles off, who held a strong fort with 200 men. The Pathan garrison, however, joined Edwardes, leaving only 100 Sikhs in Harrand fort. Mulraj's troops were encamped at Koreshi.

Edwardes and Van Cortlandt had now some 6,000 men and 10 guns in the field, and were ready for an advance; but first, in order to cause the withdrawal of Mulraj's troops from the Indus, he wished the Bahawalpur Army, known also as the Daoudputras, to cross the Sutlej and advance against and threaten Multan. With this object in view he entered into correspondence with Nawab Bahawal Khan, and at the same time wrote to the Resident at Lahore for permission to cross the Indus, to the right bank of which river he had been ordered to confine his operations. Bahawal Khan had a fine force of some 12,000 fighting Pathans. These crossed the Sutlej on the 30th and 31st May and a portion advanced northwards to Jalalpur Peronwala, 80 miles from Multan; but he split up his forces, and would not move forward on Shujabad, a measure which would have involved the retreat of the enemy at Koreshi.

Advance of the Bahawalpur force.

Edwardes, meanwhile, was given full discretion to act according to circumstances, the Resident merely indicating as his main objects the desirability of limiting Mulraj and the rebellion to as confined an area as possible, and ultimately his confinement to the fort of Multan until proper siege could be laid to that place. At the same time Lieutenant Lake of the Engineers was deputed from Lahore to accompany the Bahawalpur Army, with instructions to co-operate with Lieutenant Edwardes for the attainment of these objects. On the 10th June Edwardes made his preparations for crossing the Indus, and the same day he heard that Mulraj had ordered the retreat of the Koreshi force. He accordingly called in Van Cortlandt, leaving a garrison at Dera Gazi Khan, and a force to hold the Harrand garrison, and made the passage before nightfall with 2,500 Pathans, and 10 guns. These he encamped at Sera Diwanwala, opposite Dera Ghazi Khan, and sent his fleet back the 18 miles across the river for Van Cortlandt's force to follow, at the same time sending a message to Muzuuddin Khan, a lieutenant of Bahawal Khan, who was in the Sitpur district with 2,000 men, to reinforce Fateh Muhammad Khan Gheri, who was with the advanced portion of the Bahawalpur Army at Jalalpur Peronwala. Edwardes found that the Koreshi force had returned to Khangarh, on the right bank of the Chenab, some 20 miles distant, and 10

Edwardes crosses the Indus.

miles from Shujabad on the opposite side of the river, where Mulraj had ordered a concentration of his forces; but they soon afterwards retired to the latter place.

Advance to the Chenab.

It was not until the afternoon of the 14th that Edwardes' and Cortlandt's forces completed the passage of the Indus; the boats having to make several voyages across the 18 miles of water. On the morning of the 15th, Edwardes marched with 3,000 Pathan horse and foot and 20 *zamburaks* to Khangarh, an extensive fort, where he found that some of Mulraj's troops remained west of the Chenab. These had all been sent against Fateh Muhammad Khan, who was advancing on Shujabad with his division of the Bahawalpur Army, the intention being to defeat the latter before Edwardes could come to their assistance. Edwardes at once wrote to Muzuuddin Khan to cross the Chenab, and join Fateh Muhammad Khan, whom he at the same time enjoined not to fight a battle, but to entrench himself and stand on the defensive until he (Edwardes) joined him. On the morning of the 16th, news was received that the Bahawalpur forces had effected a junction, and thrown up entrenchments at their encampment at Guwain, 24 miles from Shujabad; and as they were 9,000 strong with 11 guns there was little fear but that they would be able to hold their own against about the same number of Mulraj's troops, who were still encamped four miles south of Shujabad.

General Cortlandt joined Edwardes at Khangarh with his guns and 1,500 regular Sikh troops on the 16th June. As soon as the moon rose, the march was resumed to Gagianwala Ferry, on the right bank of the Chenab, some 18 miles south of Khangarh.

Movements of the enemy.

On the evening of the 17th Edwardes received information that the enemy had advanced from Shujabad, and appeared to be making for the Kineri ferry, where he had intended to cross the Chenab. It thus became necessary for the Daoudputras to advance to that point to cover the crossing, moving by night. At Kineri they were joined by 3,000 Pathan levies on foot, the horses having to be left for want of boats, of which there were 47, sent up the river by Muzuuddin Khan after he had crossed.

Passage of the Chenab.

At 7 A. M. on the morning of the 18th Edwardes crossed himself, and heard heavy firing to the north-east of Kineri before he landed. Disembarking he set out for the sound of the guns, with three or four horsemen and some guides of Lieutenant Lumsden's corps. He found the Daoudputras drawn up in line on a jungly plain, with his Pathans on the left, and he rode down the line, and spoke a few words to the Bahawalpur Nawab's officers, urging them not to make a rash attack, until more men and guns should come across from General Cortlandt's camp. They promised to follow his advice, and not to advance until he gave the word. He then joined his division on the left.

The fire on both sides scarcely slackened until 3 P. M., by which hour the enemy had approached so close as to be able to reconnoitre the position, and for want of cavalry it was not possible to drive back their numerous reconnoitring parties of horse.

Battle of Kineri.

They discovered the weak (left) flank, and turned their whole fire on it. It was difficult to restrain the impatience of these untrained Pathan levies, and on that flank there were no guns to oppose the fire of the enemy; but Edwardes felt sure that General Cortlandt would not fail him, but would send the guns for which he had written, by 3 o'clock.

At half past three the enemy had pushed up to within a few hundred yards, when the guns and two regular regiments came up. A charge was carried out, followed by a hand to hand fight, while the opposing guns poured grape into each other at short range. At a little before 4, Commandant Subhan Khan made a brave sally at head of his regiment upon a single gun of the enemy, which he carried at the point of the bayonet. Confusion fell among their artillery, while Edwardes' guns advanced and poured grape into them, and although the Multan troops bravely laboured to save the two guns that were in action, they were taken. They had advanced with six in the afternoon, leaving four in rear, which they managed to carry off.

Defeat of the rebels.

The phase of the campaign which ended in the victory at Kineri is most instructive, both as regards preliminary operations and the manner in which the rivers were utilised and crossed, and in the final engagement, where Edwardes kept the Bahawalpur and his own forces on the defensive until they were sufficiently strong to assume the offensive with every chance of success. Nor is the least of its lessons to be found in the skilful training of raw levies into comparatively disciplined troops in so short a space of time.

Casualties.

In Edwardes' force the losses at the battle of Kineri amounted to 58 killed and 89 wounded. The Bahawalpur Army had about 100 casualties.

The enemy left 500 or 600 dead on the field. The routed rebels fled without halting to Multan, 46 miles distant, where they mustered some 3,000 out of 7,000 who had been in the fight.

Many no doubt went off to their homes. Had Edwardes' cavalry been present, doubtless few of the rebels would have escaped.

Results of the action.

Of the results of the action the British Resident at Lahore wrote, after commending Lieutenant Edwardes' energy, skill, and courage to the highest praise of the Government of India[1]:—

"The defeat of the enemy seems to have been complete; he showed more enterprise than I gave him credit for in marching from his position to prevent the junction of Lieutenant Edwardes' force with that of Bahawal Khan, and in attacking the latter while moving to cover the passage of Lieutenant Edwardes over the Chenab. The best disciplined native army is never attacked to so great advantage as on the line of march. The attack seems to have been well designed and well executed. The mode in which it was received, the long period for which it was sustained, till re-inforcements arrived late in the day, and subsequent advance with its results are not unworthy of the glorious anniversary on which the fight took place and the victory was won.

The neck of the Multan rebellion may be considered now broken, and having tried the result of an action on the plain and been signally beaten, the Dewan Mulraj will not, I think, be able to hold his fort for any length of time with his undisciplined and mutinous troops. If he is able to keep the garrison faithful to him till October, so much the better.

In the meantime the fort at Multan is all that remains to the Dewan; the whole of the territories are in our occupation or that of our ally, Bahawal Khan. My combinations have been everywhere successful. Shaikh Imam-ud-din, with his Muhammadan levies and two guns, is at Malsi, about thirty miles south-east from Multan, having made arrangements for the administration of the districts between Pank Pattan and that place. The rest of that Doab, to the south and south-west, has been taken up by the officers of Bahawal Khan. The force of Raja Sher Singh and his Sirdars is now at Tulamba; its fidelity may now be depended on, and it will be advanced to Sirdarpur about twenty miles from Multan. This force has been a cause of much anxiety to me. It has required constant judicious handling. The Sirdars are true I believe; the soldiers are all false I know. The Sikh army in Peshawar, Bannu, and Hazara were watching this force to take their cue from its conduct. Mulraj was anxious for its approach to Multan. My plan was to keep the attention of the Sikh Army fixed on it, and to keep it from any position in which its mettle or material could be tried, or in which Mulraj's influence on it could be brought into action till the rebels' game was lost.

In the Sind Sagar Doab, between the Chenab and the Indus, the force under Sirdar Jhanda Singh, purged of its Charanjit traitors, and no longer

[1] Edwardes was promoted to the rank of Major and made C. B. for his services. He had the advantage of writing his own despatches. No doubt his success was greatly due to Faujdar Khan and Cortlandt, who possessed an intimate knowledge of the enemy and their capacity.

doubtful, as Jowahir Mal Dutt has with him 1,500 Musalmans, is at Leia, the whole of the south of the Doab has been occupied by Bahawal Khan's officials. The trans-Indus provinces were all taken possession of by Lieutenant Edwardes and General Cortlandt, before those officers crossed that river; and arrangements for their administration made. . . . . . The Governor General will not fail to observe that, in the operations which have been undertaken for the suppression of this rebellion, the Durbar has taken no part, and that neither the Sirdars, the Durbar officials, nor the army—with the exception of General Cortlandt and his own battalions—have given any aid. What has been done has been effected by newly-raised Muhammadan levies under Lieutenant Edwardes, or in the other parts of the country by parties acting under my immediate orders, and by our ally Bahawal Khan, not only without the assistance of, but in spite of, the machinations of Durbar officials, the Sikh army, and the Sikh population, all of whom were from the first and have continued to the last thoroughly disaffected.

If therefore this rebellion is brought to a close, now or hereafter, and the delinquents to punishment, and the fort of Multan is got into our possession, the British Government will still have to call the Sikh Government to account for the murder of its officers, under circumstances of unparalleled treachery and atrocity, for which no redress has been made by them, or even, it may be said, attempted."

Advance to Shujabad.

The rear and baggage of Edwardes' force completed the passage of the Chenab on the 21st June, and next day the march was continued to Shujabad. The two armies united formed a force of 18,000 men and 30 guns. Edwardes suggested that the siege of Multan should be at once undertaken, asking for a few heavy guns, a mortar battery, some sappers and miners and the services of Major Napier* of the Engineers to plan the operations.

His opinion was supported by the Resident at Lahore, stress being laid on the importance of undertaking siege operations before the enemy had time to strengthen the fort. Government agreed with the Commander-in-Chief that, as British gunners and a British force would be necessary, the time of year was not suitable for these operations, but a force under General Wlish was eventually despatched in consideration of the evil political effect of delay.

March on Multan.

In the meantime Edwardes advanced with the intention of doing his best to take Multan, or at least to confine the enemy entirely to that place. Difficulties of supply detained him at Shujabad until the 26th June, when he marched to Sikandarabad. The spirits of Mulraj's troops were to some extent raised by the appearance at Multan of Bhai Maharaj Singh, a *chela* who had raised a following and an insurrection, and had crossed the Ravi to a place within

* Afterwards Lord Napier of Magdala.

50 miles of Lahore, where he and 500 or 600 adherents were supposed to have been driven into the Chenab and destroyed on the 1st June. His re-appearance was consequently regarded as miraculous by a people prone to superstition. Mulraj now ordered his troops out to Surajkhund, six miles from Multan, where a *nala* forty feet wide and impassable without boats or bridge, crossed the road. Here there was a bridge, which was seized by the rebels. On 1st July Edwardes advanced from Surajkhund, where he was joined by the division of Shaikh Imam-ud-din, and reached Tibi, six miles distant and four miles south-west of Multan. The whole of the infantry and artillery under command of General Cortlandt moved in order of battle, Lieutenants Edwardes and Lake bringing up the rear with all the cavalry. They reached Tibi at 11 A. M., when intelligence was received that Mulraj had recalled his troops from the Surajkhund bridge, from whence he had intended to attack the British camp at that place, and marching them parallel on the other side of the *nala*, concealed by the banks, crossed the water by a masonry bridge in front of the city of Multan and emerged on the plain three miles in front.

Action at Tibi.

Edwardes' force beat to arms, having already arrived in camp and turned out; formed line and advanced to meet the rebels in the following order:—the Daoudputras force on the right, commanded by Lieutenant Lake; Sultan Khan's Musalman Regiment, the Suraj Mukhi regiment, and General Cortlandt's ten guns in the centre, under the General; Edwardes' Pathan levies on the left centre, flanked by his Pathan cavalry; and on the left of all Shaikh Imam-ud-din's troops, whose fidelity was doubtful.

Lieutenant Lake, seeing some high mounds, the ruins of an old canal, in front of him, hurried on and took possession of them; planted his guns securely behind this natural entrenchment; and from this commanding position began the action by a heavy fire on the enemy's left, which was as heavily returned. The Daoudputras had been engaged about a quarter of an hour when the centre and left overtook them and drew off the enemy's fire. The battle then became general; Cortlandt's artillery in the centre, the Daoudputras on the right, and Shaikh Imam-ud-din's two guns being all brought to bear on the enemy, who selected his ground at the village of Saddusain, planting almost the whole line under jungle cover, with the artillery concealed in mud villages and date palm groves. A severe artillery struggle ensued, during which the infantry on both sides lay down in line behind ditches.

The enemy had 10 or 12 guns and could therefore do little against the 22 of their opponent, although the Sikh gunners stood manfully to their pieces. The rebels fought with desperate courage, the action resolving itself into a series of struggles in which they were driven back from village to village and grove to grove; their total rout was much delayed by the *nalas* and ditches with which the ground was intersected, the bridges and fords of which were known to them but not to their opponents. Thus Shaikh Imam-ud-din's guns were out of action early in the day, and the Daoudputras were long unable to extricate theirs from the bank of the canal which they first occupied; the artillery on both sides was thus equalised during the greater part of the day. The result of the action was, however, no longer in doubt; for the native army that retires is lost.

Flight of Mulraj.

At length Diwan Mulraj, who commanded in person and who had had a fall from his elephant, mounted a horse and fled precipitately from the field, carrying with him all the guns but two, which were served desperately to cover the movement. The Suraj Mukhi regiment of infantry, led by Mr. Quin, Edwardes' writer, "a young man but old soldier whose conspicuous bravery deserves special notice," finally decided the day by a brilliant charge in which they captured these two guns. A rush of the whole infantry and cavalry followed, and the broken enemy fled in irrecoverable disorder. Edwardes halted his troops under the very walls of Multan, but returned to camp as the increasing darkness did not permit him to ascertain whether they were under the fire of the fort or not.

Conduct of the troops.

The rebels numbered 11,000 or 12,000, the majority old soldiers, and two thirds Sikh and Hindu fanatics. They fought with desperation, and Edwardes attributed the victory entirely to each division of the line being led by European officers. Lieutenant Lake took up successive positions with skill and judgment, while his personal intrepidity under fire afforded a fine example to his men. General Cortlandt handled his regular regiments and artillery like a good soldier and brave man. Several Pathan Chiefs made dashing charges against Mulraj's cavalry; among others Ghulam Sarwar Khan Khagwani, who killed several Sikhs and was shot through the arm in the midst of the enemy's line. Faujdar Khan Alizai acted as Edwardes' Adjutant-General throughout the operations, and in spite of a severe sword wound received at Kineri, took command of the cavalry in this battle and directed their movements.

Casualties.

The total loss amounted to 281 killed and wounded; including several Pathans of note, Fateh Khan of Khisur, Hasan Khan Musazai, Rahim Khan Khudakka, all brave men. Captain McPherson of the Nawab of Bahawalpur's service fell at the head of his regiment. The enemy suffered severe loss, increased by a cruel and treacherous act on the part of the Diwan Mulraj. Between the field and the city ran the same large *nala* that passed by Suraj Khund and there was only one bridge across it near Sadusain. When Mulraj had passed the bridge with his artillery he planted two guns on it to prevent his soldiers from retreating. The majority forced the barrier with some loss, but many were drowned in trying to swim the *nala*. Hundreds deserted to their homes, and of the 400 Gurkhas who had deserted Vans Agnew only 150 answered their names again at Multan.

Effect of the action.

Mulraj, although defeated, retained unbroken courage.[1] Having mustered his soldiers next morning he invited them to go out with him again to fight, but when the kettledrums of Edwardes' reconnoitring cavalry were heard approaching the city, they left their ranks in confusion. The men were, in fact, greatly demoralised; numbers of Sikhs even threw their arms into the *nala* and divested themselves of every appearance of soldiers.

Now was the time when the contest should, if possible, have been pushed to a final issue, before Mulraj had time to strengthen the fortifications of the city, and before his troops could gather fresh courage and an accession of numbers after their defeats. The principal obstacle to a siege consisted in the inundations; but Lieutenant Lake wrote :—

> "I see no reason why siege operations should be impeded, as from all I can learn inundations are confined to the north side of the fort and the west side of the city. On the east and south the ground is comparatively high, and is in no way affected by the water in the surrounding canals and drains. Of four gates which the fort contains, the Khidri is the only one which will be inaccessible from water. In front of three other gates and on the city side is some very high ground which is not only above the reach of inundation but on a level with the fort itself. There is no reason why the attack should not be made from this quarter."

But Edwardes had no siege guns at his disposal.

Measures for the siege.

On Edwardes' application, the Resident on 10th July directed Major-General Whish, C.B., who was at Ferozepore, to "take immediate measures for the despatch of a siege train with its establishment

[1] On July 13th Edwardes wrote with regard to Mulraj.—"Mulraj is at his wits' end; sometimes he talks of a night attack, and sits up all night in a Hindu temple near the bridge cased in chain armour from head to foot, but nothing comes of it. One day he fortifies the city, another day he fortifies the fort. To-day he tells all his soldiers to leave him because he has no money to pay them and to-morrow keeps up their spirits by assuring them that when iron shot fail he will fire silver on the besiegers."

and a competent escort and force for the reduction of the fort of Multan."

He impressed on him the necessity for no delay in the despatch of this expedition, suggesting the employment of the second class siege train from Ferozepore, together with a complement of British and native troops of all arms. The Governor-General, on the advice of the Commander-in-Chief, did not, however, concur in the advisability of sending a force at that season of the year. Eventually, however, in view of the bad political effect of a policy of vacillation and the abstention from operations on the part of the British Government, it was decided that General Whish should take a force against Multan. The news of a British force being about to take the field had already been spread abroad, and had had a salutary effect both on the enemy in arms and on the disaffected Sikhs.

To countermand the movement would be fraught with evil consequences. As Edwardes wrote to the Resident—"Had you hesitated to take the field now my position would have been converted in a month to one of the greatest peril; the advantages I have gained would have slipped through my fingers one by one and about a fortnight or three weeks hence I should be constrained in self-defence to keep up our prestige by taking the city."

On the 22nd July the Resident at Lahore issued a Proclamation[1] regarding affairs at Multan.

It has been already related that three columns had been despatched by the Durbar to co-operate against the Multan rebels. These, under Jawahir Mal, Sher Singh, and Imam-ud-din, were now approaching Multan, and caused Edwardes some alarm owing to the disaffection existing in the Khalsa Army. On 5th July Sher Singh reached Gogran, five miles from Multan, but Edwardes wisely arranged that the Sikhs should encamp in his rear at Suraj Khund, where he could prevent their co-operating with the rebels in the city. Sher Singh's force consisted of a regular regiment of infantry, a troop of horse artillery, four guns of another troop, and some 2,500 *jagirdari* horse. So far their leaders appeared to be loyal, but the troops only awaited a favourable opportunity to break out.

Situation at Multan.

On the 20th July, Mulraj made a sortie, hoping that Sher Singh's Sikhs would join him, but the besiegers showed a bold front, the Sikhs crossing from Suraj Khund and threatening the city on the south-east, so he withdrew. On the 26th he renewed the attempt with a

[1] Appendix V.

like result. He had issued a proclamation in Multan that the Sikh army were his friends, and that the Khalsa soldiery were to have free access to the city and bazaars.

The delay in despatching a British force, and the continued defiance of the Diwan was having an unfavourable effect on the Khalsa army and country generally, and there were outbreaks at Harrand and at Bannu, while plots and intrigues were rife throughout the country from Lahore to Peshawar. These finally culminated in an uprising which resulted in the Second Sikh War and the annexation of the Punjab. In the meantime, however, General Whish was on his way to Multan at the head of a British force.

CHAPTER VII.

THE FIRST SIEGE OF MULTAN.

General Whish's force,[1] which is detailed in the margin, leftin two columns on the 24th and 26th July, moving on Multan down the rivers Ravi and Sutlej, the British troops by boat, while the native regiments marched by night, to avoid the heat, along the banks of the rivers. The 32nd Foot, however, did not embark at Ferozepore until the 11th August and joined the camp at Multan on the 25th. The right column with General Whish arrived at Sirdarpur on the 12th August, the 10th Foot leaving their boats and joining on the same date. Here a depôt with 15 days' supplies, to be replenished as required, was established, a steamer, the "Conqueror", being employed on the lines of communication. The left column reached Karampur on the 13th August, and joined the right column near Jampur on the 19th. The artillery and siege train boats were delayed by high winds and did not arrive until later. From Sirdarpur General Whish sent 100 *bildars* with tools, under the protection of a body of irregular troops and two guns, to stop the head of the canal that supplied the waters of inundation at Multan.

Advance of General Whish.

1 Brigade Cavalry.
Siege train.
Engineers.
2 Brigades Infantry.

On the morning of 18th August the right column encamped 2½ miles east of Multan, and were joined next day by the left column. They thus effected a junction with Edwardes, who had on the 16th exchanged camping-grounds with Sher Singh in order to facilitate this operation. On the 17th the enemy came out to attack General Whish's advanced guard, engaging the cavalry and piquets with a large body of horse and foot soon after 2 P. M. The piquets were reinforced by the flank companies of regiments, and the enemy retired with a loss of forty killed, many wounded, and some prisoners. On the British side six men were wounded.

On the 1st September Edwardes' force was moved from Suraj Khund to Musam Khan's well, three miles nearer Multan, to the north. During this movement General Whish and the engineer officers

Reconnaissance of Multan.

[1] For detail of force, see Appendix IV.

[2] This work was completed after much labour on 7th September.

made a close reconnaissance of the northern face of the fort. They passed half an hour unmolested near and about the Idgah (where Vans Agnew and Anderson were killed) and were retiring from it when the enemy opened a harmless fire with one or two guns. The enemy were in strong force to resist Edwardes' advance, but he gradually overcame opposition and established his camp with the centre resting upon the gardens of Kach Byragi and Khudazar, his left on the great Multan *nala*, and his extreme right half a mile to the right of the Yog Mai, a temple which his troops took possession of, but abandoned as untenable. In this operation Lieutenants Lake and Pollock distinguished themselves, as well as a party of the Daoudputras, two companies of the Surajmakhi regiment and Lieutenant Lumsden's[1] troop of the Guide Corps. Shaikh Imam-ud-din's division killed thirty or forty of the enemy, while Raja Sher Singh brought his guns into play and enfiladed the enemy for two or three hours. The construction of a rocket battery was begun the same evening in front of Edwardes' camp.

Plans of attack.

On the 4th September General Whish issued a proclamation calling on the inhabitants and garrison of Multan to surrender on the 5th—"I shall otherwise in obedience to the orders of the Supreme Government of India commence hostilities on a scale that must insure early destruction to the rebel traitor and his adherents." On this day the siege-train arrived. On the 6th a meeting of officers was held to arrange a plan of attack on the fort and city. Major Napier laid two plans before the Major-General :—

1. To take the town of Multan at all costs by a *coup-de-main* by the whole force moving down in line, getting within battering distance of the Khuni Burj and storming the breach as soon as practicable.

2. To march round to the north and attack the citadel by regular approaches.

The first plan was suggested by Major Napier on political grounds, although it would entail great loss of life to the besiegers. But affairs throughout the Punjab had become threatening, and Sirdar Chattar Singh, father of Sher Singh, had already rebelled in Hazara. Edwardes, however, to whom the matter was referred, was of opinion that the political situation did not necessiate such action. Things had gone too far to be rectified by the mere capture of Multan.[2] The second was considered by Major Napier

[1] Afterwards General Sir H. B. Lumsden.

[2] The Resident, however, considered that Major Napier had taken the more correct view of the situation, and that Lieutenant Edwardes underestimated the effect which some brilliant success to the British arms would have on the insurrectionary movement in the Punjab.

the plan most consonant with military science. But it was probable that the change of plan would be construed by the natives into a defeat. Lieutenant Lake proposed to run a trench from the battery on the extreme right of the Daoudputras, camp, north-east to a point called Ramtirat, which would be upwards of a mile; and to throw up heavy-gun batteries at such points of this entrenchment as would drive away the enemy without much loss of life and with certain success. This plan was adopted. Next day at daylight the trench was traced and opened out. The General wrote to the Resident at Lahore on the 7th September:—

The plan adopted.

Our first parallel was commenced yesterday about three quarters of a mile in advance of the small interval between us (his own and Edwardes' forces) by 1,000 of Lieutenant Edwardes' men and at intervals of six hours by 1,600 from my camp, the half thereof being at night from His Majesty's 10th and 32nd Foot; the only casualties reported are one man killed and one wounded, both of the 72nd Native Infantry. As we could thus have no battery ready and I knew the one armed with light guns, in Lieutenant Edwards' camp, was annoyed by the enemy's gun or guns 1,200 yards in its front, I directed last night two of our 8-inch howitzers to be sent thither, and went myself this morning to see them placed in position and open fire. The first round of shrapnel was fired simultaneously and followed occasionally by rounds of common shell.

Beginning of the siege.

The working parties made good progress during the next few days, and by the 9th there were established at Ramtirat, batteries of two 8-inch howitzers, and three 8-inch mortars, and at a few hundred yards from its left, a battery of four 18-pounders, while a rocket battery was added on the right of the howitzer battery that evening. On the 10th an attempt was made to dislodge the enemy from a position near that from which they were driven on the 8th. The attack was carried out with great gallantry and perseverance by Lieutenant-Colonel Pattoun, 32nd Foot, field-officer of the trenches, with detachments of the 10th Foot and 49th and 72nd Native Infantry, and two of Cortlandt's guns, but the position proved stronger than had been expected, and the detachment was withdrawn after sustaining heavy casualties.[1] Brigadier Markham was wounded later in the day.

Unsuccessful attack.

[1] *Killed.*—3 privates, 10th Foot, 1 native officer, 6 rank and file, 72nd Native Infantry. 1 havildar, 4 rank and file, 47th Native Infantry.

Wounded.—Lieutenant Hollinsworth, 12 sergeants, 34 rank and file, 10th Foot; 1 private, 32nd Foot; Lieutenants Richardson and Irwin, 1 havildar, 22 rank and file, 49 Native Infantry; 1 native officer, 7 rank and file, 72nd Native Infantry.

Missing.—3 privates, 10th Foot; 1 sepoy, 72nd Native Infantry.

PLAN No. 6

To illustrate

THE SIEGE OF MULTAN

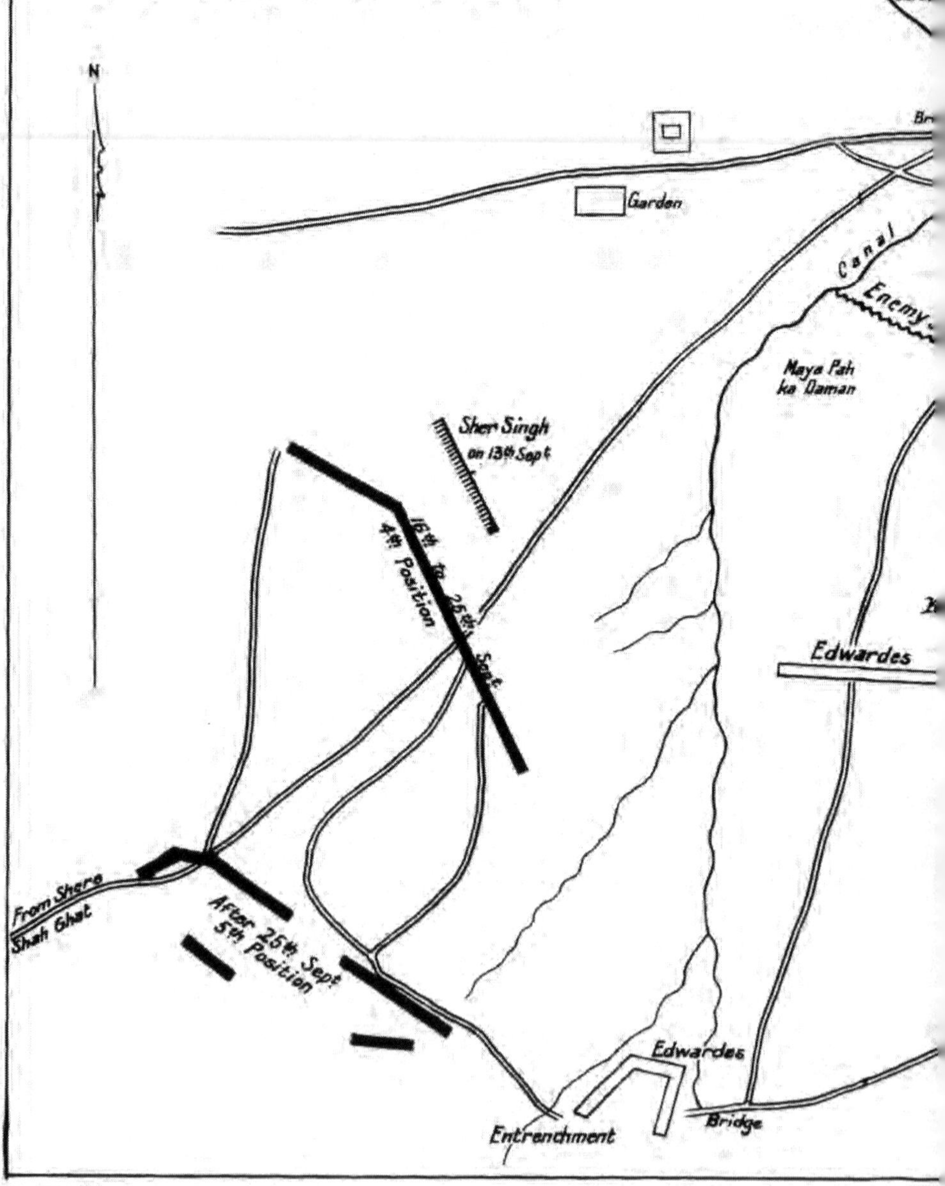

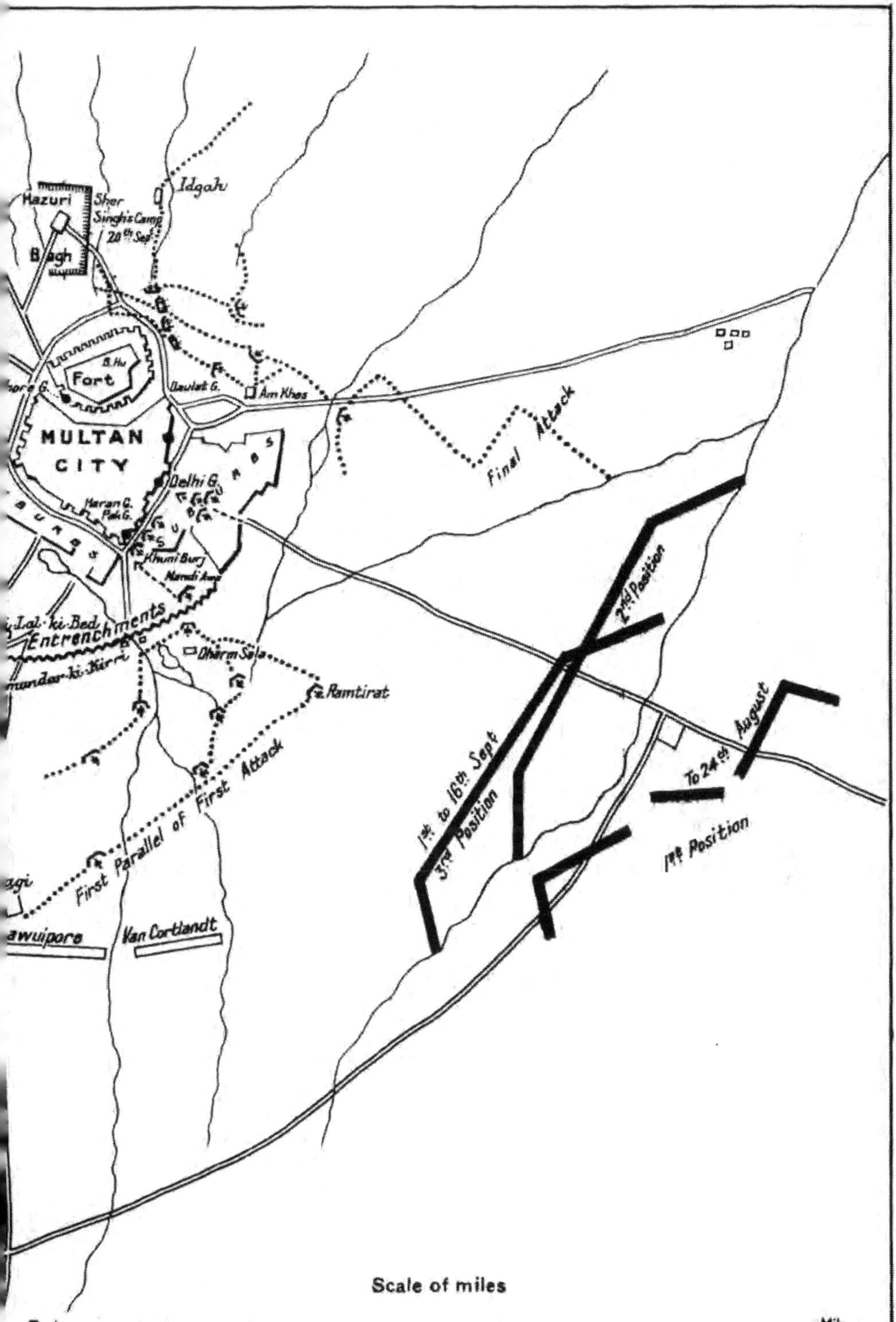

Idgah
Hazuri
Bagh
Sher Singh's Camp 28th Sept
Fort
Daulat G.
Am Khas
MULTAN CITY
Delhi G.
Haran G.
Pak G.
Khuni Burj
Mandi Awa
Lal-ki-Bed
Entrenchments
Dharm Sala
Ramtirat
Final Attack
2nd Position
1st to 16th Sept
3rd Position
To 24th August
1st Position
First Parallel of First Attack
Van Cortlandt
Scale of miles
Furlongs 8 7 6 5 4 3 2 1 0 1 2 Miles

The Chief Engineer now thought it preferable to turn the enemy's position instead of taking it by assault, and four 5½ inch mortars were brought to bear on it at 600 yards, on the left of Ramtirat.

On the 12th September the British columns advanced to the attack, the enemy's position being taken in front with the troops detailed in the margin, while Lieutenant Edwardes co-operated with his force from the left of the advanced piquet of the trenches. The troops were formed into right and left columns under Lieutenant-Colonels Pattoun and Franks, C. B., respectively.

Action of 12th September, 1846.

Brigadier Harvey.
One Troop Horse Artillery.
One Squadron each 11th Light and 7th and 11th Irregular Cavalry.
Six companies, 10th Foot.
Six companies, 32nd Foot.
8th Native Infantry.
49th Native Infantry.

The position was very strong and stoutly defended, the conflict terminating in a series of hand-to-hand encounters, and in about an hour and a half the enemy were driven back with severe loss. In this, as in many actions in India, the Horse Artillery played an important part, being brought up at an opportune moment and preventing an accession of numbers to the enemy.

The British columns stormed and captured the enemy's position, gaining half a mile of ground, while Edwardes drove back their left beyond the village of Jamundar-ki-kiri, half a mile from the southern angle of the city walls. The defenders were almost entirely destroyed, leaving 500 dead on the ground; but the British casualties were also heavy, amounting to :—

Killed.—5 British and 2 native officers, 3 sergeants, and 29 rank and file. *Wounded.*—12 British and 1 native officer, 6 sergeants, 197 rank and file.

Defection of Sher Singh.

The disaffection among the Sikh troops under Raja Sher Singh has already been referred to. But while the soldiers of the Khalsa were known to be ready for rebellion, it was supposed that Sher Singh would remain faithful to the British. On the morning of the 14th September, however, Sher Singh marched off to join the rebels at Multan, at the head of his troops, beating the Dharam ka Dhosa, or religious drum, in the name of the Khalsa. Sher Singh's father, Chattar Singh, had already broken out in Hazara, and the spread of unrest was observed throughout the Punjab. The defection of Sher Singh was, however, the event that changed the whole aspect of affairs. It now became evident that the British had to contend not merely with a rebel Diwan at Multan, but with the Sikh nation in arms.

General Whish now came to the conclusion, with the adv ce of Napier and Edwardes, that it was impossible to prosecute the siege with the force at his disposal. On the evening of the 14th he withdrew his troops, except a strong piquet with two horse artillery guns at Ramtirat. On the 15th Edwardes' force and the Bahawalpur army changed ground to Suraj Khund, and next day the British troops retired and encamped on the ground where the battle of Sadusain was fought. This move secured the ferry communication with the Leia districts, and the countries beyond the Indus, also with Sind and Bombay; whilst it preserved that with Bahawalpur and Ferozepore, and so with Lahore.

Consequent on the withdrawal of General Whish, the Commander-in-Chief ordered the 29th Foot and 31st and 56th Native Infantry to reinforce the Multan Force. A Bombay Column was also ordered up to assist him, but this did not join until the 27th December. In the meantime it is necessary to narrate the events that occurred in other parts of the country during the intervening period.

CHAPTER VIII.

THE SIKH RISING.

It has already been related that, while the events narrated in the previous chapter were taking place, rebellion had spread in Hazara under the direction of the Nazim Sirdar Chattar Singh. Major St. P. Lawrence[1] was in charge of affairs at Peshawar, his subordinate in Hazara being Captain James Abbott. On the 16th July the Resident at Lahore wrote to Government that "the Sikh troops in Hazara are described by Captain Abbott as in that state of disappointed fear which sometimes precedes desperation." But he did not consider that they would commit themselves to open revolt, in view of the trend of affairs before Multan at that time. That there was widespread conspiracy among the Sikhs has already been indicated, and the Maharani's part in this having been discovered, that lady was in July removed to Benares.

Events in Hazara.

Early in August an emissary of Mulraj was seized by one of the Yusufzai Khans in the act of inciting to rebellion, and was shortly afterwards executed. At the beginning of July, Captain Abbott reported that the Sikh force in Pakli was in a disaffected state, and on the 1st August he wrote "that the infantry of the corps had positively determined to march for Lahore" that morning. At the same time he received intelligence from Haripur that the force there and in Khatir was "expecting an immediate march to Lahore, and had received assurance of support from the Bannu force." He considered that the Sirdar Chattar Singh was the instigator of the movement. On the 6th August he wrote:—

Revolt of the Pakli Brigade.

The Pakli Brigade of about 800 bayonets, 2 troops of horse, 4 field guns and 20 *zamburaks* had broken up its bazaar, sold off its store of grain, called in its cattle, packed much of its baggage, and was actually about to march that morning for Lahore when it found that I had manned all the roads with the armed peasantry of Hazara. It is still in the same state of readiness for an immediate start, and will be joined by the Hazara, Khawta and Khatir forces, and in all probability by that of Bannu."

1 Brother of Sir J. and Sir H. Lawrence, and Commissioner in Rajputana during the Mutiny, 1857-58.

Chattar Singh refused to go to Captain Abbott and despatched his emissaries, not only to raise trouble in the Punjab, but to Kabul to invite Dost Muhammad to expel the British, receiving Peshawar in return for his co-operation. The Resident at Lahore considered that Abbott had been hasty in raising the people of Hazara, and in his treatment of and attitude towards Chattar Singh, but there can be no doubt that the latter was from the first disloyal, and in the circumstances the man on the spot was the best judge of the causes of the events which took place. On the afternoon of the 6th August an *émeute* took place at Haripur, of which Captain Abbott gave the following account :—

Abbott in Hazara.

The Sikhs have assembled in force at Haripur, by order of Sirdar Chattar Singh, to set free the brigade in Pakli who are endeavouring to effect their escape in order to march on Lahore. The Sirdar ordered out the troops from the city, contrary to my order yesterday, and directed Colonel Canora[1] to bring out his guns. The Colonel refused to do so without my order. The Sirdar sent two companies to seize them ; the *golandaz* betrayed their trust, and whilst Canora was endeavouring to defend himself he was shot dead. The Sirdar immediately ordered up the Hasan Abdal, Rawal Pindi, and Kurara forces, in all about five regiments, with a body of horse. I have ordered out the armed peasantry and will do my best to destroy the Sikh army. Colonel Canora's last act was unsurpassed by anything recorded in history. He stood alone against the whole Sikh army ; and when his dastardly *golandaz* refused to fire, took the match into his own hand.''

Later, Abbott reported that Colonel Canora wrote to him asking if he should surrender his guns, of which the Sikhs wished to get possession. He had been long apprehensive of this demand.

"In the meantime the Sirdar sent his most confidential servants to persuade him to yield, and this failing ordered two companies to take the guns by force. Canora loaded his two guns with grape, and ordered the *golandaz* to fire, but they replied that they were the Sirdar's servants. On his havildar also refusing, Canora cut him down, and seizing the match applied it to the vent. The gun burnt priming and he was shot by two of the Sirdar's servants. He attempted to rise, and cut down an officer, but his throat was severed from behind by a sabre cut. '

Chattar Singh stated that he ordered the guns out as the town was threatened by a vast concourse of armed Muhammadans, collected from the surrounding districts. They were, he said, necessary for the protection of his force, and must have fallen into the hands of the insurgents (it must be remembered that the Muhammadans had been assembled by Abbott's orders) had they remained where they were ; and he said he offered to give Canora a certificate that the

[1] An American officer in the Sikh service.

move was made by his orders and on his responsibility. Canora still refusing to move his guns was shot down by musketry. However, whether previously disloyal or not, Chattar Singh now declared himself, rewarded the men who shot Canora, and sent emissaries to raise the Sikhs in different parts of the country. Abbott had, however, blocked the passes, while Lieutenant John Nicholson was despatched from Pehsawar to Attock with an escort of 60 Jagirdari Horse and 150 Pathan levies to counteract any evil designs that Sirdar Chattar Singh might have in that direction. Moving to Hasan Abdal, Nicholson employed himself in raising militia for the protection of the country from the insurgent Sikhs, who had marched from that place to join Sirdar Chattar Singh in Hazara. He at the same time, by concentrating his levies at Margalla, took measures to prevent the march of the Sikh regiments from Karur to Hazara. By 19th August he had collected about 1,000 levies. This action, and the vigorous measures taken by Captain Abbott in Hazara, disheartened the Sikh troops for the time being.

Abbott's measures.

On 20th August Abbott heard that a regiment and two guns, with some horse and *zamburaks*, had marched from Pakli. He at once marched with all the men he had just mustered to gain the passes before the Sikhs should reach there. "A fiery march of more than thirty miles secured this object."[1] But he found that the Sikh detachment had not actually marched. He had scarcely time to make arrangements for the security of the Silhad Pass when a messenger from Nicholson brought intelligence that Sirdar Chattar Singh had marched the whole of the Haripur force for Hasan Abdal.

His march to Hasan Abdal.

In an hour he was on the move to Nicholson's aid, and having marched forty miles, halted three miles on the right rear of the Sikh force.

Nicholson, who was in a strong position on the Attock road, had entered into negotiations with Chattar Singh, and agreed that Abbott's force should withdraw to a distance; whereupon the latter selected a position overlooking the Sikh camp, which he watched during the day through his telescope. In the evening he observed the the Sikhs were about to move, so got together his levy and hastened to the Moti ravine,[2] hoping to occupy it in time to dispute the passage. Abbott wrote in his despatch—

"The Musalmans, who observe the fast rigidly, were gasping through thirst. On approaching the ravine I perceived through the twilight two

[1] Abbott's Despatch of 23rd August 1848. He marched straight off the muster parade, without even revisiting his tent.

[2] Four miles southward of Margalla.

dark masses which appeared to be elephants, and, thinking to catch those animals with the guns upon their backs, made a dash at them with my cavalry. The howitzers, however, were loaded and in position, and opened a fire which swept the whole line of my approach, so that I was obliged to draw the horsemen off to the right under cover of the village Tanda. I then returned to look after the foot, which had wholly disappeared, having dived into a small ravine when first the artillery opened upon it. In the darkness of the night it was long before I could discover a single *gole* (group or body) and very long ere any considerable portion could be thrown into the ravine. I saw a long column of dust indicating that much of the Sikh force had already passed over, and by the time that I had penetrated down the ravine to the gun road not a straggler was left on the farther side. I tried to rally my people to an attack with the sabre ; but either they had been bribed to remain inactive or their fears made them so, for neither encouragement nor taunts could persuade more than a handful to follow the Sikh march along the ravine which for half a mile ran parallel to it. I then ordered the force out of the ravine that we might unite with Captain Nicholson's camp at Pohr."

Chattar Singh's movements.

The levies had expended their ammunition, and showed their total unfitness to contend with regular troops. On the morning of the 27th Abbott and Nicholson fell back to Hasan Abdal. Chattar Singh advanced to Usman Khatir, and on the 28th Abbott started on his return to Nara. Next day Chattar Singh advanced, obliging Nicholson to retire to Burban, six miles west of Hasan Abdal, and thus obtained command of the whole line of road from Rotas to Attock, where Nicholson was on the 31st August.

Defence of Attock.

Next day Lieutenant Herbert with some levies from Peshawar arrived at Attock, where a strong fort defended the famous passage of the Indus. Nicholson provisioned the fort, placed the guns in position, and leaving Herbert in command, proceeded next day to Gondal, on the Hasan Abdal road, 7 miles from Attock, intending to keep the field with the levies which he joined there. The fort at Attock was furnished with three months' supplies for 1,000 men, and as there was plenty of ammunition he considered it secure from attack while the provisions lasted.[1]

Further movements of Chattar Singh.

It will be remembered that during this period the siege of Multan was in progress. On the 19th September Captains Abbott and Nicholson reported all well, when they had just heard of the retirement of General Whish from Multan, consequent on the defection of Sher

[1] He held out until the 3rd January 1849, when he was obliged to abandon the fort on the advance of Dost Muhammad with the Afghan Army.

Singh. On October 7th the Governor-General wrote to the Secret Committee:—

"Chattar Singh's proceedings are very unaccountable, and at present exhibit a great want of energy. He occupies the same position as he did except that by forcing the Dambur Pass he has released the Pakli Brigade, and thus strengthened himself with more men and guns, of which he is now said to be in possession of fourteen. He marches and counter-marches from place to place in the upper portion of the Sind Sagar Doab, without seeming to be able to come to any decision as to what future course to pursue".

Both the Resident at Lahore, and the officers on the spot, continued to urge the despatch of a brigade to Hazara, but the Commander-in-Chief was of opinion that the employment of detachments in this manner would be futile, and considered that an army should be assembled on the frontier. He was accordingly requested by the Governor-General to take measures for collecting at Ferozepore an army of some 13,000 men, which was eventually supplemented by additional forces, and formed the army for the conquest of the Punjab.

For a month things remained comparatively quiet in Hazara, although disaffection manifested itself among the Sikh troops at Peshawar and on 5th September Major G. St. P. Lawrence wrote that the Sikh soldiery were being invited to attack him. In the middle of October also, trouble broke out at Bannu. On the 20th October Captain Abbott wrote from Srikot in Hazara the following particulars of an affair between his levies and Chattar Singh's army:—

"It may be remembered that last year I excluded the Simalkand branch of the Tarkulli clan from the mountain of Gandgarh and built a castle in their village to secure the peace of the mountain. The garrison consisting of a company of Richpal Singh's regiment and about seventy or eighty matchlocks declared like most others in Hazara for Chattar Singh. Chattar Singh had sent a deputation of Zamindars of Hazara begging the release of the garrison, but had written by the same deputation forbidding it to evacuate the fort.[1] I had several times offered it safe conduct with arms and baggage but the offer was declined.

On the morning of the 18th Chattar Singh's camp moved up to Ghazi on the left bank of the Indus, and it was evident that his object was Simalkand. But owing to his veto to the garrison it was expected that he would endeavour by that route to carry Srikot. Simalkand being situated at the foot of the mountains, with a gun-road from the plains, it was not possible

[1] History repeats itself. In 1817, on the conclusion of treaty with Sindhia, it was agreed by the latter that certain of his forts were to be delivered up to the British. But these forts held out, and it was found that they had written instructions from Sindhia to do so, although he had concluded peace with the British.

for 1,800 matchlocks (my whole available force, inclusive of the levies of the mountain) to prevent the relief of the fort by six regiments with cavalry and artillery. But I deemed it important that the evacuation should not be effected with impunity and that no hope should be opened to Chattar Singh of ever ascending the mountain.

Long before daybreak of the 18th the Sikh army was busied in cooking food for the day's work. At about 8 A. M. the force advanced in two columns, carrying four guns, and two howitzers upon elephants. Being provided with excellent guides and having a secret understanding with the villages of Kondi and Ambar Khana, who supply some of my best matchlocks, the left column was enabled to avoid the fire of about 800 matchlocks posted upon a cliff above the gun-road under Ambar Khana. Their right column under Chattar Singh advanced without opposition at the back of the low hills and took position upon the most considerable eminence southward of the castle. But when they pushed forward their detachments the fire became hot and close and they were eventually driven back with loss.

The left column about 3,000 strong with two howitzers began the ascent of the undulations upon the crest of which was my own post, a path leading to Srikot. I had at first only 200 matchlocks to oppose to them. But as the contest grew warm about 400 of my people came up from Ambar Khana, the position avoided by the Sikhs, and the hill was disputed from rock to rock, and bush to bush, so that by 2 P. M. they had only won the foot and easiest acclivity and had still before them not only all the strong ground of my position itself but the first undulation of the mountain's base; there they turned back, retreating with much coolness under the fire of my skirmishers. Could I have persuaded the reserve to charge sword in hand, the retreat might have been converted into a rout. But my exhortations were so coldly received that I desisted. Meanwhile the garrison had evacuated and fired the fort, and had joined the relieving army. The Sikh army marched back in good order; being strong in cavalry and artillery they were secure from molestation in ground so open. They consumed fifteen of their dead in a blazing thatch upon the field, and carried away sixty bodies and about 126 wounded.''

Abbott had nine or ten killed and about as many wounded. The losses of the Sikhs were attributed to their advancing in masses against individuals scattered amongst the bushes. Chattar Singh retired in the direction of Attock.

The Sikhs rise at Peshawar.

On the 23rd October the Sikh force at Peshawar broke into open mutiny. At about 8 P. M. two shots were fired by the infantry; when the guns opened, and shot, shrapnel, and grape were poured into the Residency in rapid succession. Major Lawrence and the other Europeans escaped with some difficulty on horseback to Kohat, where the Governor, Sultan Muhammad Khan, had promised them protection. At a later date the latter, having kept them as virtual prisoners, returned them to the Sikhs at Peshawar, and they remained in captivity until the termination of the war.

Movements of Sher Singh.

While these events were in progress the Sikh rising had been proceeding apace throughout the Punjab. On the 9th October Sher Singh left Multan with his 5,000 men and 12 guns and marched rapidly up the Chenab, to effect a junction with the routed troops from Bannu, eventually concentrating the Sikh army about the fords at Ramnagar.

Revolt at Bannu.

The Bannu troops, who revolted after murdering the Muhammadan Governor, Fatteh Khan Tiwana, and Colonel John Holmes of the Sikh Army, would bring Chattar Singh's force up to ten battalions of 500 men each, with about 30 guns and 1,100 regular cavalry.

On the 21st October the Sikh troops from Bannu under Sardar Ram Singh, Chapiwala, began crossing the Indus at the Isakhel ferry, completing the passage next day. Sher Singh lingered at Jhang until the 23rd October, and Edwardes wrote:—

"The excesses which, at the request of the Hindus at Jhang, he is reported to have committed against the Muhammadans of that place are very shameful and calculated to turn the Sikh rebellion into a religious war. A *moulvi* and another learned Musalman of Jhang are reported to have been killed; a rich Muhammadan Khoja ransomed for 10,000 rupees, and the mosques of the city defiled with every indignity. The Muhammadan population are much enraged; and the proverbial fanaticism of the Sikhs was never more fully shown than in thus provoking two-thirds of the people of the Punjab to side against them in their struggle for independence."

Attack on a post near Lahore.

On the night of the 23rd a party of the enemy moving about in the district between the Chenab and the Ravi, attacked a small post of Durbar troops on the right bank of the latter river, immediately opposite Lahore, with a view to getting possession of some *zamburaks*, of which they carried off eighteen out of twenty-four, and destroyed one of the boats of the bridge just completed over the Ravi. The post adjoined a building and garden, which was occupied next day by a detachment of native infantry under a British officer.

Cureton's advance.

On the 1st November a rebel force under Lal Singh marched from Wazirabad to within nine miles of Gujranwala, while two other chiefs, Arjan Singh and Jowahir Singh, moved their forces upon the same place. In the meantime, while the army was concentrating, Brigadier-General Cureton was placed in command of all the troops of the army of the Punjab that had crossed the Sutlej. On the 2nd

November he crossed the Ravi river by the bridge-of-boats, and encamped at Parhal, about six miles north of the river on the Wazirabad road, with the troops detailed in the margin, advancing next day, with the addition of No. 10 Light Field Battery and the 14th Light Dragoons, from Lahore; and with Godby's Brigade of the 2nd European Regiment and 70th Native Infantry.

3 Troops Horse Artillery.
3rd Dragoons.
8th Light Cavalry.
12th Irregular Cavalry.

In view of the state of affairs in the Punjab, the Governor-General moved in that direction in October and arrived at Ambala on the 25th November.

CHAPTER IX.

THE SECOND SIKH WAR. THE PASSAGE OF THE CHENAB.

Reduction of the army.

On the conclusion of the first Sikh War the strength of the Bengal Army was considerably reduced from motives of economy, with the result that, when a fresh outbreak of hostilities appeared to be inevitable, it was found necessary to augment the existing corps. Regarding this measure the Governor-General, Lord Dalhousie, wrote on 7th October 1848, on receipt of the news of Sher Singh's defection :—

"No other course is open to us than to prosecute a general Punjab war with vigour, and ultimately to occupy the country with our own troops. The first step necessary for the attainment of this object is the augmentation of the army, to which we have at last most reluctantly consented. The orders which have been issued provide for an increase of about 17,000 men ; and as these will be drafted into existing regiments without adding to the number of European officers, we have observed the most economical scale by which so large an augmentation can be obtained. The recruiting depôts will be a sufficient garrison for the stations where they may be formed, and thus enable the Commander-in-Chief at once to avail himself of nearly an equal number of veteran soldiers for service in the Punjab.[1]"

The Government of Bombay, as already related, was ordered to send a Brigade through Sind to co-operate with the Punjab Army, proceeding first to Multan; and the three Bengal Infantry regiments at Midnapore, Kyouk Pyu, Chittagong and Dacca were to be relieved by three Madras regiments.

The Army of the Punjab.

On the 13th October 1848 a general order was published detailing the troops[2] which were to form "The Army of the Punjab," as follows :—

Artillery.

Brigadier-General Tennant.
8 Troops horse artillery.
3 Light field batteries.
8 Companies foot artillery.

[1] Although reductions were made in the Bengal Army on the conclusion of the first Sikh War, in July 1846, the Ferozepore and Ludhiana Sikhs (14th and 15th Sikhs) were raised, and in December of the same year a Frontier Brigade was raised as well as a corps of guides.

These still exist as the 51st, 52nd, 53rd and 54th Sikhs, and the Corps of Guides.

The hasty method of raising the strength of corps on the outbreak of war may be compared with the existing system of reinforcing from the active reserve, prepared in time of peace. But in 1847 further reduction took place.

[2] All of the Bengal Army. Detail of staff is given in Appendix VI.

Engineers.

Brigadier J. Cheape, C.B.

The corps of Sappers and Pioneers.

Cavalry.

Brigadier-General C. R. Cureton, C. B.

1st Brigade.—Brigadier M. White, C.B.

3rd Light Dragoons.

5th and 8th Light Cavalry.

2nd Brigade.—Brigadier A. Pope, C.B.

9th Light Dragoons.

1st and 6th Light Cavalry.

3rd Brigade.—Brigadier H. F. Salter.

11th Light Cavalry.

7th and 11th Irregular Cavalry.

4th Brigade.—Brigadier J. B. Hearsey.

3rd, 9th and 12th Irregular Cavalry.

Infantry.

1st Division.

Major-General W. S. Whish, C.B.

1st Brigade—Brigadier A. Mountain, C.B.

10th Foot.

8th and 72nd Native Infantry.

2nd Brigade—Brigadier F. Markham.

32nd Foot.

49th and 1st Native Infantry.

2nd Division.

Major-General Sir W. R. Gilbert, K.C.B.

3rd Brigade—Brigadier J. Eckford.

29th Foot.

31st and 56th Native Infantry.

4th Brigade—Brigadier C. Godby, C.B.,

2nd European Regiment.

45th and 70th Native Infantry.

5th Brigade—Brigadier A. Hervey.

13th, 30th and 52nd Native Infantry.

3rd Division.

Major-General Sir J. Thackwell, K.C.B.,	*6th Brigade*—Brigadier J. Pennycuick, C.B., 24th Foot. 15th and 25th Native Infantry.
	7th Brigade—Brigadier N. Penny, C.B., 20th, 22nd and 69th Native Infantry.

These arrangements were soon altered considerably. The 14th Light Dragoons were added to the 1st Brigade of Cavalry; the 29th Foot were removed from the 3rd to the 5th Brigade, their place in the former being taken by the 73rd Native Infantry from Lahore; the 15th and 22nd Infantry interchanged Brigades, and a fourth Division, the command of which was given to Brigadier-General Colin Campbell[1], had an existence of about a fortnight. This Division comprised the 8th Brigade (36th and 46th Native Infantry) and the Ninth Brigade (61st Foot and 3rd Native Infantry). On its being broken up the 61st Foot were removed to the 8th Brigade, which was then transferred to the Third Division, and the command given to Brigadier J. Hoggan, and the 3rd Native Infantry were struck off the strength of the Army of the Punjab. Major-General Sir Joseph Thackwell was appointed to command the Cavalry Division after the death of Brigadier-General Cureton in the action at Ramnagar. These and other changes will be noticed during the course of the ensuing narrative.

Effects of the insurrection at Multan.

On 4th November the Secretary with the Governor-General wrote to the Resident at Lahore :—" The insurrection at Multan having been followed by an open rebellion of the great body of the Sikh Army and the Sikh population, which has for its avowed object not only the expulsion of the British Government from that position which they hold by treaty in the Punjab, but the destruction of the British power, it is essential for the safety as well as for the honour of this Government that the hostile and treacherous attack which has thus been contemplated should at once be effectually met and that the army by which it is attempted should be dispersed and crushed.

The Governor-General hopes to learn that the Commander-in-Chief, by means of the force assembling at Ferozepore, will have been enabled without exposing to risk the position we already occupy, to attack the forces approaching from different quarters

[1] Afterwards Lord Clyde.

and to destroy them before they could effect a junction of the whole."

Early in November the Army assembled at Ferozepore was ready to take the field, and on the 9th Lord Gough crossed the Sutlej, reached Lahore on the 13th, and crossed the Ravi[1] on the 16th. Sher Singh concentrated on the fords of Ramnagar on the Chenab, where he had some 30,000 men and 28 guns. He was expecting to be reinforced by Chattar Singh, who was engaged in besieging Attock, and by Dost Muhammad, Amir of Kabul, who had been bribed to join the Sikhs by the promise of Peshawar.

Movements of the Army of the Punjab.

It has already been related that General Cureton with a portion of the Cavalry Division had preceded the army, with a view to covering Lahore, and to observe the enemy on the Chenab. On the 16th November he was joined by Brigadier Colin Campbell, who commanded the troops at Lahore, with a Brigade, and took up a position on the east bank of the river at Saharan, some 8 miles from Ramnagar.

The Chenab at this point is very wide, but at this season of the year the main river is contracted to a narrow channel running in a sandy bed and splitting up into numerous and constantly changing channels. The right bank of the river is high and commanding. Ramnagar is a walled town on the left bank of the Chenab, some three miles from it across an extensive open plain covered for a considerable distance with low scrub jungle.

Action at Ramnagar.

The Sikhs had pushed an outpost across the river to Ramnagar, communication being maintained by means of the ford at this point. Lord Gough with the main army had reached Nawala on the 21st, and at once decided to drive the Sikhs on the left bank across the river, and to capture any guns they might have on this side. For this purpose he directed Brigadier Campbell with an Infantry Brigade, accompanied by the Cavalry Division and three troops of horse artillery under Brigadier-General Cureton, to march during the night of the 21st from Saharan, four miles ahead of the main army. He himself proceeded with this force at 3 a.m. on the 22nd November to carry out what was in effect a reconnaissance in force. The remainder of the army marched at a later hour and,

[1] When Lord Gough crossed the Ravi, misrepresentations of the purposes of the British Government were being sedulously circulated by the disaffected ; and those whose interests were on the side of British supremacy in the Punjab urged the Resident at Lahore to issue a proclamation to allay the general apprehension that was felt at the advance of the Commander-in-Chief. On the 18th November Sir F. Currie accordingly issued the Proclamation reproduced in Appendix VIII.

as an officer who was present wrote, "took up a position in front of Ramnagar as spectators of the distant fight."

On reaching the high ground to the right of Ramnagar, it was seen that the Sikhs with their guns had crossed to their encampment on the opposite bank, where their whole force was in position. At the same time some small parties were observed to be retiring from the town of Ramnagar in the direction of the ford in front of their encampment, when Lieutenant-Colonel Lane's and Captain Warner's troops of horse artillery were ordered by Brigadier Cureton to pursue them and open fire on them while crossing the ford. The horse artillery in their eagerness to overtake the enemy pushed forward through the deep and heavy sand which extended for a long distance to the very margin of the water, and through which the guns could only be moved with great difficulty. Their fire inflicted considerable loss on the enemy while crossing.

In withdrawing from this position under the fire of the whole of the enemy's 28 guns, posted on the high western bank of the river, one gun and two ammunition wagons of Lane's troop got so embedded in the heavy sand behind a high bank in close proximity to the enemy's guns that they could not be recovered. The Sikhs observing this crossed with great confidence the whole of their cavalry, three to four thousand strong, which clung to the bank of the river, keeping under cover of the fire of their artillery on the opposite bank. This cavalry was charged on separate occasions by the 3rd and 14th Light Dragoons, and the 5th and 8th Regiments Light Cavalry. These charges, well and gallantly led, were in every instance successful, but were accompanied by heavy loss. Brigadier-General Cureton[1] was shot through the heart while leading a squadron of the 14th Light Dragoons to the support of the 5th Light Cavalry; Lieutenant-Colonel W. Havelock, K. H., commanding 14th Light Dragoons, and Captain Fitzgerald of the same regiment and 23 men were also killed; and 9 officers and 49 men were wounded.[2] The abandoned gun was spiked. The enemy suffered severely, numbers being precipitated into the

[1] Cureton was a fine cavalry leader, of whom Campbell wrote in his Despatch:—"In this officer the service has lost one of its most distinguished officers, and one who was beloved by the whole army." He was one of the few general officers who have risen from the ranks, having enlisted under the name of Charles Roberts in the 14th Light Dragoons, with which regiment he served throughout the Peninsular War. He commanded the 16th Lancers in the Afghan War, and a brigade in the first Sikh war.

[2] Among the killed was Subadar-Major Mir Sher Ali, Sardar Bahadur, 8th Light Cavalry, who was 78 years of age and had nearly 60 years' service. In the list of casualties (Appendix IX) will be noticed the name of Captain R. H. Gall, 14th Light Dragoons, who with his regiment performed distinguished service in the Mutiny campaign in Central India. (*See The Revolt in Central India—Division of the Chief of the Staff, 1908.*)

river and drowned. In one of the charges a silk standard was captured and the standard-bearer killed by Trooper Alif Khan, 5th Light Cavalry.

The action of Ramnagar was entirely a cavalry and horse artillery fight, and was conducted with the impetuous rashness that is so frequent in the use of those arms under a gallant leader. But it served no useful purpose; the object of the advance was already gained when the Sikhs retired from the eastern bank of the river, and it serves to illustrate the principle that while the mounted arms should be bold in their action, their leaders should avoid rushing into unnecessary and unprofitable danger, where the object to be gained is not worth the cost likely to be incurred.

It was now necessary to force the passage of the Chenab, an operation which presented no great difficulties. It was of course out of the question for Lord Gough to force the passage at Ramnagar itself, in face of an enemy occupying with guns and a large army a position on the other and higher bank. But the Chenab was fordable at other points—at Garhi-ki-Pattan, seven miles up the river from camp, but strongly guarded by the enemy; at Ranni-Khan-ki-Pattan and Ali-Sher-ki-Chak, close to each other some five miles farther up stream; and at Wazirabad, some twenty miles distant from Ramnagar, where there was also a ferry.

General Thackwell detached.

The Commander-in-Chief resolved to hold the enemy at Ramnagar, and to send a force to cross the river at the ford of Ranni-Khan-ki-Pattan if practicable and if not to move on and cross at Wazirabad. With this object in view Major-General Sir Joseph Thackwell[1] was detached with the force detailed in the margin on the night of 30th November—1st December. He was to have marched at 1 A.M., but Brigadier-General Campbell's Brigade lost the way to the starting point, and thus a delay of over two hours was caused.[2] On the night of the 30th, General Thackwell received a note from the Adjutant General in which the latter said:—

3 troops horse artillery.
2 light field batteries.
2-18 pounders.
Two companies Pioneers.
Position train.
1st Brigade Cavalry—
3rd Light Dragoons.
5th & 8th Light Cavalry.
3rd & 12th Irregular Cavalry.
3rd Brigade Infantry—
31st & 56th Native Infantry.
3rd Division Infantry—
6th Brigade Infantry.
24th Foot.
22nd & 25th Native Infantry.
8th Brigade Infantry.
6th Foot.
36th & 46th Native Infantry.

1 Sir Joseph Thackwell had fought in the Peninsular War, and lost an arm at Waterloo. He commanded the cavalry in the first Sikh War. He was now appointed 2nd in command of the Army, and to the command of the cavalry after Cureton's death.

2 An officer who was present says that the enemy must have been apprised of the movement by the clamour raised by the camp followers.

"The Commander-in-Chief hopes you understand distinctly that unless you get across the river in time to rest and breakfast your troops, so as to admit of your marching to the left of the enemy's position by 1 P.M. tomorrow, it is his wish that you should make a second day of it. The distance to the ford is now reckoned to be thirteen miles, and to cross the river, even with a good ford with the force you will have, must be a work of time... Night work is to be avoided at all times;[1] if, therefore, you cannot bring all your troops fresh and with ample daylight before them, it is much better that the attack should be deferred one day."

It was 11 A.M. on December 1st by the time Sir Joseph Thackwell reached the vicinity of the ford at Ranni-Khan-ki-Pattan, the difficulty of the march being enhanced by narrow roads (where there were any) and broken ground, and sand through which the pontoon train and guns had to be dragged. The enemy's infantry held this ford, as well as the Ali-Sher-ki-Chak, a mile higher up, which was examined by Lieutenant Paton, D. A. Q. M. G., who reported it difficult for guns and impracticable for the pontoons. The General "came to the conclusion that this ford of Ali-Sher-ki-Chak could not have artillery on the left bank of the river to cover the passage of the troops, while from the insecure bottom of the first ford, neither could the pontoon train be of much use for the same reason and the deep sands which lay between the fords. The pontoon train might have been laid over the main stream under cover of a battery, near the enemy's infantry, but beyond the river the sands seemed wet and insecure; and a branch of the river beyond them was said to be deep with a muddy bottom."

Brigadier-General Campbell[2] urged a return to camp at Ramnagar, in view of the precarious communications with the main army and of the difficulty of supply, but fortunately these cautious counsels did not prevail, and Sir Joseph Thackwell resolved to push on and cross at Wazirabad. Lieutenants Baird Smith and Yule accompanied Captain John Nicholson, who with his Pathan

[1]Those responsible for the direction of night operations are too often apt to forget their exhausting effect on the men, and the necessity for proper rest for the army. History shows many examples of both successful and unsuccessful operations of this nature, which prove that they should be undertaken only in exceptional circumstances. Here we have a whole brigade missing its way to the starting point and wandering for two hours amid the intricacies of the camp of its own army. Wellington, then Colonel Wellesley, failed in a night attack at Seringapatam in 1799 and, as he told Lord Mornington, "resolved never again to attack by night a post which had not been reconnoitred by day," a resolution embodying what is now a recognised principle. On that occasion General Harris wrote in his Diary—"no wonder night attacks so often fail." (*See Wellington's campaigns in India.—Division of the Chief of the Staff, 1908.*)

[2] The caution which characterised this general's operations in the Mutiny Campaigns in 1857 may be observed here.

levies was sent on ahead to reconnoitre that place; and the column again marched at 2 P.M., three hours having been spent in examining the fords. At 5 P.M. the leading infantry reached Wazirabad, where Captain Nicholson had already collected all the seventeen boats and staked out two fords, while his Pathans had pushed across the river and reported the other bank clear of the enemy. The river was here divided into three streams, and in no part of the ford itself did the water exceed 3 feet 10 inches in depth. Two of the streams were staked out that evening, the third was unmarked until daybreak on the 2nd owing to the pressure of work and want of materials. The ferry was about three quarters of a mile above the ford.

Passage of the Chenab.

The 6th Brigade of Infantry and some guns were passed over the Chenab immediately in the boats. The 3rd Brigade waded across by the two staked out fords, but was unable to cross the last branch of the stream, and bivouacked for the night on a sand bank. Three *risalas* of the 3rd Irregular Cavalry crossed over, but three sowars were drowned. The difficulties of the passage were described by Captain Lawrence Archer, who was present :—

"It was now a very dark night; and in the mazes of small channels and pools of water which chequered the loose sands, many a regiment lost its way, while the increasing darkness added to the general confusion, and the knowledge of abounding quicksands produced a sense of insecurity. It is hard to say what might not have befallen the force had the enemy only taken the trouble to guard this ford, or to form an ambuscade."

The commissariat arrangements were certainly defective, for apparently the men had no meal until next day, thirty-six hours or more after they had left camp at Ramnagar. The troops that had crossed the river "were obliged to pass that bitterly cold and dark night without food or fuel, and in order to escape the piercing wind, scooped out hollows in the sand in which they found a slight protection."

The pontoon train proved to be a useless encumbrance, and with the two 18-pounders was returned to camp under escort of the 12th Irregular Cavalry, 2 guns of No. 10 Light Field Battery, and 2 companies 22nd Native Infantry.

Next morning, 2nd December, the remaining troops crossed, and all the baggage and commissariat animals had passed by midday.

At 2 P.M., after the troops had had their food, the march down the right bank of the stream began. They marched in order of battle, three brigade columns of companies at half distance, left in front, at deploying interval; the 1st Brigade of cavalry in the same order on the right with strong flanking parties and rearguard, and the 3rd Irregular Cavalry on the left with orders to patrol to the river and clear the right bank, aided by infantry if necessary. They arrived at Durawal, 12 miles from the ferry, at dusk, no sign of the enemy having been seen.

Co-operation by the Commander-in-Chief.

Hearing that Thackwell had crossed the Chenab, and was moving down the right bank of the river, Lord Gough on the 2nd directed a heavy cannonade on the enemy's batteries and encampment opposite Ramnagar, which was returned by only a few guns which guarded the ford effectually and could not be silenced owing to the width of the river. In his despatch the Commander-in-Chief wrote:—"This cannonade, however, inflicted very severe loss to the enemy in their camp and batteries, and forced him to fall back [1] with his camp about two miles, which enabled me without the loss of a man to push my batteries and breastworks on the night of the 2nd to the bank of the river, the principal ford of which I then commanded. By this time I was enabled to detach another brigade of infantry under Brigadier Godby on the 3rd which effected the passage with the aid of the pontoon train six miles up the river and got into communication with Major-General Sir Joseph Thackwell." Lord Gough kept up this cannonade and demonstration on the 2nd and 3rd December, "so as to fix a large portion of the enemy there to defend that point."

In the meantime at 6 A.M. on the 3rd December Sir Joseph Thackwell marched again in the same order towards the Sikh position, intending to have reconnoitred and begun an attack on it by 11 o'clock. But when within four miles of it he received a note from the Commander-in-Chief informing him that reinforcements were being sent to him by the Garhi-ki-Pattan, and shortly afterwards another message, written at 8-15 A.M., arrived, to say that:—"When General Thackwell has taken possession of the Garhi-ki-Pattan, Lord Gough desires that he will not move his force on to the attack till reinforced from Ramnagar by a brigade of infantry and cavalry which are prepared to move at a moment's notice."[2] It then became necessary to secure that post which had been found

[1] It seems more probable that the Sikhs had fallen back to oppose Thackwell's advance, leaving a force to hold the ford opposite Ramnagar. As he "commanded the principal ford," it is not easy to understand why he did not push across and act in co-operation with Thackwell.

[2] Another note signed by Colonel Patrick Grant, the Adjutant-General, at 10 A.M. on the 3rd said:—"The Commander-in-Chief is despatching the 14th Light Dragoons, a detachment of the 9th Irregulars, and a brigade of infantry to join you at the Garhi-ki-Pattan Ghat. Our heavy guns are all in position on the river close to the ford near the clump of trees and ready to aid you as well as they can in your attack on the enemy's position."

unoccupied an hour before, but which some 600 of the enemy were now seen approaching, and General Thackwell detached two *risalas* of the 3rd Irregular Cavalry and a wing of the 25th Native Infantry, who secured the ford.

The General had halted in front of the village of Sadulapur and, as he wrote in his despatch, " this caused so much delay that enough of daylight would not be left for the advance and attack of the left and rear of the enemy's position."[1] Nicholson's Pathan Horse were sent out, and the villages of Tarwala, Ratti and Kamukhel in front were each occupied by a company of infantry. Between Sadulapur and these villages, which were surrounded by dense sugar-cane fields, was an open space about half a mile wide, in which the line had halted. At about 2 P. M. some of the enemy's guns opened on a patrol of the 5th Light Cavalry, and large bodies of cavalry and infantry were seen advancing. The picquets which occupied the three villages, being too much advanced to be supported, fell back without loss; and the enemy occupied these villages with cavalry on the right, guns, and bodies of infantry; the main body of their cavalry with horse artillery was on their left. A short retrograde movement of the British troops took place, in order to gain two hundred yards more of open space from the dense cover which surrounded the three villages. The infantry then deployed into line in front of the village of Sadulapur, the flanks extended so as not to be outflanked. This movement being taken as a retreat, the Sikhs advanced in large numbers, opening fire with their guns and threatening to envelop both flanks with their cavalry. Under this heavy fire the infantry was ordered to lie down, while the attempt on the British left was frustrated by a troop of artillery and the 5th Light Cavalry who, acting in conjunction with the 3rd Irregular Cavalry on that flank, soon caused the enemy to retire. The attack on the British right was met by the 8th Light Cavalry and 3rd Light Dragoons, supported by a troop of horse artillery, who drove the Sikh horse back on their infantry. When the enemy was well within range, the British guns opened with great effect, and the Sikhs attempted no further advance from the cover about the villages.

Action of Sadulapur.

After a cannonade of about two hours, the enemy's fire slackened, and the General directed the cavalry on the right to charge and take the guns, if possible, intending to support them by moving the brigades in echelon from the right at intervals; but as no opportunity offered for the cavalry to charge, and so little daylight remained, General Thackwell considered it safer to remain in his position

[1]Why this long halt was necessary is not, however, evident.

rather than attempt to drive back an enemy so strongly posted on their right and centre, with the prospect of having to attack their entrenched position afterwards. His infantry had no chance of firing a shot, except a few companies on the left of the line. The British loss in this action amounted to 21 killed, 51 wounded and 1 missing; 33 horses were killed and 14 wounded. The losses of the Sikhs were not ascertained, but were said to have been heavier.

Retirement of the Sikhs.

The Sikhs retired at about midnight, as was conjectured by the barking of dogs in their rear. At the same time that portion of their army which remained in front of the Commander-in-Chief also retreated to take up a new position. Lord Gough, except for a distant bombardment of the enemy's trenches, remained inactive during the 3rd December, and did not in any more decided manner co-operate with his Lieutenant while the action of Sadulapur was proceeding on the further bank of the Chenab. At dawn on the 4th he sent the 9th Lancers and 14th Light Dragoons in pursuit of the retreating enemy, and at the same time Godby's Brigade, which was to have reinforced Sir Joseph Thackwell, was still engaged in crossing at Garhi-ki-Pattan, and joined Sir Joseph between 7 and 9 A.M., having crossed in boats brought down from Wazirabad, 24 hours after he had set out from Ramnagar.

On the morning of the 4th December, Major-General Thackwell pushed on with his cavalry towards Jalalpur,[1] the infantry to follow, and not having come up with the enemy took up a position for the night 2½ miles from the village of Helan on the Jalalpur road. On the 5th he marched to Helan. The 14th Light Dragoons and 8th Light Cavalry went on to Dinghi, but returned that night to Helan, where Lord Gough directed Thackwell to form a camp. He was told that he might send his cavalry out in any direction, but that they were invariably to be sent back by dusk. On the 8th the Commander-in-Chief with the remainder of the Army crossed the Chenab, and shortly afterwards joined Sir Joseph Thackwell at Helan.

The Sikhs had retired to the Jhelum, and had taken up a position about Mung and Rasul on the left bank of that river.

[1] Jalalpur is supposed to occupy the site of Bucephala, the city established by Alexander the Great, and named after his famous horse which was mortally wounded at the battle of the Hydaspes.

CHAPTER X.

CHILIANWALA.

(*Map 7.*)

Situation of the opposing forces.

The period which elapsed between the forcing of the passage of the Chenab and the advance to the Jhelum, where the battle of Chilianwala was fought on the 13th January, was a period of inaction due to several causes. Lord Gough was himself of opinion that he was not strong enough, and that it would be best to await the fall of Multan, which would release the troops there engaged, before attacking the Sikhs. And the Governor-General wrote to the Secret Committee on the 22nd December 1848:—

"Being satisfied that in any extended advance which His Excellency might attempt to make, he would experience very great difficulty in procuring supplies for the army, I requested His Excellency on no consideration to advance into the Doab beyond the Chenab, except for the purpose of attacking Sher Singh in the position he held, without further communication with me.

This injunction is based on certain circumstances, and is to continue in force only while those circumstances remain unchanged. The information which I have since received has led me to believe that in many material respects they have undergone a change. I have, therefore, acquainted His Excellency that if he can satisfy his own judgment regarding the state of his supplies, his supports, and his communications, if the intelligence he may receive and the reconnaissances he may be able to make, shall satisfy him that the enemy may be attacked with success, with such force as he may have safely disposable, and without heavy loss, in such case I should be happy indeed to see a blow struck that would destroy the enemy, add honour to the British arms, and avoid the prospect of a protracted and costly war."

It does not appear what the circumstances were or what was the information to which Lord Dalhousie referred. But he may have foreseen the fall of Attock, bringing with it the advance of Chattar Singh and Dost Muhammad's Afghans to reinforce Sher Singh. For in the same despatch, written from Camp, Ludhiana, he says that on the 6th December, Lieutenant Herbert's "tenure of the fort of Attock had become very precarious. He had been blockaded for twenty-seven days, and his troops were showing strong symptoms of insubordination."[1] He may also have considered the situation at Lahore, where the Chiefs professedly loyal to the Maharaja and to the British Government were, with one or two exceptions, disaffected; and where constant vigilance was necessary for the protection of the Maharaja. The removal of Brigadier-General Campbell and two regiments from the garrison made the protection of the city and cantonments a very responsible charge; "while the intrigues of all at Lahore and the neighbourhood, and the disposition to rise on any opportunity being given, render constant and anxious vigilance indispensable."

Moreover, the effect of prolonged inaction on the whole of India had to be considered; for the enemies of British rule were again standing at gaze as they had stood when the British and Sikhs faced each other on the Sutlej three years before.

The British camp at Helan was distant only some ten miles from that of the Sikhs, so it was inevitable that during this period of inaction some desultory operations such as skirmishes between patrols, should take place. On the 18th December, Sher Singh advanced 10,000 men to Dinghi, seeming to threaten a movement on Wazirabad which would have menaced the British communications. A small force was accordingly despatched to occupy the fords over the Chenab at that point.

The fall of Attock.

On the 10th January news of the fall of Attock was received, with intelligence of the advance of Chattar Singh, thus released to reinforce the Sikh army on the Jhelum, which already amounted to some 30,000 men with 62 guns. It became imperative to attack the Sikhs before they received this reinforcement, and on that date Major Mackeson, the Governor-General's Political Agent with the Commander-in-Chief, wrote to the latter—"I would urge, in the event of your Lordship's finding yourself strong enough, with the army under your command, to strike an effective blow at the enemy in our front and that the blow should be struck with the least possible delay."

Advance of Lord Gough.

The Commander-in-Chief concurred with this view of the situation, considering himself "perfectly competent effectually to overthrow Sher Singh's army,"[2] with the 12,000 men and 66 guns which he had at his disposal. At daylight on the 10th January 1849 Lord Gough moved from Lawa Tibi (adjacent to Helan) twelve miles to Dinghi, where he learnt from his spies and other sources of informa-

[1] Herbert held out a month longer.

[2] This being the case it is not quite clear why he did not feel himself strong enough before, as his inaction must have had its influence both on his army and on that of the Sikhs

tion that Sher Singh still held with his right the villages of Lakhniwala and Fateh Shah-ki-Chak. The main Sikh force was at Lalianwala, with the left at Rasul on the Jhelum strongly occupying the southern extremity of a low range of difficult hills, intersected by ravines, which extended nearly to that village. Lord Gough made his arrangements accordingly that evening and communicated them to the commanders of the several divisions. But to ensure correct information as to the nature of the country, which he believed to be excessively difficult and ill-adapted to the advance of a regular army, he determined upon moving on Chilianwala with a view to reconnoitre. A memorandum of the enemy's strength on 12th January, apparently in the handwriting of Colonel Patrick Grant, Adjutant General, is as follows:—[1]

The Sikh position.

At Lakhniwala (the right of their position): the Bannu troops under Ram Singh, one regiment of cavalry, four of infantry, and eleven guns.

Fateh-Shah-ki-Chak: Sirdar Atar Singh and Lal Singh, with two regiments of cavalry, six old and four new corps of infantry, and seventeen guns.

At Lalianwala: Sher Singh with one regiment of cavalry, five old and four new regiments of infantry, and twenty guns, with main body of Ghorcharras, about 4,000.

At Rasul (the extreme left) are two new infantry corps and seven guns.

At Mung: Surat Singh with three guns in—(remainder illegible).

The villages that have been mentioned were situated in an arc along the left bank of the river Jhelum, Chilianwala being about the centre of the circle, with Rasul due north, and something over 2 miles distant. The range of hills referred to by Lord Gough presented a sloping aspect to the plains, where the hills terminated in precipitous heights overhanging the river. The spurs of the hills were crowned by extensive earthworks. A wide, thorny jungle of varying density, consisting of bushes which were sometimes seven or eight feet high,[2] stretched in a south-westerly direction, being less dense towards Dinghi, and losing its wild character at the village of Chilianwala.

At 7 A.M. on the 13th January, a still and almost cloudless morning, the army advanced, says Sir Joseph Thackwell, "in brigade column of cavalry, artillery and infantry towards the Sikh position. Each column formed its own advanced guard, and the heads of

Advance on Chilianwala.

[1] Life of Lieutenant General Sir Joseph Thackwell. By Colonel H. C. Wylly.
[2] Mostly thorny *acacia*, or *babul*.

columns were to be one hundred yards from each other. The right wing moved in column, left in front, and the left wing right in front, directed by the heavy battery, in front of which was the Commander-in-Chief."

A considerable detour was made to the right, partly to distract the enemy's attention, but principally to get, as far as possible, clear of the jungle, on which it appeared the enemy mainly relied.

The army approached Chilianwala at about 12 noon; a strong piquet of the enemy found on a mound close to the village was at once dislodged, and from the mound a very extended view of the country was obtained. The enemy could be seen drawn up in battle array, having during the night or in the early morning moved out of his positions and occupied the ground in front, which was a difficult jungle, his right in advance of Fateh-Shah-ki-Chak, and his left on the furrowed hills about Rasul.

It will be remembered that the Commander-in-Chief's intention on this day was not to fight but to reconnoitre, and the day being so far advanced, he decided to take up a position in rear of the village, in order to reconnoitre to the front, finding that he could not turn the enemy's flanks, which rested on a dense jungle extending nearly to Helan, and upon the hills near Rasul, without detaching a force to a distance; which he considered both inexpedient and dangerous.

The engineer department had been ordered to examine the country in front, and the Quartermaster-General was in the act of taking up ground for the encampment when the enemy advanced some horse artillery, and opened a fire on the skirmishers in front of the village. Lord Gough immediately ordered them to be silenced by a few rounds from the heavy guns, which advanced to an open space in front of Chilianwala. This fire was instantly returned by that of nearly the whole of the enemy's field artillery, thus exposing the position of his guns which the jungle had hitherto concealed. It was now evident that the enemy intended to fight, and would advance his guns, so as to reach the encampment during the night. To encamp was, therefore, manifestly impossible. Retreat was out of the question, and a battle was inevitable.

Battle of Chilianwala.

It was now about 2 o'clock. The Commander-in-Chief drew up in order of battle. The infantry was ordered to lie down, while the heavy guns opened a well-directed and powerful fire on the enemy's centre, where his guns appeared principally to be placed. This fire was supported on the flanks by the field batteries of the infantry divisions.

After about an hour the fire of the enemy appeared to be sufficiently subdued to justify an advance upon his position and guns.

British dispositions.

The troops advanced in the following order, the left division moving off first, as it had to traverse a greater extent of ground, in front of which the enemy appeared not to have many guns:—

Second (Right) Division.

Major-General Sir W. R. Gilbert

3rd (Right) Brigade.	4th (Left) Brigade.
Brigadier Godby.	Brigadier Mountain.
2nd Bengal Europeans.	29th Foot.
31st and 70th Native Infantry.	30th and 56th Native Infantry.

The division was flanked on the right by Brigadier Pope's (2nd) Brigade of Cavalry (the 9th Lancers, 1st and 6th Light Cavalry, and the 14th Light Dragoons, and three troops horse artillery under Lieutenant-Colonel Grant).

The heavy guns under Major Horsford were in the centre, between the two divisions.

Third (Left) Division.

Brigad ier-General C. Campbell.

5th (Right) Brigade.	7th (Left) Brigade.
Brigadier Pennycuick.	Brigadier Hoggan.
24th Foot	61st Foot.
25th and 45th Native Infantry.	36th and 46th Native Infantry.

with the 15th and 69th Native Infantry under Brigadier Penny in reserve. The left was flanked by three troops horse artillery under Colonel Brind and Brigadier White's (1st) Brigade of Cavalry (3rd Light Dragoons, 5th and 8th Light Cavalry.)

The field batteries were with the infantry divisions, between the intervals of brigades. No. 17 Field Battery under Captain Dawes was between the two brigades of the Right Division. No. 5 Field Battery, Captain Mowatt, and half No. 10 Field Battery, Lieutenant Robertson, were with the Left Division; and Brigadier-General Campbell posted the former between the two brigades, and the latter on the extreme left

The whole line fronted the centre of the Sikh position, which overlapped both flanks. It was about 3 o'clock when the Left (Campbell's) Division was ordered to advance. The same orders were shortly afterwards given to the Right (Gilbert's) Division.

Before the advance began, Brigadier-General Campbell came to the conclusion that, owing to the density of the jungle, he could not possibly direct personally the attack of both brigades of his division. He accordingly remained with his left (Hoggan's) brigade, which he led throughout the battle. In addressing the men of the right brigade, prior to the advance, and before riding off to head the left brigade, he told the 24th Foot that "there must be no firing, the bayonet must do the work."

Movements of. Campbell's Division.

We will now follow Pennycuick's Brigade. Captain Lawrence Archer, who was present with the 24th Foot,[1] gives the following account of the movements of that regiment, on which the movements of the Brigade mainly depended: —

Movements of Pennycuick's Brigade.

"Immediately after Brigadier-General Campbell had addressed the 24th, that regiment was put in motion, and when the right had cleared the village of Chilianwala, just where the jungle began to increase in density, the ground was taken more than once to the right flank by echelon of companies, and in consequence under the circumstances as each company was of unusual strength, in reforming line overlapping occurred by the loss of distance, while the long rows of loose thorny hedges clinging to the men's legs and dragging after them increased the unsteadiness primarily caused by the impossiblity to hear, at the extremities of the line, the words of command, as they were given from the centre of the corps...............At length the jungle became denser at every step and the *keekur* and *kureel* bushes higher. The advance was continued at a rapid pace and in such alignment as the various companies, now broken into sections or files, could manage to preserve, acting on the independent judgment of individuals, and the habit of previous training. After this advance almost at random had been continued for about 1800 paces, the jungle suddenly ceased; and when the regiment, pounded incessantly with round shot by an unseen enemy, emerged from it, rapid discharges of grape and canister swept away whole sections."

Mowatt's guns were apparently soon masked by the brigade during the advance, and so were unable to support the infantry by keeping down this desolating fire. "In front, the enemy's position was protected by a natural glacis, a gentle grassy incline, forming a gradient of about six feet in fifty yards, rising from a network of pools of water with abrupt margins, and between these were many trees with pendant branches, almost entirely denuded of foliage.

There was no time to pause and take breath even had that been necessary, and the line, now dispersed and broken in the advance, made a rush for the guns. Many fell at this moment under

[1] The 24th was the centre regiment of the Brigade, having the 25th and 45th Native Infantry on the right and left.

discharges of grape, and but for the rapidity of the onset many more must have fallen. The pools of water in front of the enemy's battery obliged some to make a detour, and in doing so a few began to load and fire. All order in the wild *mêlée* was gone amongst the confused and scattered groups as they rushed upon the enemy, and in a short fierce struggle, enveloped in the gloom of the smoke which clung about the guns, captured the latter at the point of the bayonet.

Attack by the 24th Foot.

So impetuous was the assault that the enemy at once gave way, while the men of the 24th, instead of following up their success committed the error of staying to spike the guns. The delay was fatal to the victors, for the vanquished, now realising the paucity of their attackers, quickly rallied, and re-inforced by infantry from behind, recovered possession of the battery in a short and violent hand-to-hand conflict." The 24th, having suffered terrible loss, were driven back into the jungle and retreated to the village from which they had advanced, pursued a short distance by the Ghorcharras. The regiment had suffered a loss of 204 killed, including 11 officers, and 276 wounded, including 10 officers. Among the killed were Brigadier Pennycuick and his son,[1] both of the 24th.

Repulse of the brigade.

The native infantry regiments which supported the attack on either flank were driven back at the same time, but although their losses were considerable, they were slight in comparison with those of the 24th.

In his despatch the Commander-in-Chief wrote :—

This brigade, I am informed, mistook for the signal to move in double time the action of their brave leaders, Brigadier Pennycuick and Lieutenant-Colonel Brookes (two officers not surpassed for sound judgment and military daring in this or any other army) who waved their swords over their heads as they cheered on their gallant comrades. This unhappy mistake [2] led to the Europeans outstripping the native corps, which could not keep pace, and arriving completely blown at a belt of thicker jungle, where they got into some confusion, and Lieutenant-Colonel Brookes, leading the 24th, was killed between the enemy's guns. At this moment a large body of infantry which supported their guns opened upon them so destructive a fire that the brigade was forced to retire, having lost their gallant and lamented leader Brigadier Pennycuick, and the three other field officers of the 24th and nearly half the regiment when it gave way ; the native regiment when it came up also suffered severely.

[1] Both fell just as they reached the guns. A stalwart Sikh was inflicting gashes on the body of the former, who had been shot, when his son, a boy of seventeen who had that morning come off the sick list, rushed forward to avenge his father, but was overpowered and killed.

[2] But Captain Lawrence Archer, who was present with the 24th, said that the regiment did not break into a double until they got clear of the jungle, when they charged the enemy's guns. And he adds that in any case, owing to the height and thickness of the bush, this waving of swords could not have been seen by the regiment.

The Sikhs had little opportunity of following up this success for they had now to turn and meet the attack of Hoggan's and Mountain's brigades.

Led by Brigadier-General Campbell, the Divisional Commander, Hoggan's brigade soon lost touch with that of Pennycuick on its right. But it pushed steadily on and in good order to the front, aided by Mowatt's guns, which had been masked by Pennycuick's rapid advance, and by Robertson's guns and the horse artillery under Colonel Brind on the left. These guns silenced the Sikh heavy battery, which would otherwise have enfiladed the brigade during its advance.

Movements of Hoggan's Brigade.

General Campbell gave the following account of the action of Hoggan's brigade :—

Although the jungle through which the 7th Brigade passed was close and thick, causing frequent breaks to be made in the line, yet by regulating the pace so as to make allowance for these obstructions, the left brigade, after an advance of half a mile, reached a comparatively open tract of country in a tolerably connected line. On this open tract we found formed in our front a large body of cavalry and regular Sikh infantry which had played upon us during our advance. H. M.'s 61st Regiment charged this cavalry and put it to an immediate and disorderly flight, while the 36th Native Infantry on the right made an attack on their infantry, which, however, was not successful, and in consequence they came down accompanied by two guns upon the 36th Regiment, obliging it to retreat in rear of H. M.'s 61st.

The two right companies of the 61st were instantly made to change front to the right, and while the remainder of the regiment was ordered to form rapidly in the same direction, the two right companies charged the two guns and captured them. The fire of these two companies upon the enemy who were in pursuit of the 36th compelled them to desist and retreat.

While the remainder of the 61st was forming on those two companies, the enemy brought forward two more guns and fresh infantry, upon which those who had desisted from pursuit of the 36th again formed, and the whole opened a heavy fire; this force was likewise charged by H. M.'s 61st Regiment, put to the rout, and the guns captured. At the same time the 46th Native Infantry in its movement to form on the left of the 61st was attacked by a large body of the enemy's cavalry which it gallantly repulsed.

The formation of the brigade on the flank of the enemy's line now being completed, it moved forward driving everything before it, capturing in all thirteen guns, until it met with Brigadier Mountain's brigade[1] advancing from the opposite direction. The enemy retreated upon their guns, which were in position along their line in twos and threes, which they defended to the last moment in succession, and were only obtained possession of by us after a sharp contest such as I have described in the capture of the first two

[1] The left brigade of Sir W. Gilbert's Division. The gap between was left by the repulse of Pennycuick's brigade, already described.

guns, and they were all charged and taken by H. M.'s 61st Regiment. During these operations we were on two or three occasions threatened by the enemy's cavalry on our flank and rear, and were obliged to face about and drive them off. The guns were all spiked, but having no means with the force to remove them and it being too small to admit of any portion being withdrawn for their protection, they were, with the exception of the last three taken, unavoidably left upon the field.

Meanwhile the cavalry on the British left under Brigadier White had been thrown back at the beginning of the action, and as Campbell's Division advanced and bore off to the right, the interval between the cavalry and the infantry of Hoggan's Brigade on that flank increased. Brind's three horse artillery batteries engaged the enemy's heavy guns on this flank for about three quarters of an hour and thus materially assisted the advance of the infantry, as already related. Lieutenant Robertson's guns co-operated with the horse artillery, and, owing to a misunderstanding, moved off to the left, instead of advancing with and directly assisting the advance of Hoggan's Brigade. Robertson stated that a staff officer, who was never identified, ordered this movement; and it appears that Brigadier-General Campbell gave no order to his guns, which were thus left behind and far to the flank during the advance.

Action of Robertson's guns.

With regard to this incident, Robertson wrote to Brigadier-General Campbell:—

I received the following order:—'Take your guns to the left and assist the horse artillery in silencing those guns,' from a staff officer who rode up to me when I had advanced with the line about 200 yards ....I accordingly trotted out to the left—probably 500 yards................ I dispersed a considerable body of horsemen there, and after having fired about twenty rounds, I limbered up and proceeded in the direction indicated by the mysterious staff officer as the whereabouts of the horse artillery.

A shot or two evidently fired at the infantry of your left or your right brigade informed me of the position of the enemy at last, and as these shots hopped along my front, I brought up my right shoulder and unlimbering found myself opposed to a string of guns which were busily engaged directly with the horse artillery, but occasionally wheeled round a gun in acknowledgment of my attacks on their left flank which, being unprotected, enabled me to enfilade the whole string of them. I think we were engaged here half an hour and then the enemy's fire slackened and ceased. The Adjutant of the artillery rode up from the horse artillery (which I never saw though I knew its position) and told me that my fire had been of great service to them, that Brind was about to advance and wished to know what I intended to do. Having done as I was ordered I said I would rejoin my own division. When we limbered up we heard the rattle of the musketry on the left,[1] as we guessed, at 1,200 yards distance.

It will thus be seen that Robertson played an independent part, for he never placed himself under Colonel Brind's orders, and his action presumably contributed to the widening of the gap between the infantry and the cavalry.

Cavalry action on the British left.

The cavalry on this flank were in the meantime actively employed. The Sikhs had assembled a large body of cavalry on their right, with which they threatened to turn the British left. Perceiving this, Sir Joseph Thackwell, the commander of the cavalry division, who accompanied White's Brigade, ordered a squadron of the 3rd Light Dragoons and the 5th Light Cavalry to charge and drive back the Sikh horse, and then endeavour to take the guns in flank. The 5th were repulsed by heavy musketry fire and were rallied again on the 8th Cavalry. The charge of the squadron of the 3rd Dragoons was thus described by its commander, Captain Unett[2]:—

Charge of the Light Dragoons.

On returning from reporting myself to the officer commanding the 5th Light Cavalry, I saw the enemy's line who had just commenced to open fire at a distance of about seventy or eighty yards at the edge of a low, thorny jungle. We were on low ground but open to the enemy, and had just passed through jungle with stunted trees, in line with the 5th Light Cavalry, the same as one regiment. Their bugle sounded the charge and we instantly started and drove through the centre of the enemy's *gole* at the utmost speed the formation of the enemy and nature of the ground where they stood would admit of. They closed in on our flank, and it was "pell-mell". I had received three blows from different men on my left when engaged on my right front. We then got pretty clear of the enemy and I killed a *ghorcharra* at least 900 yards in rear of their *gole*......I then found myself entirely alone, and the first man I saw was Private Galloway. We rallied a few more as we were dreadfully broken up and instantly charged back through the enemy to our old ground. They did not offer so much opposition but opened out and abused us as we passed .... We could not, from the casualties, confusion and jungle, all meet and come back at the same time, but we were pretty near the three officers with parties. I think this caused greater panic and dismay to the enemy, for they could not tell at what point we were coming through them, and on our reforming they retired off the field. As to the 5th Light Cavalry, we never saw anything of them, and by Captain Wheatley's official report they were repulsed and driven back. Out of my squadron of 106 men, including 3 officers, we had 23 killed and 17 wounded (2 officers wounded) with 18 horses killed and 8 wounded, and on reforming we had only 48 men in their saddles."

[1] Meaning presumably the left of the British infantry.

[2] Quoted in the Military Memoirs of Lieutenant-General Sir Joseph Thackwell.

After this charge, Sir Joseph Thackwell detached a troop of horse artillery and a squadron of the 8th cavalry to join Hoggan's infantry brigade, and with the remainder of the left cavalry brigade took ground to the right to cover the left flank of Campbell's division. He eventually formed up in rear of Hoggan's and Mountain's brigades when these joined, as already described.

While this battle of the British left division and their left flank cavalry and guns was proceeding, Sir W. Gilbert's division, kept well in hand by its commander, advanced steadily through the jungle, Godby's brigade on the right and Mountain's on the left. The right of this division was covered by Pope's cavalry brigade with three troops horse artillery, under Colonel Grant. It has already been observed that their superior numbers caused the Sikhs to overlap both flanks of the British, and the right as well as the left was thus threatened. Seeing a large body of Sikh horse towards Rasul, Brigadier Pope detached a wing each of the 9th Lancers and 1st and 6th Light Cavalry and some guns under Colonel Lane to protect that flank. He then advanced with the remainder of his brigade (14th Light Dragoons, and a wing of each of 9th Lancers and 1st and 6th Light Cavalry) in line with the infantry. Finding a body of Sikh cavalry in front, he pushed forward his guns, but at the same time advanced with his cavalry in one line, with no supports or reserves, masked the fire of his guns, and moved forward at a trot with the 9th Lancers on the right and the 14th Light Dragoons on the left. Now occurred one of those extraordinary panics which sometimes overtake the best troops. In the words of Hope Grant, who commanded the squadrons of the 9th Lancers, they "were proceeding on steadily and changing their direction a little to their left when the native cavalry began to cheer and charge. I confess at the time I could see no enemy except a party of about fifty horsemen a good deal to our right flank, which I took to be some of our own Irregular Horse." The cause of the disaster which ensued is involved in obscurity. Brigadier Pope was disabled by a wound. It is said that the word "threes about" was given, and it has been conjectured that Pope, realising that he was masking the guns, gave the word "threes right" to clear their front, and that this command was misunderstood. The British officers of native cavalry were, according to another account, far ahead of their men, and their action in hurrying back, either on this command or with a view to give orders for a charge may have added to the misunderstanding. At any rate the whole of the cavalry turned and stampeded to the rear, galloping through and upsetting their guns, and leaving the right flank of the infantry exposed; and did not draw rein

Panic of Pope's cavalry.

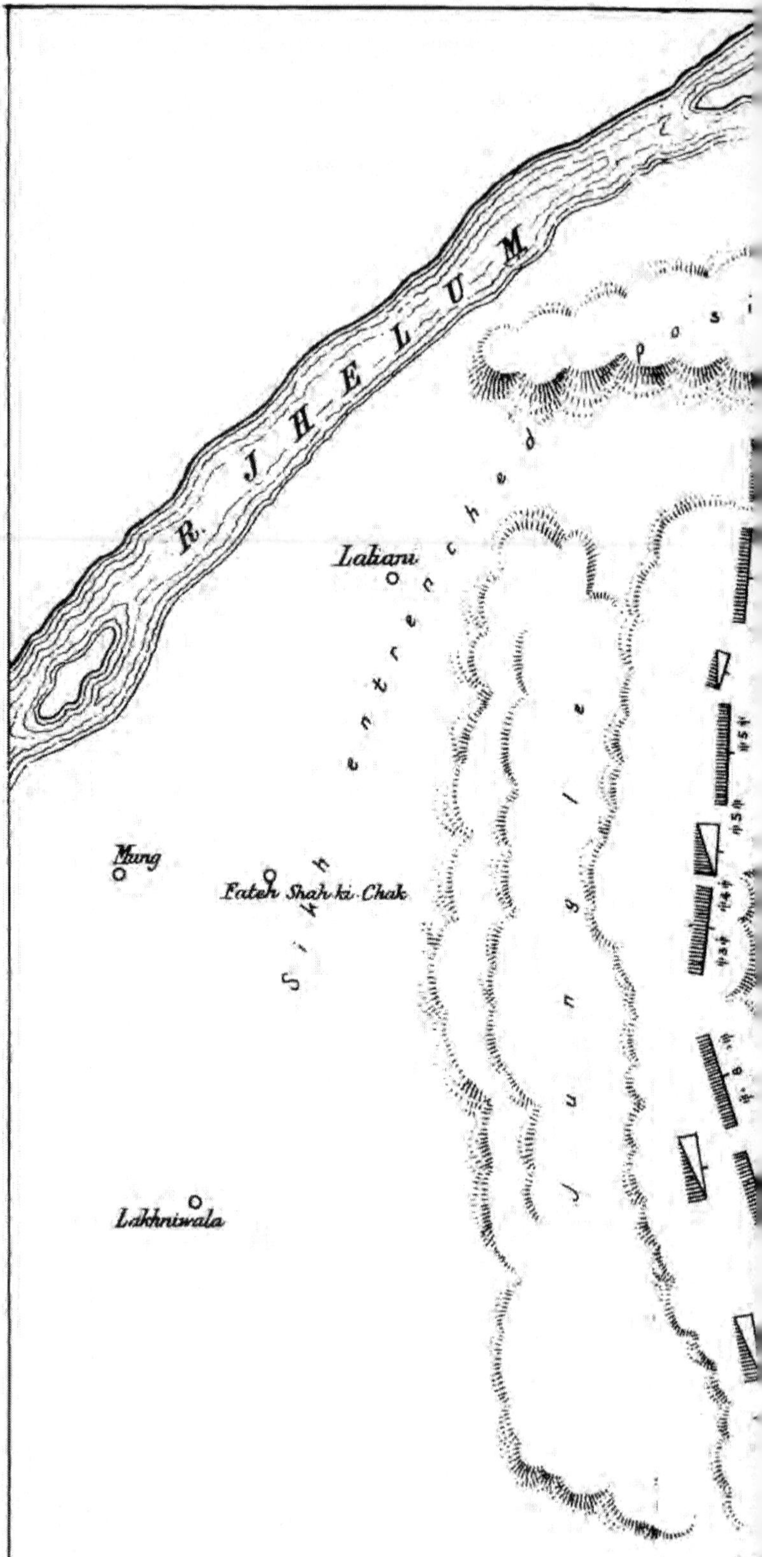
R. JHELUM
Laliani
Sikh entrenched
Mung
Fateh Shah-ki-Chak
Jungle
Lakhniwala

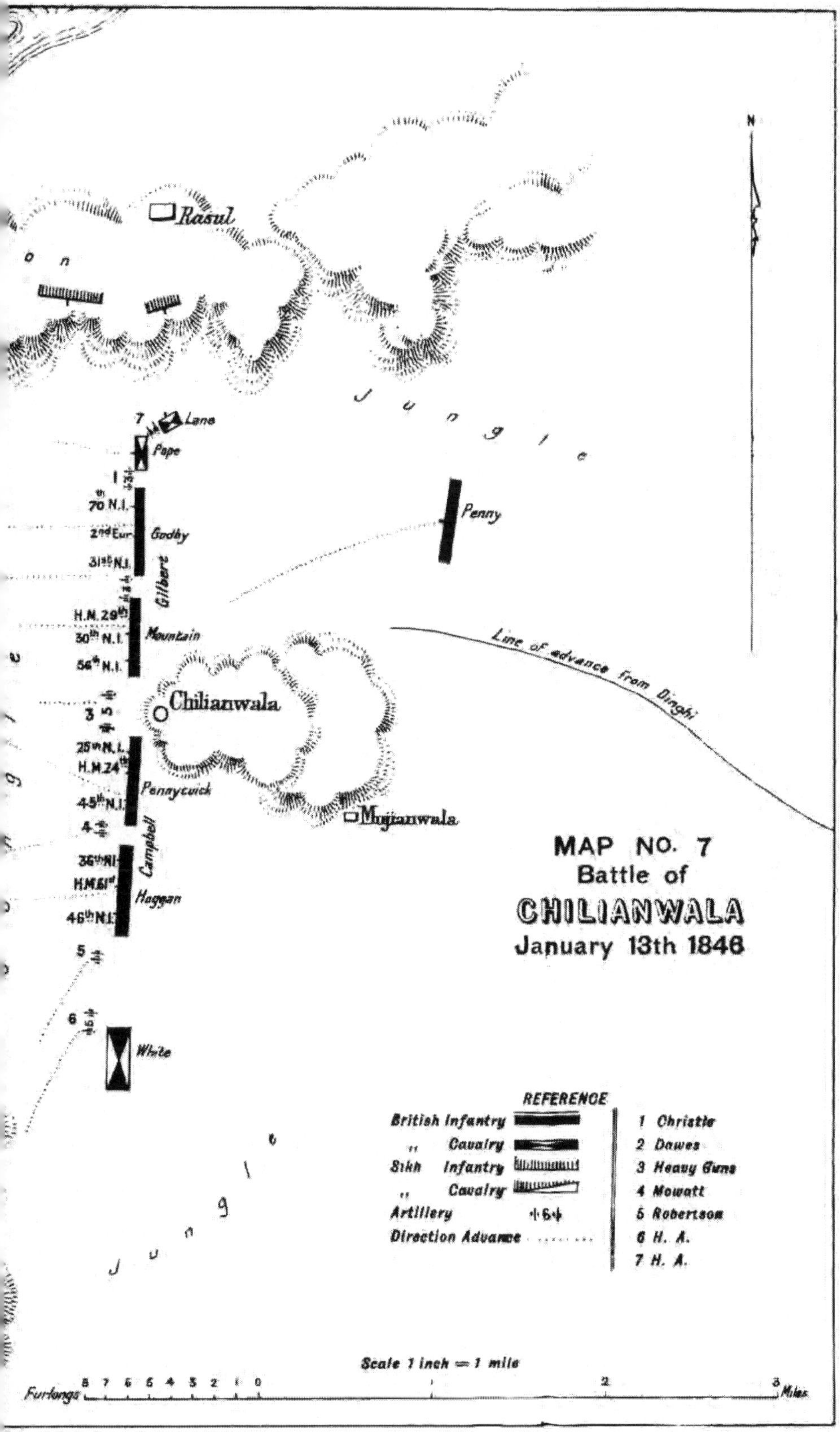

Rasul
Jungle
7
Lane
Pope
1
70th N.I.
2nd Eur.
Godby
31st N.I.
Gilbert
Penny
H.M. 29th
30th N.I.
Mountain
56th N.I.
Line of advance from Dinghi
3
5
Chilianwala
25th N.I.
H.M. 24th
Pennycuick
45th N.I.
Mujianwala
4
Campbell
36th N.I.
H.M. 61st
Hoggan
46th N.I.
5
6
White
MAP NO. 7
Battle of
CHILIANWALA
January 13th 1846
REFERENCE
British Infantry
,, Cavalry
Sikh Infantry
,, Cavalry
Artillery
Direction Advance
1 Christie
2 Dawes
3 Heavy Guns
4 Mowatt
5 Robertson
6 H. A.
7 H. A.
Scale 1 inch = 1 mile
Furlongs 8 7 6 5 4 3 2 1 0 1 2 3 Miles
N

until they were clear of the field, where they were rallied by Colonel Patrick Grant and other officers on the Staff. A body of Sikh cavalry followed, cut down many of the gunners, mortally wounded their commander, Major Christie, and carried off four guns and two wagons, with 53 horses.

Movements of Gilbert's division.

Colonel Lane, who had been detached with some cavalry and horse artillery towards Rasul as already related, appears to have last touch entirely with his main body. No instructions were sent him, and he knew nothing of this disaster. There was consequently a wide unguarded gap between his detachment and the right flank of Sir W. Gilbert's division. That division behaved splendidly and retrieved the battle which had thus been so adverse on either of its flanks. The troops continued to advance steadily, Godby's brigade on the right and Mountain's on the left, covered by the fire of No. 17 Field Battery[1] under Major Dawes. Godby's brigade was somewhat thrown back, to protect the exposed flank, while the division advanced on the villages of Kot Baluch and Tupai; and Mountain's Brigade consequently first came into action. They carried the enemy's battery in front of the village of Laliani at the point of the bayonet, and Godby's brigade then also took the guns in their front. The heavy casualties show the hard fighting in which these brigades were involved and the resistance they encountered.

Penny's reserve brigade had been ordered to retrieve the disaster to Pennycuick's brigade; but inclined too much to the right; and after some sharp fighting eventually reached Godby's brigade, with which it co-operated during the remainder of the day.

Advance of the 2nd Europeans.

The "Journal of a Subaltern" of the 2nd Europeans (afterwards 104th Foot and now Royal Munster Fusiliers) which formed part of Godby's Brigade, gives some interesting details which enable us to realise the work in the ranks—

The word came for the infantry to advance, and into the jungle we plunged with a deafening cheer, the roll of musketry increasing every moment. On we went at a rapid double, dashing through the bushes and bounding over every impediment; faster rolled the musketry, crash upon crash the cannon poured forth its deadly contents. On swept our brigade and gaining an open space in the jungle, the whole of the enemy's line burst on our view. "Charge!" ran the word through our ranks, and the men bounded forward pouring in a murderous fire. The enemy's bullets whizzed above our

[1] Now the 53rd Battery, Royal Field Artillery.

heads. The very air seemed teeming with them. Man after man was struck down. On we went with a steadiness which nothing could resist. The enemy fired a last volley, then wavered, turned and fled. Pursuit in a jungle like that, where we could not see twenty yards before us, was useless; so we halted and began to collect our wounded, when all of a sudden fire was was opened on us in our rear. A large body of the enemy had turned our flank in the jungle and got between us and the rest of the troops. Another party was on our left, and we found ourselves with our light field battery completely surrounded, and alone in the field. The word was given "Right about face", and we advanced steadily loading and firing as we went. Captain Dawes' battery was the saving of us. As the cavalry was bearing down, the Brigadier shouted—"A shower of grape in there," and a salvo was poured in that sent horse and man head over heels, in heaps. The fire was fearful; the atmosphere seemed alive with balls."

The Sikhs, sword in hand, charged more than once, and tried to break through the British line, which had to turn in different directions to resist attack, but they were at length driven from this part of the field.

Repulse of the Sikh Army.

The Sikh right had now been rolled up by Campbell's left brigade, many guns had been taken, and the enemy driven from the field. But if a victory at all, it was a Pyrrhic one, for the victors had probably lost more than the vanquished, and could not even hold the ground on which they stood, or the guns which they had taken. The enemy retreated on Rasul, passing across the front of Lane, who commanded the cavalry and horse artillery beyond the British right, and who dispersed them with the fire of his guns. But while the Sikhs had been driven back to the Jhelum, the British were obliged from want of water to withdraw from the field of battle to the village of Chilianwala, and to relinquish the spiked and captured guns. Under cover of darkness parties of the enemy returned and carried off all the guns that had not been brought into camp.

Thus ended one of the hardest fought battles ever contested on Indian soil. The British loss[1] amounted to over 2,000 men, six guns, and several stands of colours. The Sikhs lost no prestige; their casualties are not recorded; twelve of their small field-pieces were captured.

Comments.

This battle is instructive as showing the difficulty and the necessity of maintaining inter-communication between the component parts of a force, particularly when in thick cover. The want of success was due to this among other causes, including the relinquishing by

[1] For detail of casualties, see Appendix IX.

Brigadier-General Campbell of the command of his whole division for that of a brigade, and the panic on the right flank owing to Brigadier Pope's faulty disposition of his cavalry. The guns of Campbell's division did not co-operate as they might have done, largely owing to the above mentioned cause, and apparently to the absence of any orders from the divisional commander, who discovered this defect too late. The soldiers, both British and native, fought heroically, and by their steady and gallant bearing retrieved the fortunes of the day, and averted what might well have been a great disaster.

CHAPTER XI.

THE SECOND SIEGE OF MULTAN.

(*Map 6.*)

Situation at Multan.

It was related in Chapter VII that General Whish had been compelled to abandon the siege of Multan, owing to the inadequacy of his force after the defection of Raja Sher Singh. He fell back on the 16th September, and remained inactive for some weeks, awaiting reinforcements which were being sent to him from Bombay. Sher Singh marched from Multan on 9th October, as related in Chapter VIII, to raise the Sikhs throughout the Punjab, and the Sikhs generally ceased to consider Multan as the place where the battle of their faith was to be fought. Sher Singh's departure was followed by an extensive desertion of Mulraj's cause by his Sikh soldiers, horse and foot. The general idea was that all Sikhs were to assemble and fight the battle of Khalsa independence in the neighbourhood of Lahore.

The weakening of Mulraj by the departure of the Sikhs eventually enabled General Whish to resume the offensive, although he was not strong enough to carry the city and fort until the arrival of the Bombay column, which did not reach him until 22nd December. On the 1st November, Mulraj, assuming the offensive, established himself on the raised banks of a dry canal which intersected the British lines, and for some days kept up a constant artillery fire on the camp.

Action of Suraj Khund.

On the 7th November General Whish attacked the enemy's position outside the walls of Multan. The British force was drawn up at 6 A.M. on the eastern side of the Grand Canal, which flanked Edwardes' position at Suraj Khund. The infantry columns were to make a detour to the right, to take the enemy's position in flank, and the cavalry and horse artillery to make a corresponding movement and on nearing the enemy to act according to circumstances. The allies (Edwardes and Cortlandt with the Darbar troops and levies, and the Bahawalpur Contingent) were to move forward, or act on the defensive as directed by Edwardes, up the left bank of the canal. During the night several hundred men of one of Van Cortlandt's regiments[1] deserted to the enemy.

General Whish himself remained in camp, thinking it undesirable that he should leave in view of the defection of the Sikhs. The troops for the attack were detailed as follows:—

2 squadrons, 11th Light Cavalry, completed to 160 rank and file.

2 squadrons, 7th Irregular Cavalry, completed to 220 rank and file.

2 squadrons, 11th Irregular Cavalry, completed to 220 rank and file.

4th Troop, 3rd Brigade Horse Artillery.

BRIGADIER MARKHAM, COMMANDING INFANTRY.

Lieutenant-Colonel Franks, C.B.

6 companies, 10th Foot, completed to 400 rank and file.

companies, 8th Native Infantry, completed to 512 rank and file.

8 companies, 52nd Native Infantry.

Lieutenant-Colonel Brooke.

6 companies, 32nd Foot, completed to 500 rank and file.

8 companies, 49th Native Infantry, completed to 352 rank and file.

8 companies, 51st Native Infantry, completed to 560 rank and file.

Brigadier Markham wrote in his report:—

"According to arrangements, I proceeded with the force under my command across the bridges over the nullah on the right of the allied camp in the Suraj Khund, in open column flanking the enemy's position, and brought our shoulders forward to the left, proceeding directly across their rear. When we had advanced sufficiently far to insure overlapping the most distant part of their position, we wheeled into line, three guns on the right, three on the left, the whole of the cavalry, with the exception of a small party with the guns, on our right flank between the line and the Sultan Sadula Gardens.

The reserve, in quarter distance column in rear of the centre of the right brigade, advanced steadily in echelon of brigade at fifty paces distance from the right, under a smart fire of grape and round shot. At this moment I ordered the cavalry to attack a large body of the enemy who were moving to our right and to prevent their moving the guns."

The cavalry under Major Wheler were getting clear of the jungle on to open ground, when they saw on their right front a body of the enemy with a standard, a mass of his cavalry in and around some villages a little further retired on tolerably good ground, and his batteries in the distance. Major Wheler at once made up his mind to attack, and with a cheer his men charged with the utmost precision and rapidity, carrying all before them. But rapid and good as the charge was in itself, it was so timed

[1] The number of deserters was 220, all Hindus, and chiefly from Lucknow.

as to be of essential service, for some of the squadrons charged immediately in rear of the enemy's guns, preventing the line of infantry from being enfiladed. More than this, the enemy's mass of cavalry, apparently unaware of their proximity, were staggered by this sudden advance and never made a stand in a body, though parties of them showed a good front until the horsemen were among them. Some squadrons charged repeatedly, while others charged only once, but prevented the guns from being carried off. Lieutenant Vibart, 11th Light Cavalry, captured a standard. As the cavalry cleared the front the horse artillery opened fire, the line charged and took the position with the whole of the guns on the bank of the nullah, driving the enemy across and up it with considerable loss. The batteries were then destroyed, and the force returned to camp, the engagement having lasted only about an hour.

The allied forces under Edwardes and Lake co-operated in the attack, and were at first subjected to offensive operations on the part of the enemy, who drove back 500 Pathans forming an advanced post on the nullah, and turned the inner flank of an eight gun battery at a well 400 yards in front of the camp. The gunners at this moment behaved well, drawing back their guns from the embrasures, and, bringing them to bear on the enemy issuing from the nullah, discharged grape so rapidly as to check the attack. Both sides were now reinforced, and a desperate conflict took place, until the defenders, being reinforced by two of General Cortlandt's regiments and a large body of Daoudputras, after a sharp fight of half an hour expelled the enemy from the nullah and drove and pursued them right up to their entrenchments. The allied forces subsequently advanced and co-operated in the final attack.[1] In this action the British force had 3 killed and 58 wounded; the allies lost 39 killed and 172 wounded. The enemy's casualties are not recorded, but five guns were taken.

Arrival of the Bombay column.

The long expected Bombay column[2], which has already been referred to, did not join General Whish until the 22nd December, and until then a period of inaction ensued, during which, however, the enemy's

[1] During this advance some of Edwardes' Pathans captured a gun, when fire was opened on them by some of the British sepoys, who mistook them for enemies. At this juncture a brave soldier, Private Howell of the 32nd Foot, leaped down into the canal, and, standing in front of the Pathans, faced the British troops waving his shako at the end of his bayonet, as a signal to cease firing. Thus many friendly lives were saved.

[2] The Bombay column under command of Brigadier the Hon. H. Dundas consisted of one troop horse artillery, two companies foot artillery, two light field batteries, 2 companies sappers, 1st Bombay European Fusiliers, Her Majesty's 60th Foot, 1st Bombay Light Cavalry, Sinde Horse, 3rd, 4th, 9th and 19th Bombay Infantry. This brought the total force under General Whish to a strength of 15,648.

position was thoroughly reconnoitred by Colonel Cheape, the Chief Engineer, who arrived on November 30th. On the 25th the original position before Multan was occupied and on the 27th December the operations were resumed in accordance with the following Division Orders, issued to the Multan Field Force by Major-General Whish on the 26th :—

"A wing of Her Majesty's 10th Regiment and a regiment of native infantry from the 1st Brigade will proceed at a quarter of an hour after noon precisely to take possesstion of the brick kilns to the north-west of camp. Brigadier Cheape will attach an engineer to the party and a company or two of pioneers.

A squadron of cavalry and four horse artillery guns will accompany this party to act according to circumstances.

Three companies of Her Majesty's 32nd Regiment and six companies native infantry from the 2nd Brigade to parade at the advance picquet of that Brigade a quarter of an hour before noon to accompany heavy ordnance to the front.

The portion of the force not ordered on other duties will be ready to stand to arms from noon until dismissed.

The Officer Commanding the Bombay Division is requested to have prepared two columns of a wing of European and a regiment of native infantry each, accompanied by a squadron of cavalry and light field battery each, at 11 A.M. The batteries to open on the enemy's positions at Mandi Awa and Sidi-lal-ki-bed precisely at noon, and to be followed up by the infantry and artillery, according to the effect produced on the enemy, to the taking of those two positions if facilities offer, for which purpose a company of sappers should be attached to each columnwith entrenching tools to secure the posts if taken.

The column acting on the left of the Bombay Division should be warned that Major Edwardes' force co-operates with this attack, on the west of the canal (or large nullah), to whose troops a few of the Bengal Cavalry, Regular and Irregular will be attached to facilitate their being recognised as allies."

In accordance with these orders, the columns detailed in the margin moved to the attack on the 27th December, the first two composing the Bombay Column under Brigadier Dundas, the remainder forming the Bengal Column in support under Brigadier Stalker. On leaving camp the left centre column proceeded towards the Mandi Awa, guided by Captain Abercrombie of the Engineers

Left Column.

Brigadier, the Hon'ble H. Dundas, C.B.
5 Companies, 1st Bombay Fusiliers, Major Miguan.
4th Bombay Rifles, Major Honner.
No. 7 Light Field Battery, Captain Turnbull.
Squadron, Sinde Horse, Lieutenant Merewether.
1 Company Sappers, Lieutenant Kendall.

Left Centre Column

Brigadier Capon.
5 Companies, Her Majesty's 60th Rifles, Major Dennis.

3rd Bombay Infantry, Major Hallett.

No. 5 Light Field Battery, Captain Bailey.

Squadron, 1st Bombay Lancers, Captain Curtis.

1 Company Sappers, Lieutenant Walker.

Right Centre Column.

Lieutenant-Colonel Nash, C.B.,

3 Companies, Her Majesty's 32nd Regiment, Major Case.

6 Companies, 72nd Bengal Infantry, Captain Lloyd.

4 guns, Horse Artillery, Captain Anderson.

3rd Company Pioneers, Lieutenant Gordon.

Right Column.

Lieutenant-Colonel Young.

5 Companies, Her Majesty's 10th Foot, Captain Longden.

52nd Bengal Infantry, Captain Jamieson.

4 guns, Horse Artillery, Captain Mackenzie.

1 squadron, 11th Irregular Cavalry, Captain Dowson.

2nd Company Sappers, Lieutenant Grindall.

Movement of the left centre column.

and two companies, 60th Rifles, took possession of the building called Ramtira , under fire of round shot and shrapnel from the city. The battery opened on the enemy at the Mandi Awa at 700 yards. This column then advanced in line covered by skirmishers whose fire soon subdued that of the enemy. After twenty minutes a general rush to the mound (Mandi Awa) took place, and the enemy evacuated it and fled towards the suburbs, followed by the greater part of the 60th Rifles, while the 3rd were engaged in pursuing some of the enemy who had taken shelter in a mosque and under hedges and walls. Here they charged and drove the defenders into the city.

The troops were recalled from the pursuit, and the light field battery brought into position on the mound. As part of the Bengal Column on the right now approached, Brigadier Capon resolved that the suburbs should be held in front and on both flanks of the mound (Mandi Awa) as far as possible.

The suburbs were reoccupied without much resistance by the 60th Rifles and part of the 3rd Bombay Infantry, in conjunction with a portion of the Right Centre (Bengal) Column, consisting of three companies, 32nd Foot, under Major Inglis, and part of the 51st Bengal Infantry under Major Finnis. About this time a shrapnel shell from the town burst over one of the 9-pounder guns, which had begun to reply to the enemy's fire, killing Lieutenant Younghusband, 9th Bombay Infantry, and two artillerymen, and severely wounding Lieutenant Hill, field engineer. The 9-pounder guns soon silenced the enemy's howitzer or mortar and only round shot were subsequently fired at the Mandi Awa, with little effect except that Captain Bailey had his arm carried off, and an artilleryman was mortally wounded. Just before this, Major Gordon, 60th Rifles, when in command of a party clearing the suburbs in front of the mound, fell mortally wounded by a matchlock ball fired from one of the houses, when crossing an open space ; no other casualties occurred, owing to the skill of the men in taking cover during the advance.

A chain of posts was then established in the suburbs, in co-operation with the column on the right flank.

Movements of the left column.

In the meantime the left column, guided by Lieutenant Pollard, Bengal Engineers, passed over very broken ground, intersected by deep nullahs. The enemy's advanced piquets being distinctly seen, the advanced guard extended, and as soon as the 4th Bombay Rifles had disentangled themselves from the nullahs, the skirmishers advanced and drove in the defenders. The column moved on to the left until the head had passed the left of the old entrenchments, when the 1st Bombay Fusiliers formed in the parallel, while the 4th Bombay Rifles lay down under a bank in front of a white building or mosque. The battery was placed in position and opened on the mound of the Sidi-lal-ki-bed, from which the enemy retired. A few rounds were fired at the mosque, from which the 4th Bombay Rifles then drove the enemy, as well as from a large one with adjoining buildings where they had two guns. A general advance then took place, the 1st Bombay Fusiliers passing the mound to the right and the 4th Rifles to the left. The advance was continued over very strong and difficult ground, the enemy being driven from every point where they attempted to make a stand, the 1st Fusiliers pursuing them through a deserted village into the suburbs and the 4th Rifles following them and driving them out of the large enclosure of the Bhigi Bagh and quite into the suburbs. The guns were placed in position at the Sidi-lal-ki-bed, but could produce little effect owing to the distance of the city wall, which was scarcely perceptible. While the guns were being brought up to the hill, a retrograde movement was made by the troops, owing to the 4th Rifles having imprudently advanced too far and expended all their ammunition. The greater number of casualties occurred at this time, but the Fusiliers, falling back gradually and keeping up a steady fire, checked the advance of the enemy and covered the retreat of the 4th Rifles.

Both regiments having formed under the hill, the ammuniton was replenished, when the Fusiliers moved to the right and quickly drove the enemy from the deserted village, under cover of which they then formed, keeping skirmishers out to the front.

The 4th Rifles reoccupied the Bhigi Bagh.[1] The object of the attack in distracting the enemy having been attained, no further advance took place. The troops maintained their positions until dark, a constant cannonade being kept up from the battery. At dark, the Bhigi Bagh being very extensive and thickly studded with

[1] They were relieved in the afternoon by a wing of the 19th Bombay Infantry, who repulsed all attempts of the enemy to regain possession of the place.

trees, it was deemed advisable to retire from it. The Sappers having made several large openings in the wall, to facilitate reoccupation, if necessary, a position was taken up in rear, the left being thrown back and resting on the large mosque, the right extending to the right of the Sidi-lal-ki-bed. The enemy kept up an ineffective fire of matchlocks during the night.

Movements of the Bengal division.

While the operations that have been described were in progress, the Bengal Division, forming the Right and Right Centre Columns, co-operated on their side, and drove the enemy before them into the city, losing 12 killed and 70 wounded; the Bombay Column had 14 killed, 98 wounded and 18 missing.

Sortie by the enemy.

At 3 P.M., on the 28th, Edwards and Lake with the auxiliaries relieved the Bombay Column of charge of the Sidi-lal-ki-bed, and all the posts on the left of it, including the Bhigi Bagh, the villages of Dera, Jog and Marja. They remained undisturbed during the night, but were attacked at about 1 P.M., on the 29th by 2,000 of the enemy, almost all on foot, and chiefly regulars, among whom the deserters of the 7th November were conspicuous. They issued from the Delhi Gate, filed behind the suburbs in front of the Sidi-lal-ki-bed, and made their appearance suddenly on the left front of the allies, pushing boldly on into the gardens which were unoccupied, and opening a heavy musketry fire from behind the walls, a position, however, from which they were rapidly dislodged by Edwardes' Rohillas and other irregulars, aided by two companies of General Cortlandt's regiment, who expelled them and followed them up to the city walls. Among those who distinguished themselves in this action were two volunteers, Messrs. Quin and MacMahon, the latter of whom killed the leader of the enemy's infantry, a powerful Sikh, with one blow which divided his head.

General Whish now made arrangements for assaulting the city of Multan. At 9 A.M., on the 30th December the enemy's principal magazine in the citadel was blown up by a shell from one of the mortars, the explosion destroying the grand Masjid and many houses and other buildings in the vicinity.

Establishment of breaching batteries.

General Whish had now the following batteries :—

Six 8-inch mortars	.. ..	opened on	28th	December.
Three 10-inch ,,	.. ..	,,	,,	,,
Four 5½-inch ,,	.. ..	,,	,,	,,
Six 18-pounders, on the Khuni Burj		,,	29th	,,

Two 8-inch howitzers }
Two 10 inch ,, } with the mortars in the first line, opened
Two 24-prs. } on 29th.

And five 8-inch mortars were laid down on the 30th near the 10-inch mortars.

The fire from the citadel was quite subdued on the 30th. On the morning of the 31st a small gun was occasionally used, but the enemy appeared to have gone into the city, where a few of them kept up a smart matchlock fire on the breaching batteries.

On the 2nd January 1849, General Whish issued the following orders:—

"It being the Major-General's intention to assault the city to-day, it will be effected by two columns constituted as follows:—

From the Bengal Division:—

Her Majesty's 32nd Regiment, 49th Regiment, Native Infantry; 72nd Regiment, Native Infantry; right column under the command of Brigadier Markham.

From the Bombay Division:—

1st Bombay Fusiliers; 4th Bombay Native Infantry (Rifles); 19th Bombay Native Infantry; left column under the command of Brigadier Stalker, C.B. Each column to be conducted by an officer of Engineers and to be accompanied by a sergeant and 12 artillerymen, furnished with gun-spikes, and to have a complete company of sappers and pioneers in attendance.

The columns will leave their respective lines at noon precisely and halt in the vicinity of the Mandi Awa.

The troops now on duty there and in the suburbs between it (the Amkhas inclusive) augmented on either flank by two guns of horse artillery and a squadron of cavalry (the Bombay Division providing for the left and the Bengal Division for the right) will form the reserve under the command of Brigadier Hervey.

Brigadier the Hon'ble H. Dundas is requested to send the Sinde Horse to Bakurabad at noon, with two guns of horse artillery; and Brigadier Salter will attach a regiment of Irregular Cavalry towards the north-west angle of the fort, Major Garbett placing two horse artillery guns at his disposal to accompany the same. One *risala* to be told off to the guns with orders not to quit them on any account

Officers commanding columns will be furnished with particular instructions for their guidance, and outline plans of the city.

Officers commanding companies to be impressed with the necessity of preventing their men separating in search of plunder or on any other pretext.

The camps will be under charge of Brigadiers Capon and Salter respectively, who will order the troops in them to stand to their arms from 1 P.M.

In accordance with these orders, the columns assembled at the Mandi Awa, and at 2 o'clock orders were issued for the assault on the two breaches, the right column having first to proceed to the Delhi Gate. At about 3 o'clock, on the signal of a salvo fired from the Delhi Gate battery, the two columns moved to the attack. Two companies of the 32nd Foot under Captain Smyth proceeded to storm the breach. Upon passing the broken ground and ruined outworks of the gate under a heavy fire of matchlocks they descended a deep hollow and found to their surprise the city wall in front, about thirty feet in height, unbreached and totally impracticable, being fairly concealed from view from the nature of the ground until they came close upon it.

Movements of the right column.

Captain Smyth immediately and with great judgment and promptitude decided to retire, and rejoined the column with the loss of several men. Brigadier Markham at once proceeded to the breach at the Khuni Burj, which he found had already been entered by the left column, and from thence to the part of the city close to the Daulat Gate and directly in front of the fort. The enemy offered considerable opposition in the narrow streets and on the ramparts, which were strongly barricaded; but the troops carried all before them, and before dark that part of the city was in their possession, and their posts connected up with those of the left column.

The loss of the right column amounted to 4 killed and 26 wounded.

In the meantime the left column, which was drawn up in three columns in rear of the Mandi Awa, had moved down to storm the left breach at the angle of the Khuni Burj. The distance to the breach was about two hundred yards, the approach being fully exposed to fire from musketry and *zamburaks*. The storming party, three companies 1st Bombay Fusiliers under Captain Leith, mounted the breach at 3-15, but when they reached the summit found themselves in a sort of enclosure, from which there was only one regular exit by a narrow lane on the right, and over a low house into the Khuni Burj. The first to mount the breach was Colour-Sergeant John Bennet, who planted the Union Jack on its crest, and stood beside it until the whole brigade had passed. The colour and staff were riddled with bullets. The enemy had retrenched the breach and dug deep ditches into which several of the leading men and officers fell. Captain Leith was dangerously wounded soon after crossing the breach, and the column was detained nearly twenty minutes by the obstacles at the top. The storming party pushed down the lane to the right, under Lieutenant Gray, to clear away obstacles between the breach and the

Movements of the left column.

point at which the Bengal column was to enter, and was in part the cause of the enemy abandoning the Khuni Burj. Fortunately, two short ladders were procured and placed by the Bengal Sappers under Lieutenant Oliphant against the house on the left, just as the enemy found their communication with the town threatened; they were, therefore, obliged to defend both the lane and the tower, and their resistance was consequently less energetic.

Capture of the town.

The Brigade, in three columns, proceeded—the 1st column under Major Mignan to the left, clearing the ramparts, the others under Majors Mant and Honner pushing for the centre of the town, where they established themselves in the grain market. The narrowness of the streets rendered regular formation impossible, and the enemy was followed up by the troops in the best mode in which they could move, and without giving him time to halt, until the town was completely carried, and the several columns established, the left having succeeded in reaching the Lahore Gate. A company was left at the Lahore Gate, and all the columns similarly established advanced posts, and then retired to the more open ground in the centre of the town. The town was completely cleared by dark. During the night one of the enemy's powder magazines blew up, burying several men in the ruins. Had the assault taken place earlier in the day, this explosion might have been avoided. The enemy's ammunition was lying about in great quantities, and there was nothing to distinguish their magazines from the other houses. In the morning Lieutenants Pollard and Maxwell of the Bengal Sappers removed a considerable quantity of powder from another magazine close to a burning house and threw it over the wall where it exploded harmlessly.

In his report Brigadier Stalker wrote:—

Brigadier Stalker's report.

"The Pak Gate was cleared during the night by the Bengal Sappers, the Haran Gate by the Bombay Sappers, and the Behar Gate was nearly opened when the explosion took place, which rendered it impossible to go on. It was opened next morning by the Bengal Sappers.

It is quite impossible to say where the engineer officers were: the troops were so scattered by the narrow lanes that there were no distinct columns. The only real guide was to follow the retreating enemy, which was done. Not only are the ramparts so incomplete as to render a passage round them by a column of men quite impracticable, but the parts which are complete were at the time of the assault crossed by traverses and cut up by small trenches. The night closed before the communication between the different bodies could be effected, but by morning the troops were in communication with each other.

It is to be regretted that we had not a couple of hours daylight as we should then have probably avoided the explosion of the magazine; but the town was as completely cleared of the enemy by dark as it is at the present moment.

The steady and well-directed fire of the 60th Rifles kept down that of the enemy very considerably while the troops were approaching the breach, and a discharge of grape thrown on the top of the breach by Lieutenant Keir, Bombay Artillery, just over the heads of the Fusiliers as they advanced was of the utmost value to us; but when the top was gained and our men became mingled with the enemy the fate of the day depended on the steadiness and courage of the Fusiliers, and both men and officers responded nobly to the call.''

Lessons of the assault.

These operations illustrate the difficulties to be encountered in street fighting, and show the advisability of beginning an action early in the day so as to conclude it before nightfall. The same defect of beginning the action too late occurred at the battle of Ferozeshahr. The value of supporting and covering fire both by rifles and artillery during the advance is also emphasised in Brigadier Stalker's despatch, and has been experienced on many occasions both before and since the siege of Multan. It is to-day one of the first principles in the attack of a position.

The losses in the assault on the city of Multan amounted to 30 killed, 218 wounded, and 1 missing.*

Action of the auxiliaries.

The forces under Edwardes and Lake, prior to and during the assault, created a diversion on the south and west of the city. Lieutenant Lake threw out a large skirmishing party directly in his front close up to the Pak Gate; General Cortlandt another on the left of the Daoudputras; and Edwardes a third on the left of General Cortlandt; thus opening a smart fire nearly down to the Bohar Gate, and securing the attention of a large portion of the enemy's soldiers on the walls. Edwardes also moved out a large body of cavalry and a troop of horse artillery in front of the village of Dera, while the remainder and main body of the infantry were in reserve at the Bhigi Bagh and Sidi-lal-ki-bed.

At about 1-30 P.M. the Daoudputras under direction of Lieutenant Lake, and the remaining auxiliaries under the direction of Lieutenant Young of the Engineers, Mr. Hugo James, and Mr. Quin, opened their fire from the most advanced suburbs, and drew fire from the ramparts and the guns on the Moti bastion until the advance of the British on the breach. After the capture of the city Lieutenant Lake occupied the Pak Gate with the Daoudputras

*For detail of casualties during the operations before Multan, see Appendix VI.

and a small party of the 3rd Bombay Infantry. When the skirmishers of the auxiliaries had been withdrawn, Edwardes ordered the cavalry from Dera to patrol to the westward, where they intercepted a party of the enemy's infantry who had escaped from the city, killed twenty and took the rest prisoners.

Siege of the citadel.

The number of the enemy now confined to the citadel as a result of the operations of the 2nd January was estimated at from 2,000 to 2,500.* Close siege was laid to this last stronghold. On the morning of the 4th January a brigade of the Bombay Column was marched to a site on the north-west angle of the fort, to take immediate possession of Hazuri Bagh. Two 5½-inch mortar batteries were established in the advanced trench and zig-zag, which by the 6th reached the glacis east of the fort; and to facilitate operations Brigadier Cheape established himself at Wazirabad with the Sappers and Miners. On that day Edwardes wrote to the British Resident at Lahore:—

"The garrison of Multan is now in the last extremity. The gunners are unable to serve their guns, from incessant shelling; the buildings are almost all unroofed from the same cause, and afford but little shelter; Dewan Mulraj himself has sought refuge in the gateway of the Sukkee Gate; and every soldier is obliged to grind the wheat for his own dinner, all the flour having been blown up in the explosion of the Jumma Musjid."

Progress of the siege.

In this extremity Mulraj opened negotiations, asking for terms, but was told that nothing less than unconditional surrender would be considered. On the 8th, the seven 18-pounder battery opened within 200 yards of the fort, and a mortar battery of three 10-inch howitzers. On the same day, a battery for six 24-pounders and six 18-pounders was begun, and trenches were widened. The object of this battery was to keep down the fire of the citadel opposite it and eventually to breach at the north-east angle; the sap begun on the 6th was carried on, the object being to blow in the counterscarp. On the 9th the sap was advanced ninety-five feet; the seven 18-pounder battery, constructed of fascines and sand-bags, was set on fire at about 3.30 P. M. by one of the enemy's shells, and burnt down. The guns and powder were saved by the sailors of the Indus flotilla, who had been working the guns.

The enemy, observing the occurrence, kept up a heavy fire, and several men were wounded. A position was prepared in the city for six guns and four 5½-inch mortars, and roads leading to it were widened. On the night of the 10th, 110 gabions were

* An incorrect estimate, as nearly 4,000 eventually surrendered.

added in continuation of the sap, bringing it near the foot of the glacis. The enemy were alarmed and kept up a heavy fire throughout the night, impeding the work. After daylight the fire was kept down by riflemen, for whom advantage had been taken of a hill to construct cover which flanked the head of the sap. On the night of the 18th January 130 of the garrison surrendered, and on the 20th another 300 were taken by the cavalry. Mulraj's followers were leaving him in large numbers, and he continued negotiations for surrender, but attempted to obtain terms which could not be granted. On the 21st January General Whish wrote:—

"The rebel is reduced to the last extremity; he was all yesterday endeavouring to rally the garrison, but they told him plainly that he must do one or the other of two things; sally out at the head of his troops and cut his way through the besiegers, or immediately surrender, as it was impossible for the soldiers to stand the shelling any longer."

Next day Mulraj surrendered, and the garrison, numbering between 3,000 and 4,000, laid down their arms.

Mulraj was tried and sentenced to imprisonment which lasted until his death not long afterwards.

Gudhar Singh, who murdered Mr. Vans Agnew, was subsequently hanged in Multan.

CHAPTER XII.

OPERATIONS IN THE JULLUNDUR DOAB.

Insurrection in Nurpur.

We find that, in consequence of the trend of events in the Punjab, the moveable column which was stationed at Jullundur under Brigadier Wheeler was ordered early in September to be ready to take the field in the Jullundur Doab, between the Sutlej and Beas rivers. At that time Ram Singh, son of Shama, one of the hereditary wazirs of Nurpur, crossed the frontier and attacked several posts on the customs line in the vicinity of Pathankot and Nurpur. A force of the 15th Irregular Cavalry and 29th Native Infantry under Major Fisher was accordingly sent against him and crossed the Beas at Katgarh on the 9th September. Early on the 10th Major Fisher marched to Pathankot, where arrangements were made for attacking the rebels who were reported to be in possession of the neighbouring fort of Shahpur. As the force approached that place a body of men was seen on the hill overlooking the fort; these were charged and dispersed by the cavalry. When the party neared the fort, a heavy fire of musketry was opened from the walls, by which a few sowars were wounded. Fire continued until dusk, and during the night the rebels evacuated the fort, escaping by a precipitous path leading to the Ravi, which flowed several hundred feet below.

On the 10th September, Mr. J. Lawrence,* Commissioner of the Jullundur Doab, reached Kangra, and on the 13th arrived at Nurpur, where he heard that Ram Singh occupied a long narrow hill in the immediate vicinity of the town. He had perpetrated several dacoities and had written circular letters to the headmen of villages, inviting them to join him. On the morning of the 14th, Mr. Lawrence and Major Fisher reconnoitred the enemy's position, and the surrounding country, which was difficult. It was found that cavalry could act with difficulty on the south, a wide ravine, interspersed with rice fields, running along that side; on the north the country was much more difficult, being broken in every direction into hundreds of little spurs running out from the main chain on which the insurgents were posted. Reinforcements were brought up, and on the morning of the 19th, Ram Singh and his followers were dispersed. The force with Mr. Lawrence consisted of 360 men of the 1st Sikh Regiment, under Major Hodgson, of whom 300 attacked on one side;

Attack on Ram Singh.

*Afterwards Lord Lawrence, Governor-General of India.

two companies 29th Native Infantry under Lieutenant Johnston, who went up on another side; four companies 71st Native Infantry, under Captain Rind, and 150 men of the Kangra Regiment, under Lieutenant Wallace made a long detour, and mounting the eastern extremity of the hill, gained possession of the heights. Major Fisher commanded the whole force, and with the 15th Irregular Cavalry guarded the southern and western sides of the hill. The casualties amounted to one sepoy killed and 9 wounded; the enemy sustained considerable loss.

After this action Major Hodgson returned to Hoshiarpur with the 1st Sikh Local Infantry; a garrison was left at Nurpur, and Mr. Lawrence proceeded to Pathankot with Major Fisher and the cavalry.

The Jullundur Moveable Column.

As the tranquillity of the Jullundur district depended on that of the country on the right bank of the Beas, Brigadier-General Wheeler* was directed to move with the Jullundur Moveable Column to Tanda on the banks of the Beas, with the exception of one corps, sent to Amritsar to occupy the fort of Govindgarh. There he was to collect boats for crossing at any point, and await orders, according to the trend of events.

The spread of the Sikh insurrection soon lent a greater importance to the operations of the Jullundur Moveable Column.

On 7th October 1848, the Resident wrote to Brigadier C. Campbell, who commanded the troops at Lahore, and under whose orders the Column was acting:—

"'It is of the last importance that coercive measures should be promptly adopted in regard to some petty chiefs residing in the Bari Doab, who have joined the rebellion set afoot by Sirdar Chattar Singh and Raja Sher Singh, and are endeavouring to bring the insurrection to our neighbourhood. The presence of Brigadier Wheeler in the neighbourhood of two of these insurgents affords an ample opportunity of reading the disaffected a lesson without moving troops from Lahore. The chiefs themselves are in open rebellion at Multan; the attachment of their houses and property has been ordered by the Government. They have forcibly resisted this attachment; their representatives have garrisoned their dwelling houses, and have replied to the Government order that their castles stand or fall with Multan.'

These parties, if they refuse to surrender when the troops arrive, must be coerced; their castles be forcibly entered; all persons offering opposition be treated as rebels."

Reduction of Rangar Nagal.

The first place to be reduced in pursuance of these orders was Rangar Nagal, against which Brigadier Wheeler at once marched, and encamped

*Brigadier-General H. M. Wheeler, C.B., murdered at Cawnpore in 1857.

on the 14th October in a good position, just clear of the enemy's fire, to the south-east of the fort. This place was situated fifteen miles from the Ghat at Shri Hargovindpur, directly opposite Brigadier Wheeler's position at Tanda. The premises were extensive, enclosed by a stone wall with a gateway, and having a double fausse-braie with a wide and deep ditch and a garrison of upwards of a hundred men, but not disciplined soldiers, for there was not yet a Sikh force of any kind on the Lahore side of the Jhelum, except at Multan.

Having sent the cavalry round to the northern and western faces to take up distant positions and watch any attempt to escape, Brigadier Wheeler proceeded with the artillery to drive the enemy from the village, when they at once took refuge in the fort, pressed by a party of the Guide Corps under Lieutenant W. S. R. Hodson.* Fire was now opened on the fort with shell from two 24-pounder and one 12-pounder howitzers, with an occasional shot from a battery of 9-pounders. The occupation of the village enabled the attacking force to line the wall and two high houses with Lieutenant Hodson's Rifles, and a company of the 3rd Native Infantry, whose fire kept down that of the garrison. At 10 o'clock in the morning Brigadier Wheeler drew off, leaving two companies of the 3rd Native Infantry in the village, aided by a party of the Corps of Guides. Finding that the western gate of the town commanded the gate of the fort, the Brigadier had two embrasures made through the wall, and at 4 P.M. opened a destructive fire on the gate and its defences. At sunset the force was withdrawn, two companies, 61st Foot and one of the 3rd Native Infantry being left in the village. A little after midnight the fort was evacuated and taken possession of by a party of the Guides. In this action Lieutenant Hodson by his daring boldness and that of his men gained the admiration of all. One sowar of the 2nd Irregular Cavalry was killed by a round shot from a British 9-pounder which passed clear over the place; four men were wounded.

Capture of Morari and Kalalwala.

On 25th October Brigadier-General Wheeler was in camp near Morari, six miles north of Dinanagar, and five south of the Ravi; the fort of Morari had been evacuated by insurgents during the night.

On 23rd November he reduced the strong fort of Kalalwala, killing some 300 of the enemy, and losing only one killed and five wounded.

On the 30th November the Resident wrote to him that it was desirable that he should move across the Ravi, or detach a party

* Hodson of Hodson's Horse, killed in 1857. He had invested the fort before the arrival of General Wheeler's force.

with Lieutenant Hodson towards Dinanagar, the insurgents being "for the most part a mere rabble, requiring for their coercion but a small body of regular troops."

On that day he reached Kelaspur after a long march, and found that the enemy had retired to Nerot, nine miles farther north. They then left their camp, with the alleged object of attacking the column, whereupon Brigadier-General Wheeler moved out with his force. The enemy turned, but were pursued by a party of the 2nd Irregular Cavalry under Captain Jackson; a division of the regiment commanded by Naib Risaldar Mirza Hyder Beg came up with them, and killed eight, routing a body of four times his strength with a loss to his own party of only four wounded. He himself lopped off the head of a Sikh horseman with one sweep of his sword.

Rout of the Raja of Amb.

On 2nd December Major Simpson, commanding a detachment in the Jaswan Valley, routed the mob of the Raja of Amb, which had assembled on the heights above Ambota. The heights were stormed by five companies, 29th Native Infantry, and the enemy, consisting of 400 men armed with *jezails* and matchlocks, were driven off with loss, Lieutenant Faddy and 9 men being wounded. Thirty-eight prisoners were taken. Other desultory operations took place from time to time under the direction of Mr. J. Lawrence, in the British trans-Sutlej territories, where all disturbances were suppressed.

Action of Dalla Mountain.

On the 8th January Brigadier-General Wheeler marched from Pathankote against a body of insurgents under Ram Singh, who had taken up a position on the Dalla Mountain north of Shahpur. He sent the 4th Native Infantry and a *risala* of Irregular Cavalry under command of Lieutenant-Colonel D. Downing, up the bed of the Chaki river, to take post at the opposite end of the mountain where the ascent was easier than on the Shahpur side. At Shahpur he found that a range of hills had to be crossed to reach the Dalla Mountain. He had hoped to avoid this range by marching up the bed of the river Ravi, but it was found that the fords were too deep and the stream too rapid, so a road was made across a gorge which crossed the intervening hills, the work occupying three days. At the foot of the Dalla Mountain three days were employed in reconnoitring, and on the 15th and 16th January three columns marched to different points, from which a simultaneous attack was made on the latter date. The enemy were driven from their stronghold with considerable loss, 35 bodies being counted. On the British side Cornet Christie, 7th Light Cavalry, and Jemadar Ram Kishen Singh, 1st Sikh Local Infantry, were killed, and Lieutenant Peel, 2nd-in-command of the latter corps, was wounded.

CHAPTER XIII.

GUJERAT.—THE END OF THE WAR.

After the battle of Chilianwala the Sikhs withdrew to Tupai on the Jhelum and to Rasul. On the night of the battle and on the succeeding three days heavy rain prevented a renewal of the engagement, under circumstances that might have offered a chance of decisive success. A few days after the battle the Sikhs were reinforced and a royal salute in the enemy's camp announced the arrival of Chattar Singh with his army and Afghan levies, released by the fall of Attock. The Commander-in-Chief accordingly entrenched himself at Chilianwala, resolving to await reinforcements which would march to join him after the surrender of Multan, an event daily expected, but which did not take place until the 22nd January 1849.

Position after Chilianwala.

In the meantime, some reconnoitring and skirmishing took place, the British patrolling parties occasionally encountering those of their opponents. On the 30th January, Lieutenant Chamberlain* with a party of the 9th Irregular Cavalry intercepted a body of the enemy's horse, killing sixteen, and being himself wounded in the combat. On the 5th February it was found that the Sikhs had abandoned a portion of their position at Rasul. According to an officer who was present, the earthworks were admirably constructed. "The embrasures were strengthened by forked trunks of trees, like the letter Y, beneath which the ground was excavated for the reception of ammunition, and for protection. Beyond this, the ground was deeply rent in every direction, forming precipitous ravines; while on an isolated little plateau stood the mud village of Rasul, connected with the adjacent parts by an extremely narrow neck of land, slightly protected with wood; on the opposite side a deep escarpment was presented to the Jhelum."

While the Commander-in-Chief deemed it advisable to await the arrival of reinforcements from Multan before attacking the Sikhs, this delay gave the enemy fresh confidence and enabled them to receive a considerable accession of strength. Nor was this the only danger of delay. Dost Muhammad had advanced

*Afterwards Field Marshal Sir Neville Chamberlain.

to the Indus, and was raising fresh levies in rear, and although only some 1,500 horse under his brother Akram Khan had joined the Sikh Army, the Afghan danger was a very real one.

The Sikhs retire to Gujerat.

On the 11th February and subsequent days the enemy abandoned their position, and withdrew towards Gujerat, where they threatened the British communications with Lahore.

On the 11th Sher Singh made a demonstration of attack on the British left, probably with a view to covering the retirement at night; this was met by a few squadrons of the British cavalry.

On the 13th Brigadier Cheape† arrived in camp from Multan with some squadrons of irregular cavalry; and on the 14th intelligence was received that the Sikh Army had taken up their position at Gujerat.

British march on Gujerat.

On the 15th February the Commander-in-Chief broke up his camp between Chilianwala and Mujianwala, and marched to Lasuria, moving next day to Pakka Masjid and on the 17th to Kunjah, from whence the enemy could be seen in the direction of Gujerat. On the 18th the army moved to Trakhur, in rear of the position occupied by the Sikhs in the action of Sadulapur. On the 20th the army marched to Shadiwala, where the piquets were in touch with those of the enemy, and by this date the whole of the troops from Multan joined the camp, Brigadier-General Dundas having arrived on the 19th, and Brigadier Markham on the following day.

Colonel Byrne.
53rd Foot.
13th Native Infantry.
12th and 13th Irregular Cavalry.
4 Guns.

While at Ramnagar, Major-General Whish had wisely detached the force detailed in the margin to Wazirabad, where 6,000 Sikhs made a demonstration of crossing the Sudra ford, but withdrew to Gujerat when the British troops drew up to dispute the passage.

Disposition of the Sikh army.

The Sikhs, who by their march to Gujerat had threatened the safety of the British communications, were drawn up in battle array on the 21st February, in the form of a crescent facing south, and a mile to the south of Gujerat. Their regular troops were in the centre behind the fortified villages of Kalra and Chota Kalra in an open space between the town and the deep and winding bed of the Dwara river, which was now dry and sandy, and which covered their right. Their left rested on the Katela stream, while on either flank, beyond

† Chief Engineer.

these water-courses, which were some three miles apart, was disposed their cavalry, the Afghan Horse on their right. They were estimated at 60,000 strong and had 59 guns disposed between the intervals of their bodies of infantry.

To oppose them Lord Gough was able to put about 20,000 men into the field, and 96 guns, being thus for the first time superior to the Sikhs in artillery.

Position of the British.

The British force ‡ which had undergone some changes in organisation, was drawn up at 7 A.M., a fine and bright morning, on both sides of the Dwara *nala*, which thus divided their centre. The right was protected by a troop of horse artillery and two brigades of cavalry under Colonels Lockwood and J. B. Hearsey. On the right was Whish's Division. In the centre Gilbert's Division, the brigades of Penny on the right, and Mountain on the left, being divided by the Dwara *nala*; next came the eighteen heavy guns; then Campbell's Division, and on the left the Bombay Brigade. The left flank was protected by White's Brigade of Cavalry. The ground between the watercourses was open, and a dead level, broken only by the villages which stood on rising ground in the Sikh position.

British plan of action.

The Commander-in-Chief's plan of action was to penetrate the centre of the enemy's line so as to turn the position of their force in rear of the Dwara *nala*, and thus enable his left wing to cross it with little loss, and in co-operation with the right to double up on the centre the wing of the enemy's force opposed to them. At 7-30 the army advanced in the order above described, with the precision of a parade movement.

Battle of Gujerat.

The enemy opened fire at a long distance and thus unmasked both the position and range of their guns. The infantry was thereupon halted just out of fire, while the whole of the artillery advanced, covered by skirmishers.

‡ *Cavalry.*

Lieutenant-General Sir J. Thackwell, K.C.B.
1st Brigade—
Colonel Lockwood.
14th Light Dragoons.
1st Light Cavalry.
2 Risalas, 11th Irregular Cavalry.
2 Risalas, 14th Irregular Cavalry.
2nd Brigade—
Colonel J. B. Hearsey, C.B.,
3rd and 9th Irregular Cavalry.
3rd Brigade—
Brigadier White.
3rd and 9th Light Dragoons.
8th Light Cavalry.
Sindh Horse.
2 troops, Horse Artillery.

1st Infantry Division.

Major-General Whish.
Brigadier Hervey.
10th Foot.
8th and 52nd Native Infantry.
1 Troop, horse artillery.
1 company, Pioneers.
Brigadier Markham.
32nd Foot.
51st and 72nd Native Infantry.
2 troops, horse artillery.
Dawes Light field battery.
2 troops, horse artillery in reserve.

Reserve.—5th and 6th Light Cavalry, 45th and 69th Native Infantry, one Bombay light field battery.

2nd Infantry Division.

Major-General W. R. Gilbert.
Brigadier Penny.
2nd Europeans.
31st and 70th Native Infantry.
Brigadier Mountain.
29th Foot.
30th and 56th Native Infantry.

3rd Infantry Division.

Brigadier-General C. Campbell.
Brigadier Carnegy.
24th Foot.
25th Native Infantry.
Brigadier McLeod.
61st Foot.
36th and 46th Native Infantry.
2 light field batteries.
Bombay Brigade.
Brigadier Dundas.
60th Rifles.
1st Bombay Europeans.
3rd and 19th Bombay Native Infantry.
1 Bombay light field battery.

A great and terrible cannonade was now opened on the Sikhs, who served their guns with their accustomed rapidity, and well and resolutely maintained their position, but after an obstinate resistance the overwhelming fire of the British artillery obliged them to fall back.

Advance of the infantry.

This cannonade lasted between two and three hours, when the infantry was deployed, and a general advance ordered, the movement being covered by the artillery. The village of Bara Kalra, the key of the position, in which the enemy had concealed a large body of infantry, and which was flanked by two batteries, lay immediately in the line of Major-General Sir Walter Gilbert's advance. That General ordered Brigadier Penny to attack the village, whereupon the Brigadier led the 2nd Europeans, supported by the 31st and 70th Native Infantry, to storm the place, which was carried after an obstinate resistance. The Sikhs on the other side of the village covered with their fire the retreat of their comrades; many shut themselves up in the small mud houses, but the doors were burst open, and fire poured in until the defenders perished, fighting bravely to the last.

In the meantime part of Brigadier Hervey's Brigade, led by Colonel Franks, C.B., 10th Foot, with that regiment and the 8th Native Infantry, supported by Fordyce's troop of horse artillery, carried the village of Chota Kalra, under a heavy fire from loopholes, which caused many casualties in the infantry and decimated the horse artillery.

The heavy guns in the centre continued to advance with extraordinary celerity, taking up successive forward positions, driving the enemy from those they had retired to, whilst the rapid advance and excellent practice of the horse artillery and light field batteries under Brigadier Brooke and Lieutenant-Colonel Brind broke the ranks of the enemy at all points. The whole line of infantry now rapidly advanced, and drove the enemy before it, the *nala* was cleared, the guns that were in position carried, the camp captured, and the enemy routed in every direction, the British troops passing in pursuit to the eastward and westward of the town.

Action of the cavalry.

Throughout these operations the cavalry brigades on the flanks were threatened and occasionally attacked by vast masses of the enemy's horse, which were in every instance put to flight, with the aid of the horse artillery. Regarding the action of the cavalry on the British left, where Sir Joseph Thackwell was, that officer wrote in his diary:—

"Large bodies of Sikh cavalry showed themselves in front and on the rising ground on our left flank, and this occasioned the cavalry to form line, as the infantry had already deployed. This induced the enemy to open fire from four guns, which obliged White to retire his left. I, however, soon remedied the mischief by directing Duncan's troop to advance within four or five hundred yards of the enemy's cavalry and he opened a well-directed fire upon them. Huish's troop also advanced and opened fire, and as the enemy's cavalry were advancing to outflank my left, the Lancers, who had thrown back the left, were formed to the front, and I ordered the Sindh Horse and a squadron of Lancers, supported by another squadron in echelon to the right, to charge the enemy's right, which they did in fine style, and drove this Afghan body and *Ghorcharas* opposed to them back with considerable loss. Meanwhile our line and guns were advanced, and cannonaded the enemy with good effect, and the Sikh cavalry were driven with loss beyond the Bara Darri, losing a gun * which had belonged to Captain Huish's troop. The infantry of the left being well up, I continued my movement to the left of the above place, where the tents of Sher Singh and others with their entire camp were left standing, and opened my twelve guns on the retreating enemy, and continued this, inclining well to the left, by which movement an immense body was cut off from the road to Jhelum, and eventually from that to Bhimber. They were several times charged by the 9th Lancers and 8th Light Cavalry, and a good deal cut up by Duncan's, Huish's and latterly Blood's battery, until the horses had no longer a trot in them. A great number of men were killed in the pursuit, which lasted for nearly twelve miles from Bara Darri.''

Flight of the Sikh Army.

The retreat of the Sikh army became a flight when the general advance of the British line took place; they dispersed in every direction, throwing away their arms, and the track of the fugitives was marked by dead, wounded, and articles of equipment. The total British loss in this action amounted to 96 killed and some 700 wounded†. The Sikh loss in men does not appear to have been very heavy, but 53‡ guns and several stand of colours were taken.

The battle of Gujerat was a skilfully planned and decisive engagement. Wisely waiting until he had sufficient reinforcements, particularly in guns, to ensure complete success, the Commander-in-Chief so hemmed in the Sikhs by his movements that they were forced to fight. He was at length superior in artillery, and he used

*Taken by the Sikhsat Chilianwala

†For detail of casualties see Appendix IX.

‡42 were taken on the field of battle. 9 were afterwards taken by the 1st Light Cavalry, accompanied by Captain J. Nicholson as Political Officer, and Campbell's division took two more during the subsequent pursuit.

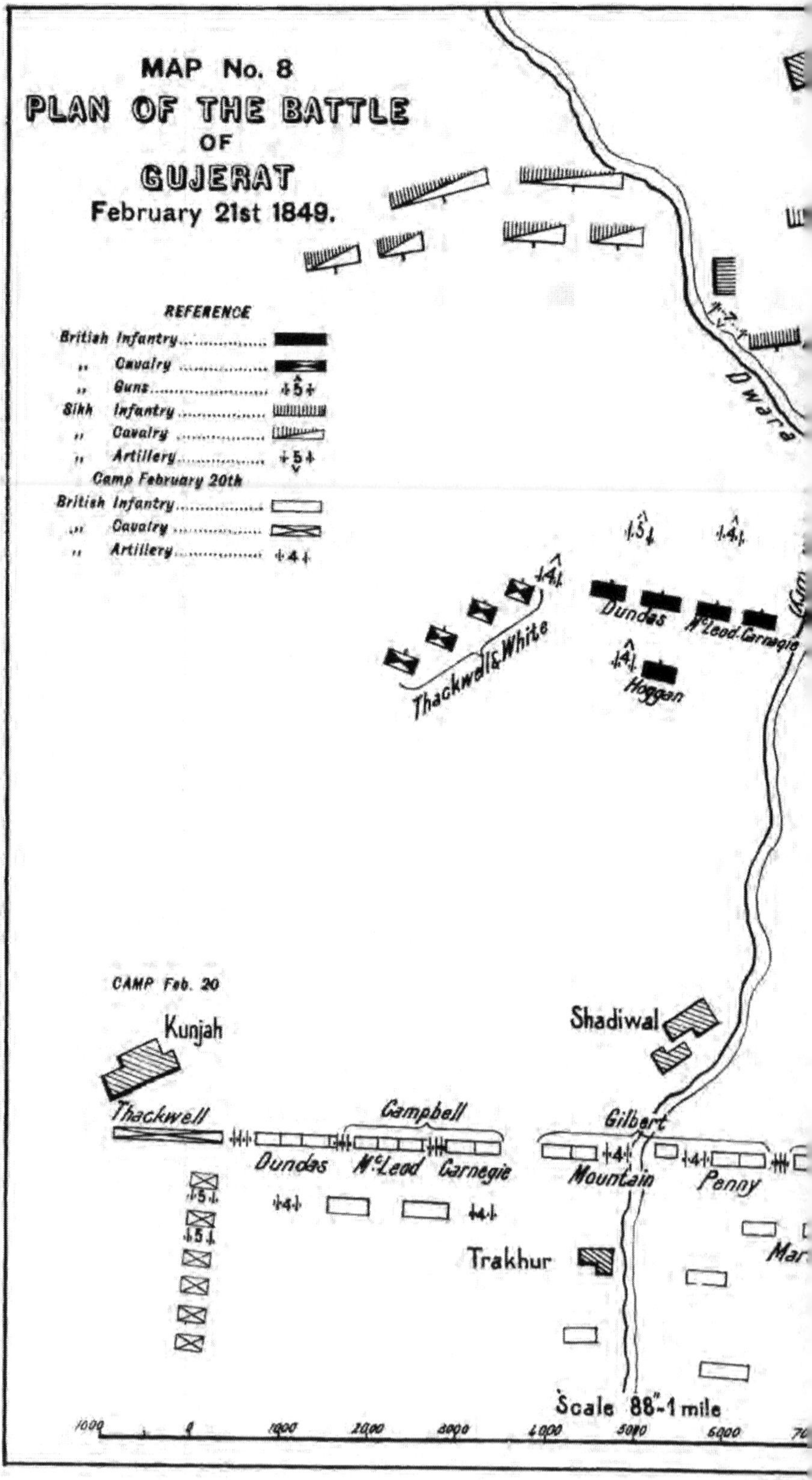
MAP No. 8
PLAN OF THE BATTLE
OF
GUJERAT
February 21st 1849.
REFERENCE
British Infantry
" Cavalry
" Guns
Sikh Infantry
" Cavalry
" Artillery
Camp February 20th
British Infantry
" Cavalry
" Artillery
Dwara
Thackwell & White
Dundas
McLeod
Carnegie
Hoggan
CAMP Feb. 20
Kunjah
Shadiwal
Thackwell
Campbell
Gilbert
Dundas
McLeod
Carnegie
Mountain
Penny
Trakhur
Scale 88"-1 mile
1000
0
1000
2000
3000
4000
5000
6000

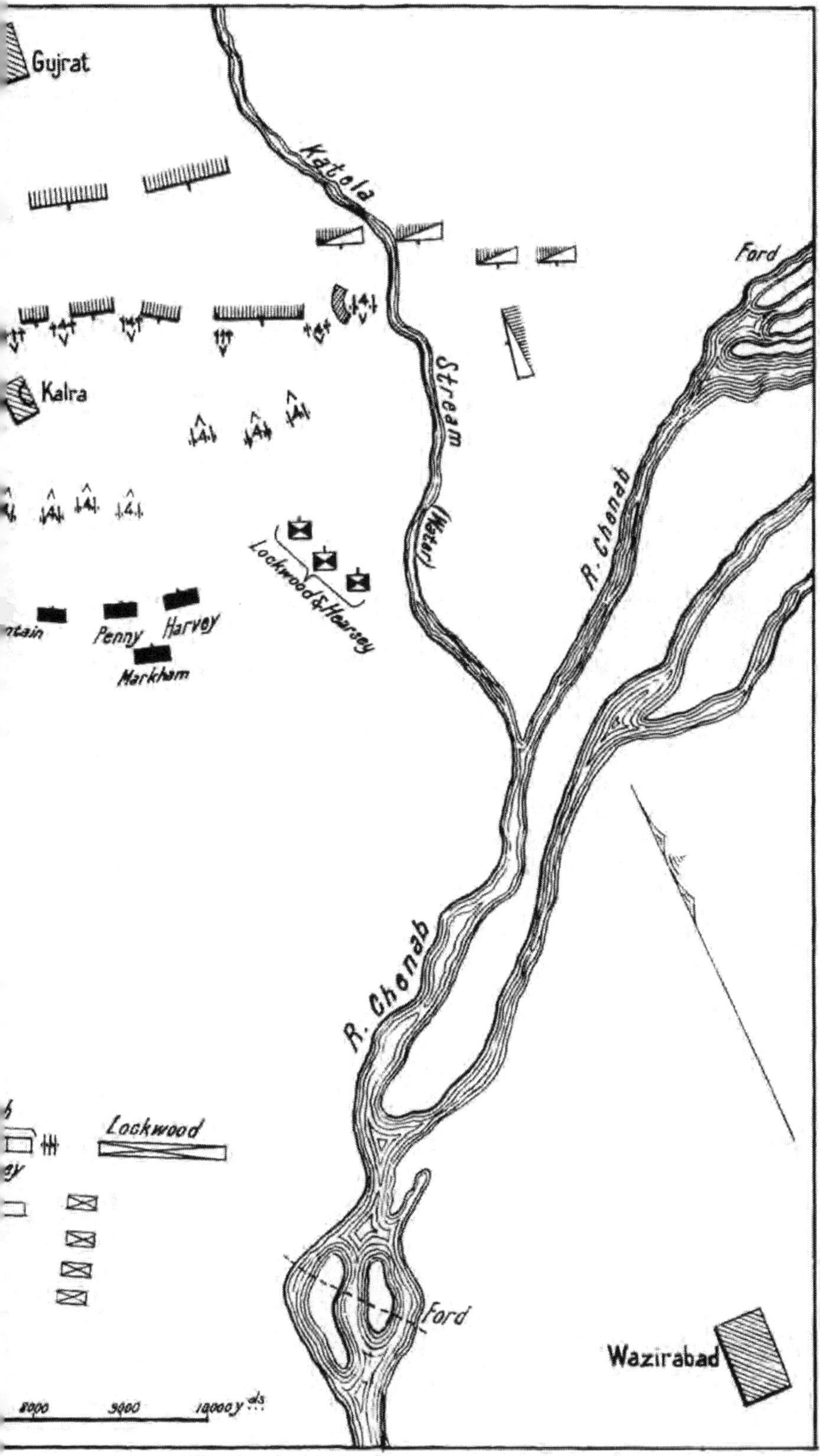

Gujrat
Katola
Ford
Stream
(Water)
R. Chenab
Kalra
Lockwood & Hearsey
Penny
Harvey
Markham
R. Chenab
Lockwood
Ford
Wazirabad
8000
9000
10000 y^ds

his guns to break down the defence before launching his infantry to the attack. The action throughout showed a skilful combination of the three arms, which were all used most effectually.

At daylight on the 22nd, the Commander-in-Chief despatched Major-General Sir W. R. Gilbert, with the force detailed in the margin, to pursue the enemy and effect the passage of the Jhelum.

The pursuit.

Fordyce's Troop, Horse Artillery.
Dawes Light Field Battery.
14th Light Dragoons.
11th Irregular Cavalry.
2nd Infantry Division.

The 3rd Infantry Division under Brigadier-General Campbell was at the same time detached to follow up a portion of the Sikh Army supposed to have fled towards Bhimber, and to drive them from the plains, should they attempt to rally in that direction. The exact quarter to which the enemy had fled was unknown, but they appeared to have dispersed in every direction, while the Afghan Horse crossed the Jhelum on the night of the battle. Campbell returned on the 25th, having found two abandoned guns; he had scoured the country in every direction until he could find no trace of the enemy.

Gilbert's pursuit of the Sikhs.

On the 23rd February, Sir Walter Gilbert arrived at Puran, having marched the first day 17½ miles to Sikri Wala, and 18 miles the second day. On the 24th he marched 14 miles to Naurangabad, and hearing on the way that the enemy were in the act of crossing the Jhelum with their remaining guns, he moved on rapidly with his mounted troops to the ferry, where he found that they had all crossed, taking with them the ferry boats which they were engaged in burning and cutting to pieces. The enemy appeared some 20,000 strong on the opposite bank, all apparently irregulars from Bannu, as there were no red coats among them. At his camp here General Gilbert was joined by Brigadier J. B. Hearsey, with the 3rd and 9th Irregular Cavalry.

Passage of the Jhelum.

On the 27th he marched to Sukhlajpur, leaving the 3rd Cavalry to watch the enemy's movements. He then proceeded to reconnoitre the river Jhelum and its fords, taking 2 guns Horse Artillery, the 9th Irregular Cavalry, and the 31st Native Infantry. He found the river running in three distinct streams, the current being very rapid in all, and especially in the middle one, where the depth was so great as to make the ford almost impracticable for infantry. Having taken possession of the large island between the first and second streams, he returned to camp, leaving his escort which he reinforced with 4 guns Fordyce's troop, Dawes' Field Battery, the left wing of the 2nd Europeans, and the remainder of the 31st to hold the island during the night. At sunset the enemy were seen in large numbers at Pakhawal, just above the ford, but the occupation of the island appeared to have alarmed them, for they abandoned their position during the night. On the 28th, Sir Walter Gilbert crossed the Jhelum to Pakhawal, and the same day the town of Jhelum was taken possession of by a party of the 9th Irregular Cavalry. Continuing the pursuit, Sir Walter Gilbert arrived on the 8th March within 31 miles of Rawal Pindi, where the enemy had halted to the number of 16,000. That day the British prisoners,* captured at Peshawar and elsewhere, came in accompanied by Raja Sher Singh, Lal Singh Moraria, and 450 followers. On the following day Sher Singh returned to Rawal Pindi to arrange with his troops for unconditional capitulation. Sir Walter Gilbert, however, continued his advance, and closed up his rear division for the purpose of moving on the enemy's position. On the 10th he was at Manikyala, where Sirdar Khan Singh Majitiya tendered his submission, with 1,000 armed retainers and some guns. On the 12th at Hurmuk on the left bank of the Sohan river Chattar Singh, Sher Singh, and other Sirdars and officers of the Sikh Army, gave up their swords and 17 guns. On the 14th the General reached Rawal Pindi, and received the surrender of the whole Sikh Army. Forty-one guns were in all given up, and over 20,000 stand of arms were laid down.

Submission of the Sikhs.

But although the Sikh Sirdars and army had surrendered, the war could not yet be regarded as concluded, until Dost Muhammad Khan and the Afghans were driven from the province of Peshawar, or destroyed within it. On the 15th March Sir Walter Gilbert marched 17 miles to Jani-ki-Sang, and on the 16th fourteen miles to Wah. At that place he heard that the bridge over the Indus was still standing, and that Attock was occupied by the Afghan troops. Seeing the importance of securing the bridge-of-boats at Attock, the General resolved to make a forced march of 31 miles. He left Wah on the evening of the 16th, bivouacked a few hours at Burhan, and reached Shamsabad at sunrise. After feeding the horses he pushed on with his cavalry and artillery to Attock, where he arrived with the cavalry at half past eleven, the guns coming up at one o'clock. He found the fort evacuated, and the rear guard of the Afghan army in the act of crossing the bridge-of-boats.

Gilbert's pursuit of the Afghans.

His troops had hardly shown themselves when the bridge was broken up and many of the boats floated down the river. The Afghans were drawn up in force on the right bank, and on the slop-

* Major George Lawrence and his family; Lieutenant Herbert, and others.

ing ground extending from the river to the hills in their rear. On the riverbank they had placed three batteries, two of them of three guns each, the third or right battery consisting of a larger number of guns. Outside the fort of Khairabad to their right they had placed two guns. Each battery was supported by a regiment of regular infantry; and crowds of irregulars, both cavalry and infantry, were formed on the sloping ground in rear of the guns.

But although showing so imposing a front, and having a rapid river to protect them, the Afghans showed no fight, and moved off before the British guns arrived. On the 19th Sir Walter Gilbert crossed the Indus, and on the 21st he entered Peshawar. The Afghan Army under Dost Muhammad had two days before evacuated that place and fled headlong through the Khyber.

Termination of the war.

The last struggle in the British conquest of India thus terminated in the final defeat of the most warlike enemy hitherto opposed to our arms and in the annexation of one of our finest provinces. And it is noteworthy that the noble people who stood so manfully against us on the banks of the Sutlej and the Jhelum have since supplied so many of the best soldiers to the ranks of the Indian Army, and less than nine years later served with valour and fidelity beneath our colours in the great struggle of the sepoy war.

APPENDIX I.

Proclamation by the Governor-General of India.

(*Camp, Laskari-Khan-ki-Serai, dated the 13th December 1845.*)

The British Government has ever been on terms of friendship with that of the Punjab. In the year 1809 a treaty of amity and concord was concluded between the British Government and the late Maharaja Ranjit Singh, the conditions of which have always been faithfully observed by the British Government, and were scrupulously fulfilled by the late Maharaja. The same friendly relations have been maintained with the successors of Maharaja Ranjit Singh by the British Government up to the present time.

Since the death of the late Maharaja Sher Singh, the disorganized state of the Lahore Government has made it incumbent on the Governor-General in Council to adopt precautionary measures for the protection of the British frontier: the nature of these measures and the cause of their adoption were at the time fully explained to the Lahore Durbar.

Notwithstanding the disorganized state of the Lahore Government during the past two years and many most unfriendly proceedings on the part of the Durbar, the Governor-General in Council has continued to evince his d sire to maintain the relation of amity and concord which has so long existed between the two states, for the mutual interests and happiness of both. He has shown on every occasion the utmost forbearance, from consideration to the helpless state of the infant Maharaja Dhalip Singh, whom the British Government had recognized as the successor to the late Maharaja Sher Singh.

The Governor-General in Council sincerely desired to see a strong Sikh Government re-established in the Punjab, able to control its army, and to protect its subjects; he had not up to the present moment abandoned the hope of seeing that important object effected by the patriotic efforts of the Chiefs and people of that country.

The Sikh army recently marched from Lahore towards the British frontier, as it was alleged, by the orders of the Durbar, for the purpose of invading the British territory. The Governor-General's Agent by direction of the Governor-General demanded an explanation of this movement, and no reply being returned within a reasonable time, the demand was repeated. The Governor-General, unwilling to believe in the hostile intentions of the Sikh Government, to which no provocation had been given, refrained from taking any measures which might have a tendency to embarrass the Government of the Maharaja or to induce collision between the two States. When no reply was received to the repeated demand for explanation, while active military preparations were continued at Lahore, the Governor-General considered it necessary to order the advance of troops towards the frontier, to reinforce the frontier posts. The Sikh army has now without a shadow of provocation invaded the British territories.

The Governor-General must therefore take measures for effectually protecting the British provinces, for vindicating the authority of the British Government, and for punishing the violators of treaties and the disturbers of the public peace. The Governor-General hereby declares the possessions of the Maharaja Dhalip Singh on the left or British bank of the Sutlej confiscated and annexed to the British territories. The Governor-General will respect the existing rights of all jagirdars, zemindars, and tenants in the said possessions, who by the course they now pursue evince their fidelity to the British Government.

The Governor-General hereby calls upon all the Chiefs and Sardars in the protected territories to co-operate cordially with the British Government for the punishment of the common enemy, and for the maintenance of order in these States. Those of the Chiefs who show alacrity and fidelity in the discharge of their duty which they owe to the protecting power will find their interests enhanced thereby ; and those who take a contrary course will be treated as enemies to the British Government and will be punished accordingly.

The inhabitants of all the territories on the left bank of the Sutlej are hereby directed to abide peaceably in their respective villages, where they will receive efficient protection by the British Government. All parties of men found in armed bands who can give no satisfactory account of their proceedings will be treated as disturbers of the public peace. All subjects of the British Government and those who possess estates on both sides of the river Sutlej, who, by their faithful adherence to the British Government, may be liable to sustain loss, shall be indemnified and secured in all their just rights and privileges.

On the other hand all subjects of the British Government who shall continue in the service of the Lahore State, and who disobey the proclamation by not immediately returning to their allegiance, will be liable to have their property on this side of the Sutlej confiscated, and themselves declared to be aliens and enemies of the British Government.

APPENDIX II.

The Army of the Sutlej—1845-46.

ARTILLERY.

Brigadier G. Brooke—7 troops horse and 7 companies foot artillery.

ENGINEERS.

The Corps of Sappers and Miners.

CAVALRY.

Brigadier D. Harriott.

1st Brigade; 3rd Light Dragoons, 8th Light Cavalry, 9th Irregular Cavalry.

2nd Brigade; Body Guard, 5th Light Cavalry, 8th Irregular Cavalry.

3rd Brigade; 4th Light Cavalry, 2nd and 3rd Irregular Cavalry.

INFANTRY.

1st Division.

Major-General Sir H. Smith, K.C.B.

1st Brigade; 31st Foot, 24th and 47th Native Infantry.

2nd Brigade; 50th Foot, 42nd and 48th Native Infantry.

2nd Division.

Major-General W. R. Gilbert

3rd Brigade; 29th Foot, 41st and 45th Native Infantry.

4th Brigade; 1st European Light Infantry, 2nd and 16th Native Infantry.

3rd Division.

Major-General Sir J. M'Caskill, K.C.B.

5th Brigade; 9th Foot, 26th and 73rd Native Infantry.

6th Brigade; 80th Foot, 11th, 27th and 63rd Native Infantry.

4th Division.

Major-General Sir J. Littler, K.C.B.

7th Brigade; 62nd Foot, 12th and 14th Native Infantry.

8th Brigade; 33rd, 44th and 54th Native Infantry.

Reorganised on 1st January 1846.

ARTILLERY.

Brigadier G. E. Gowan, C. B., 11 troops horse, 8 companies foot, Artillery 4 Light Field batteries and an elephant battery.

Engineers.

Lieutenant-Colonel E. J. Smith, C.B., The Corps of Sappers and Miners.

Cavalry.

Major-General Sir J. Thackwell, K.C.B.

1st Brigade; 3rd Light Dragoons, 4th and 5th Light Cavalry, 9th Irregular Cavalry.

2nd Brigade; 9th Light Dragoons, 11th Light Cavalry, 2nd and 8th Irregular Cavalry.

3rd Brigade; 16th Light Dragoons, Body Guard, 3rd Light Cavalry. 4th Irregular Cavalry.

4th Brigade; 1st and 8th Light Cavalry, 3rd Irregular Cavalry.

Infantry.

1st Division.

Major-General Sir H. Smith, K.C.B.

1st Brigade; 31st Foot, 24th and 47th Native Infantry.

2nd Brigade; 50th Foot, 42nd and 48th Native Infantry.

2nd Division.

Major-General W. R. Gilbert.

3rd Brigade; 29th Foot, 41st and 45th Native Infantry.

4th Brigade; 1st European Light Infantry, 2nd and 16th Native Infantry.

3rd Division.

Major-General Sir R. H. Dick, K.C.B.

5th Brigade; 9th Foot, 26th and 73rd Native Infantry.

6th Brigade; 80th Foot, 11th and 33rd Native Infantry.

7th Brigade; 10th Foot, 43rd and 59th Native Infantry.

4th Division.

Major-General Sir J. H. Littler, K.C.B.

8th Brigade; 62nd Foot, 12th and 14th Native Infantry.

9th Brigade; 27th, 44th and 54th Native Infantry.

5th Division.

Major-General Sir John Grey, K.C.B.

10th Brigade; 53rd Foot, 30th and 68th Native Infantry.

11th Brigade; 6th, 9th, and 38th Native Infantry.

12th Brigade; 55th and 63rd Native Infantry. The Nasseri and Sirmoor Battalions.

APPENDIX III.

Casualties in the First Sikh War.

(At Mudki, the 18th December 1845).

Personal Staff.—2 officers killed; 2 officers wounded; Major Herries, A. D. C., and Captain Munro, killed; Captains Hillier and Edwardes, wounded.

General Staff.—1 officer killed ; 1 officer wounded; Major-General Sir R. Hill-Sale, G.C.B., killed ; Major P. Grant, wounded.

Artillery Division.—2 officers, 4 sergeants, 13 rank and file, 8 followers, 45 horses, killed ; 4 officers, 1 native officer, 2 sergeants, 42 followers, 25 horses, wounded; Captain J. Trower and Lieutenant Pollock, killed ; Captain F. Dashwood (mortally), Lieutenants Cox, Wheelwright, and Bowie, wounded.

Cavalry Division.—3 officers, 6 sergeants or havildars, 1 trumpeter, 71 rank and file, 164 horses, killed ; 9 officers, 1 native officer, 6 sergeants or havildars, 1 trumpeter, 70 rank and file, 63 horses, wounded.

Staff.—Brigadier Mactier, Captain T. L. Harrington, Volunteer A. Alexander, wounded.

3rd Dragoons.—Captain G. Newton, and Cornet E. Worley, killed ; Lieutenants Fisher, Swinton and E. B. Cureton, wounded.

Body guard.—Lieutenant Fisher, killed ; Captain Dawkins and Lieutenant Taylor, wounded.

5th Light Cavalry.—Major Alexander and Lieutenant Christie, wounded.

1st Infantry Division.—4 officers, 1 native officer, 4 sergeants or havildars, 69 rank and file, killed ; 18 officers 2 native officers, 20 sergeants or havildars, 299 rank and file, wounded.

Staff.—Captain Van Homrigh, A.D.C., killed. Brigadier S. Bolton, C.B., Captain E. Lugard, D.A.A.G., Lieutenant E. Nicolls, A.D.C., wounded.

1st Brigade.—31st Foot :—Lieutenant H. W. Hart, killed ; Lieutenant-Colonel Byrne, Captain Willes, Captains Bulkeley, G. D. Young, Lieutenant Pollard, Lieutenant Brenchley (mortally), wounded. Assistant-Surgeon R. B. Gahan, 9th Foot, wounded. Lieutenant J. F. Pogson, 47th Native Infantry, wounded.

2nd Brigade.—50th Foot.—Assistant Surgeon Graydon, killed. Captain Needham, Lieutenants Carter, Bishop, DeMontmorency and Young, wounded,

24nd Native Infantry :—Lieutenant J. Spence, killed ; Ensign Holt, wounded.

2nd Infantry Division.—I native officer, 17 rank and file killed ; 4 officers, 5 native officers, 10 sergeants or havildars, 81 rank and file, wounded ;

Major R. Codrington, A. Q. M. G., Captains Bolton and Gifford, Ensign Warden, wounded.

3rd Infantry Division.—1 officer, 1 sergeant or havildar, 6 rank and file, killed. 1 officer, 4 sergeants or 73 rank and file, 1 lascar, wounded;

Major-General Sir J. M'Caskill, K.C.B., K.H., killed: Ensign Hanham, 9th Foot, Lieutenant-Colonel Bunbury, 80th Foot, wounded.

T TAL—215 killed; 657 wounded.

(*At Ferozeshahr, 21st and 22nd December 1845.*

Staff.—Killed, Captain W. Hore; wounded, Lieutenant-Colonel R. B. Wood, A.D.C., Lieutenant F. P. Haines, A.D.C., Major Fitzroy Somerset, M.S. (mortally).

Artillery Division.—2 officers, 2 native officers, 1 sergeant, 26 rank and file, 10 followers, 118 horses, killed. 4 officers, 2 warrant officers, 10 sergeants, 61 rank and file, 11 followers, 75 horses, wounded.

Captain Todd and Lieutenant Lambert, Horse Artillery, killed; Captains Warner and Mackenzie, Lieutenants Paton and Atlay, wounded.

Cavalry.—3 officers, 2 native officers, 4 havildars, 1 trumpeter, 78 rank and file, 172 horses, killed; 9 officers, 2 native officers, 1 warrant officer, 9 havildars, 133 rank and file, 114 horses, wounded;

Lieutenant-Colonel D. Harriott, Captain C. F. Havelock, 9th Foot, D.A., Q.M.G., Lieutenant-Colonel White, C.B., wounded.

3rd Dragoons.—Captain J. E. Codd and Cornet Ellis, killed; Major Balders, Lieutenants Morgan, Burton, Orme, White, Rathwell, wounded; Cornet G. W. K. Bruce, 16th Lancers, killed.

1st Infantry Division.—4 officers, 6 native officers, 5 sergeants or havildars, 1 drummer, 119 rank and file, killed; 19 officers, 21 sergeants or havildars, 8 drummers, 399 rank and file, wounded.

Staff.—Captain Lugard; Lieutenants Galloway and Holdich, wounded;

31st Foot.—Lieutenants Pollard and Bernard, killed; Major Baldwin, Lieutenants Plaskett and Pilkington, Ensigns Paul and Hutton, wounded.

50th Foot.—Captain Knowles, Lieutenants Mouat, Chambers and Barnes, Ensigns White and Mullen, wounded.

24th Native Infantry.—Major Griffin, killed; Lieutenant Grubb, wounded.

42nd Infantry.—Lieutenant Wollen, killed; Lieutenant Ford and Ensign Wardlaw, wounded.

48th Native Infantry.—Lieutenants Litchford and Taylor, wounded.

2nd Infantry Division.—8 officers, 3 native officers, 6 sergeants or havildars, 150 rank and file, killed; 13 officers, 9 native officers, 26 sergeants or havildars, 8 drummers, 365 rank and file, wounded.

Staff.—Captains Lucas and Burnet, killed; Lieutenant-Colonel Taylor, wounded.

29th Foot.—Captain Molle and Lieutenant Simmons, killed; Major Congreve and Captain Stepney, wounded.

1st Europeans.—Captain T. Box and Ensign Moxon, killed; Captains Clark and Kendall, Lieutenants Beatson (1st Native Infantry, Interpreter) and Fanshawe, Ensigns Salisbury and Wreford, wounded.

2nd Native Infantry.—Ensign Armstrong, killed; Captain Bolton and Ensign W. S. R. Hodson, wounded.

16th Native Infantry.—Major Hull, killed; Ensign O'Bryen, wounded.

45th Native Infantry.—Lieutenant C. V. Hamilton, wounded.

3rd Infantry Division.—11 officers, 1 native officer, 2 sergeants or havildars, 2 drummers, 111 rank and file, killed; 9 officers, 2 native officers, 13 sergeants or havildars, 3 drummers, 215 rank and file, 1 lascar, wounded.

Staff.—Lieutenant-Colonel L. Wallace, killed.

9th Foot.—Lieutenant-Colonel A. B. Taylor, Captains S. Dunne and J. F. Field, killed; Captain A. Borton, Lieutenants Taylor, Vigors, Sievwright, Cassidy, and Ensign Forster, wounded.

80th Foot.—Captains Best and Scheberras, Lieutenants R. G. Warren, G. Bythesea, killed; Major Lockhart, Captain Fraser (mortally), Lieutenant Freeman, wounded.

26th Native Infantry.—Lieutenant G. A. Crowly and A. C. Eatwell, killed.

73rd Native Infantry.—Captain R. M. Hunter, killed.

4th Infantry Division.—8 officers, 3 native officers, 9 sergeants or havildars, 115 rank and file, killed; 21 officers, 5 native officers, 20 sergeants or havildars, 5 drummers, 323 rank and file, wounded.

Staff.—Lieutenant Harvey, killed; Captains Egerton and Burnet, Lieutenant-Colonel Reed, wounded.

62nd Foot.—Captains Clarke and Wells, Lieutenants Scott, M'Nair, Gubbins, Kelly and Sims, killed; Captains Graves, Sibley and Darroch, Lieutenants Gregorson, Ingall and Craig, Ensigns Roberts and Hewett, wounded.

12th Native Infantry.—Lieutenant-Colonel L. Bruce, Captain Holmes, Lieutenant Tulloch and Ensign Ewart, wounded.

14th Native Infantry.—Captains Struthers and Walsh, Lieutenants Wood and Lukin, Ensign Weld, wounded.

Total.—694 killed; 1,721 wounded.

(At Aliwal, 28th January 1846.)

Artillery.—3 men and 30 horses, killed; 15 men and 9 horses, wounded.

Cavalry.—3 officers, 2 native officers, 94 men, 145 horses, killed; 8 officers, 4 native officers, 134 men, 70 horses wounded; 1 man missing.

16th Lancers.—Lieutenant H. Swetenham and Cornet G. B. Williams, killed; Major Smyth, Captains Bere, Fyler, Lieutenants Arme, Patte and Morris, wounded; Lieutenant Smalpage, 4th Irregular cavalry, killed. Cornets Beatson and Farquhar (mortally), 1st Light Cavalry, wounded.

Infantry.—1 officer, 1 native officer, 47 men killed ; 17 officers, 2 native officers, 233 men wounded, 16 men missing. Captain P. O. Hanlon, Brigade-Major, wounded. .

31st Foot.—Lieutenant Atty, wounded.

24th Native Infantry.—Lieutenant Scott, wounded.

50th Foot.—Lieutenant Gremes, killed ; Captains Knowles and Wilton, Lieutenants Frampton, Bellers, Elgee, White, Vernett, Purcell and Ensign Farmer, wounded.

48th Native Infantry.—Captains Troup and Palmer, Lieutenant Wall, and Ensign Marshall, wounded.

36th Native Infantry.—Ensign Bagshaw, wounded.

TOTAL.—151 killed ; 413 wounded ; 25 missing.

(*At Sobraon, 10th February 1846.*)

Staff.—Lieutenant Colonels S. B. Gough, C.B., and M. Barr, wounded.

Artillery.—1 officer, 3 rank and file, 3 drivers, 17 horses, killed ; 1 officer, 1 sergeant, 33 rank and file, 10 followers, 23 horses, wounded. Lieutenant H. S. Y. Faithfull, killed ; Major C. Grant, wounded.

Engineers.—2 rank and file killed ; 3 officers, 1 native officer, 16 rank and file, wounded. Captain Abercrombie, Lieutenants Becher and Herbert, wounded.

Cavalry.—6 rank and file, 13 horses, killed ; 4 officers, 2 trumpeters, 36 rank and file, 53 horses, wounded.

3rd Dragoons.—Lieutenants Hawkes and White, Cornet Kauntze, Quartermaster Crabtree, wounded.

1st Infantry Division.—2 officers, 1 native officer, 97 rank and file, killed ; 28 officers, 13 native officers, 489 rank and file-wounded.

Staff.—Lieutenant-Colonel Penny, Captain Garvook, Lieutenant Holdich, wounded.

31st Foot—Lieutenants Law, Elmslie, Timbrell, Gabbett, Tritton (mortally), Bolton, and Ensign Jones, wounded.

27th Native Infantry.—Lieutenant Renny and James ; Ensigns Walcot and Ogston, wounded.

50th Foot.—Colonels Ryan and Petit, Captains Tew, Bonkam, Needham and Wilton, Lieutenants Hough, Smyth, Mount and Tottenham, Ensign Slessor, wounded

42nd Native Infantry.—Major Polwhele and Lieutenant Macqueen wounded.

Nasiri Battalion.—Captain O'Brien, wounded.

2nd Infantry Division.—5 officers, 1 native officer, 5 sergeants, 109 rank and file, killed ; 38 officers, 12 native officers, 46 sergeants, 2 drummers, 685 rank and file, wounded.

Staff.—Major-General Gilbert, Lieutenant-Colonel Maclaren, C.B., Lieutenants Gilbert and Jones, wounded.

29th Foot.—Captains Stepney, Young and Murchison, Lieutenants Henry, Duncan, Kirby, Macdonnell, Walker, Nugent, Henderson, and Scudamore, Ensign Mitchell, wounded.

41st Native Infantry .—Ensign Scratcherd, killed ; Captains Halford, Cumberlege and Stephen, Lieutenants Onslow and Kemble, Ensigns Aikman and Bennet, wounded.

68th Native Infantry.—Lieutenant Robertson and Ensign Dorin, wounded.

1st Europeans.—Captain Magnay, Lieutenants Patrello, Lambert, Denniss, Hume, Staples, Beatson (14th Native Infantry), Ensigns Palmer, Davidson (mortally), and Innes, wounded.

16th Native Infantry.—Captain Balderston and Ensign W. S. R. Hodson, wounded.

3rd Infantry Division.—5 officers, 1 native officer, 3 sergeants, 1 drummer, 75 rank and file, killed ; 25 officers, 13 native officers, 27 sergeants, 3 drummers, 573 rank and file, wounded.

9th Foot.—Lieutenant Daunt, wounded.

26th Native Infantry.—Lieutenant Mackenzie and Ensign White, wounded.

62nd Foot.—Lieutenant Haviland, wounded.

80th Foot.—Captain Cookson, Lieutenants Crawley, Kingskley and Ensign Wandesforde, wounded.

33rd Native Infantry.—Lieutenant Tullok, wounded.

63rd Native Infantry.—Captain Ormsby, Lieutenant Morrison and Ensign Barber, wounded.

10th Foot.—Lieutenants Evans and Lindham, wounded.

43rd Native Infantry.—Captain Lyell and Ensign Munro, wounded.

59th Native Infantry.—Lieutenant H. B. Lumsden, wounded.

53rd Foot.—Lieutenant-Colonel Gold, Captain Smart, Lieutenants Chester, Stokes, Breton, Clarke, Ensigns Dunning and Lucas, wounded.

APPENDIX IV.

THE MULTAN FIELD FORCE.

Commanding.

Major-General Whish, C.B.

Deputy Quartermaster General—Colonel Drummond, C.B.
Chief Engineer.—Major R. Napier.
Assistant Quartermaster General—Major Becher.
Assistant Adjutant General—Captain Whish.

TROOPS.

Cavalry.

Lieutenant-Colonel H. Salter.

7th Irregular Cavalry.
11th Irregular Cavalry.
11th Light Cavalry.

Artillery.

Major H. Garbett.

Two troops, horse artillery.
Four companies, foot artillery.
One second class siege train.

Engineers.

Three companies, sappers.
Two companies, pioneers.

First Brigade.

Lieutenant-Colonel A. Hervey.

10th Foot.
8th Native Infantry.
52nd Native Infantry.

Second Brigade.

Lieutenant-Colonel F. Markham.

32nd Foot.
49th Native Infantry.
51st Native Infantry.
72nd Native Infantry.

APPENDIX V.

PROCLAMATION.

Lahore, 22nd July 1848.

The crimes and offences of Diwan Mulraj, the former Nazim of Multan, his rebellion against the Government of the Maharaja Dhalip Singh, his treacherous murder of the British officers, and his schemes and plots for the subversion of the Khalsa Government are matters of notoriety.

Diwan Mulraj and his force have been twice beaten in two general actions by the troops of the Maharaja under the command of Lieutenant Edwardes and General Cortlandt and the army of the Nawab of Bahawalpur; and the rebel has betaken himself to the city and fort of Multan.

A large British force of all arms with an efficient siege train is now moving on Multan for the reduction of the fort and city, and the full and complete punishment of the rebel and his associates. This army will not return to its cantonments till these objects are fully accomplished and such condign punishment has been inflicted on the rebels to the Maharaja's Government and the insulters of the British power as will be a warning to all people.

But while the British Government will take ample and awful vengeance on the guilty in this rebellion, it is desirous that the innocent should not be involved in the ruin which awaits the rebel and his followers, and that those who have only joined the rebel standard as mercenaries should have an opportunity of escaping the vengeance which will be visited on all those found in arms, aiding and abetting the rebel when the British force arrives in Multan.

Notice is therefore now given to the people in arms at Multan and the inhabitants of the city. The former are warned to lay down their arms and depart to their homes. Those who are not the actual perpetrators and abettors of the outrage committed on the British officers, or servants and soldiers of the Maharaja who have deserted their colours or His Highness's service, and joined the rebellion against the Khalsa Government will be permitted if they depart at once to go away unmolested.

When the British army arrives before Multan, it will be too late; the hour of grace will have passed away. The inhabitants of the city and those who possess property therein are warned that if, on account of armed opposition, it becomes necessary to take forcible possession of the city by storm, it will be impossible to save their lives, or those of their families, or protect their property. The city will, of necessity, it is to be feared, be involved in bloodshed, plunder, and ruin.

On the arrival of the British army before Multan, if the city has been peaceably surrendered the fort only will be attacked. If the fort be not unconditionally surrendered with those therein to the British power it will be besieged, and on being captured by storm the garrison will be put to the sword.

This proclamation is issued now with a view to save unnecessary bloodshed, and that all concerned may be fully informed of what will assuredly take place and that they may act accordingly.

APPENDIX VI.

Casualties in the operations before Multan, 1848-49.

Corps	Killed. Officers.	Killed. Sergeants and Havildars.	Killed. Rank and file.	Wounded. Officers.	Wounded. Sergeants and Havildars.	Wounded. Rank and file.	Remarks.
Bengal Division.							
Engineer Department ..	..	..	18	8	5	34	Major Napier. Lieutenants Lake, Garforth, Taylor, Gulliver, Pollard, Garnett.
Artillery	1	2	10	4	3	62	*Killed.*—Lieutenant J. Thompson, *wounded* Lieutenants Bunny, Hunter. Sankey, Graham.
11th Light Cavalry ..	..	..	..	..	..	6	
7th Irregular Cavalry ..	..	..	2	2	..	4	2 Native Officers wounded.
11th Irregular Cavalry ..	..	..	..	1	1	6	One Native Officer wounded.
H. M.'s 10th Foot	1	..	13	4	5	108	*Killed.*—Major G. S. Montizambert. *wounded.*—Lieut. Hollinsworth (mortally). Capts. Macgreger and Moore. Lieut. Herbert.
H. M's. 22nd Foot ..	2	1	16	11	3	103	*Killed.*—Lieut. Col. Pattoun, Quartermaster Taylor. *wounded.*—Brigadier Markham; Major Case; Capts. Balfour, King (twice), Smyth, Brine. Lieuts. Swinburne, Birtwhistle, Straubenzee, Maunsell.
8th Native Infantry ..	1	..	3	4	2	56	*Killed.*—Lieut. Cubitt; *wounded.*—Lieuts. Richardson and Irwin.
49th Native Infantry ..	1	2	8	2	2	57	*Killed.*—Major Lloyd; *wounded.*—Captain Wroughton; Lieuts. Drew and Turnball, 1 native officer.
51st Native Infantry ..	..	2	7	1	1	21	*Killed.*—Lieut. Cubitt. *wounded.*—Lieut. Richardson and Irwin. Lieut. Tyrwhitt.
52nd Native Infantry ..	1	..	7	1	4	38	*Killed.*—Lieut. Playfair; *wounded.*—1 Native Officer.
72nd Native Infantry ..	1	..	24	7	2	47	*Killed.*—1 native officer, *wounded.*—Lieut.-Col. J. Nash, C.B., Captain Maitland; Lieuts. Gillon (mortally) Ensign MacDougall; 3 native officers.
Bombay Division.							
Staff	..	..	..	1	..	..	Captain Tapp, Deputy Assistant Adjutant General.
Engineer Department ..	..	..	12	3	2	53	Lieuts. J. Hill and Fuller; 1 Native Officer.
Artillery	..	..	9	2	2	25	Captain Bailey (mortally); 2nd Lieut. Henderson.
H. M's. 60th Rifles ..	1	1	9	2	..	28	*Killed.*—Major Gordon. *wounded.*—Major Dennis, 2nd Lieut. R. W. Brooke.
1st Bombay Fusiliers ..	..	..	16	6	6	80	Capt. Leith; Lieuts [illegible], Gray, Dansey, Herne, Law.
3rd Native Infantry ..	..	..	1	2	2	18	Lieut. [illegible]; 1 Native Officer.
4th Native Infantry ..	..	1	28	2	2	70	Lieut. Warden; 1 native officer.
9th Native Infantry ..	1	..	1	2	2	8	*Killed.*—Lieut. Younghusband; *wounded.*—Lieuts. Baugh and Fanning.
19th Native Infantry ..	..	..	6	2	4	37	Ensign Gordon; 1 native officer.
Indian Navy	..	1	..	1	1	3	Acting Master Elder; Quartermaster A. Johnstone, (mortally); H. Sandford; J. Chandler; H. Jones.
TOTAL	10	10	190	68	49	864	

APPENDIX VII.

Staff of the Army of the Punjab, 1848-49.

Lord Gough, Commander-in-Chief.

Lieutenant-Colonel Gough, C.B., Quartermaster General.

Lieutenant-Colonel P. Grant, Adjutant General.

Major Kins, Deputy Adjutant General.

Major Lugard, Acting Adjutant General.

Major Tucker, Assistant Adjutant General.

Captain Otter, Acting Assistant Adjutant General.

Lieutenant-Colonel Garden, C.B., Quartermaster General.

Lieutenant Tytler, Assistant Quartermaster General.

Lieutenant Paton, Deputy Assistant Quartermaster General.

Lieutenant-Colonel Birch, Judge Advocate General.

Captain Ramsay, Deputy Commissary General.

Captain P. Haines, Military Secretary.

Cavalry Division.

Brigadier-General Cureton, C.B.

Captain Pratt, Deputy Assistant Adjutant General.

Lieutenant Tucker, Assistant Quartermaster General.

1st Division.

Major-General Whish.

Captain Whish, Assistant Adjutant General.

Lieutenat-Colonel Becher, Assistant Quartermaster General.

2nd Division.

Major-General Sir W. R. Gilbert, K.C.B.

Major Chester, Assistant Adjutant General.

Lieutenant Galloway, Assistant Quartermaster General.

3rd Division.

Major-General Sir Joseph Thackwell, K.C.B.

Major Ponsonby, Assistant Adjutant General.

Ensign Garden, Assistant Quartermaster General.

APPENDIX VIII.

Proclamation by the Resident at Lahore, dated the 18th November 1848.

To the subjects, servants, and dependents of the Lahore State, and the residents of all classes and castes, whether Sikh, Musalman, or other, within the territories of Maharaja Dhalip Singh, from the Beas to the mountains beyond Peshawar. Whereas certain evil-disposed persons and traitors have excited rebellion and insurrection and have seduced portions of the population of the Punjab from their allegiance, and have raised an armed opposition to the British authority ; and whereas the condign punishment of the insurgents is necessary ; therefore the British Army under the Command of the Right Hon'ble the Commander-in-Chief has entered the Punjab districts. The army will not return to its cantonments until the full punishment of all insurgents has been effected, all armed opposition to constituted authority put down, and obedience and order have been re-established.

And whereas it is not the desire of the British Government that those who are innocent of the above offences, have taken no part, secretly or openly, in the disturbances, and who have remained faithful in obedience to the Government of Maharaja Dhalip Singh, be they Sikh or be they of any other class, should suffer with the guilty ; therefore all persons who are not concerned directly or indirectly in the present disturbances, are assured that they have nothing to fear from the coming of the British Army. Such persons are exhorted to remain without apprehension in their villages and homes, and, as loyal subjects of the Maharaja, to give every aid by providing carriage, supplies and the like, to the army which has entered the Lahore territories, not as an enemy to the constituted government, but to restore order and obedience.

Furthermore all classes of the community, be they Sikh or be they of any other caste or tribe, who merely through ignorance may have been led away by the false statements of the evil-disposed and insurgent Sirdars and others and have left their homes and assembled themselves under the standard of rebellion, are hereby admonished instantly to separate themselves from the insurgents and to return to their villages. If they do so now without hesitation or delay, no injury will happen to them ; if they neglect this warning and advice, certain destruction will come upon them in common with the other insurgents and rebels, and disturbers of the public peace.

APPENDIX IX.

Casualties in the Second Sikh War.

(At Ramnagar, 22nd November 1848.)

Staff.—Ensign G. N. Hardinge, wounded.

Horse Artillery.—2 killed, and 7 wounded.

Cavalry.—Brigadier-General C. R. Cureton, C. B., killed.

3rd Light Dragoons.—1 killed, and 5 wounded; 6 horses killed, 12 wounded.

5th Light Cavalry.—9 men killed. Lieutenant-Colonel W. Alexander, Captains Ryley and Wheatley, 1 native officer, and 12 men, wounded; 18 horses killed, 22 wounded.

8th Light Cavalry—2 killed, 2 wounded, 4 horses killed, 3 wounded.

14th Light Dragoons.—Lieutenant-Colonel Havelock, Captain Fitzgerald and 12 men killed; Captains R. H. Gall and Scudamore, Lieutenant McMahon, Cornet Chetwynd, and 31 men wounded.

12th Irregular Cavalry.—Lieutenant J. G. Holmes, wounded.

(At Sudulapore, 3rd December 1848.)

Artillery.—6 killed; Captain E. G. Austin, Lieutenant E. J. Watson and 14, wounded.

CAVALRY.

3rd Light Dragoons.—1 wounded.

5th Light Cavalry.—1 wounded.

8th Light Cavalry.—1 killed.

3rd Irregular Cavalry.—3 killed; Lieutenant Gibbings and 3 wounded.

12th Irregular Cavalry.—1 killed.

INFANTRY.

31st Native Infantry.—1 havildar, 6 men wounded.

24th Foot.—2 killed, 4 wounded.

22nd Native Infantry.—1 killed; Jemadar Sudar Khan and 2 wounded.

25th Native Infantry.—Jemadar Thannu Ram and 4 killed; 8 wounded.

61st Foot.—2 killed; 9 wounded.

36th Native Infantry.—2 killed; Lieutenant Garstin and 2 wounded.

46th Native Infantry.—1 wounded.

(*At Chilianwala, the 13th January 1849.*)

Staff.—Major Ekins, D.A.G., killed ; Major Tucker, A.A.G., and Lieutenant Paton, D. A., Q.M.G., wounded.

Horse Artillery.—Major Christie, Lieutenant Manson, and 22 killed ; 20 wounded.

Foot Artillery.—3 killed ; Captain Dawes, Lieutenant Dundas, and 19 wounded.

Engineers.—3 wounded.

CAVALRY.

3rd Light Dragoons.—24 killed ; Captain Unett, Lieutenant Stisted and 14 wounded.

14th Light Dragoons.—Lieutenant A. J. Cureton* and 1 killed ; Major C. Stewart, and 14 wounded ; 2 nursing.

5th Light Cavalry.—6 killed ; Lieutenant Christie, Elliot and 14 wounded.

8th Light Cavalry.—8 killed ; 2 wounded.

2nd Brigade.—Brigadier Pope, C.B., wounded.

9th Lancers.—4 killed ; 8 wounded.

1st Light Cavalry.—4 killed ; 5 wounded.

6th Light Cavalry.—Lieutenant Shepherd and 6 killed ; Lieutenants Boys, Grindlay and 7 wounded.

INFANTRY.

2nd European Regiment.—6 killed ; Lieutenants Nightingale, Bleaymire and 59 wounded.

31st Native Infantry.—3 killed ; Captain Dunmore and 14 wounded.

45th Native Infantry—17 killed ; Captain R. Haldane, Lieutenant Palmer Ensigns Combe and Trotter, and 55 wounded ; 3 missing.

70th Native Infantry.—5 killed ; 20 wounded.

29th Foot.—31 killed ; Major Smith, Lieutenants Monoton and Metge, Ensign Nevill, and 203 wounded ; 3 missing.

30th Native Infantry.—Captain Ross, Lieutenant de Morel, and 65 killed ; Major Loftie, Captains Campbell, Ewart, Fenwick and Morrison, Lieutenant Swinhoe, Ensigns Pierce, Wood, Leicester, and 209 wounded.

56th Native Infantry.—Lieutenant Warde, Ensign Robinson and 43 killed ; Major Bamfield (mortally), Lieutenants Gott, Jones, Jervis, Bacon, Delamain and 227 wounded ; 38 missing.

Staff.—Brigadier Pennycuick, C.B. and Captain Harris, killed ; Br. Campbell, C.B., and Captain Morris, wounded.

24th Foot.—Lieutenant-Colonel R. Brooks, Major Harris, Captains Lee, Shore, Travers, Lieutenants Phillips, Payne, Woodgate, Phillips, Collis and

* Son of Brigadier Cureton, who was killed at Ramnagar.

Ensign Pennycuick and 193 killed ; Major Paynter, Captains Brown, Bazalgette, Lieutenants Williams, Croker, Berry, Thelwall, Hartshorn, Macpherson, Archer (96th Foot) and 266 wounded ; 38 missing.

25th Native Infantry.—Lieutenant Money, and 98 killed ; Lieutenants Sutherland, Jeune and 90 wounded ; 12 missing.

15th Native Infantry.—8 killed; Lieutenants Anderson, Shaw, Ellice and 45 wounded.

69th Native Infantry.—4 killed ; Captain James, Lieutenant Nisbett, and 61 wounded.

61st Foot.—11 killed ; Captain Massey, Ensigns Nagle, Parks, and 100 wounded.

36th Native Infantry.—28 killed ; Captain Carleton, Lieutenants Thompson (mortally), Weston, Magnay, Ensigns Bagshaw, Godley and 71 wounded.

46th Native Infantry 3 killed ; 51 wounded.

Total 602 killed ; 1,651 wounded ; 104 missing.

(At Gujerat, 21st February, 1849.)

Staff.—Provost-Marshal Budd, wounded.

Horse Artillery.—Captain J. Anderson and 22 killed ; 58 wounded ; 1 missing.

Foot Artillery.—Lieutenant Day and 5 killed ; Major Sir R. Shakespear and 25 wounded.

Engineers.—Lieutenant Hutchinson and 8 wounded.

CAVALRY.

Lieutenant Lloyd, 14th Light Dragoons and 2 killed ; Captains Goddard and Scudamore, 14th Light Dragoons, Lieutenant Stannus, 5th Light Cavalry and 37 wounded ; 1 missing.

INFANTRY.

10th Foot.—7 killed ; Captain Best and 53 wounded.

8th Native Infantry.—Ensign Cox and 4 killed ; Major Farquharson, Ensign Griffiths, and 63 wounded.

52nd Native Infantry.—5 killed ; Captain Jamieson, Lieutenants Lowther, Smith and 31 wounded.

32nd Foot.—1 killed ; Lieutenant Jeffrey and 4 wounded.

51st Native Infantry.—5 killed ; Lieutenant Darnell and 48 wounded.

72nd Native Infantry.—1 killed ; 8 wounded.

2nd Europeans.—Lieutenant Sprot and 8 killed ; Captain Boyd, Lieutenant Elderton, Ensigns Toogood, Sandford, Matheson and 135 wounded ; 3 missing.

31st Native Infantry.—11 killed ; Ensign Gully and 131 wounded.

70th Native Infantry.—10 killed ; Major McCausland, Captain Edwards, Lieutenant Fytch, Ensigns Whiting, Murray, and 39 wounded.

29th Foot.—2 killed ; 6 wounded.

30th Native Infantry.—3 wounded. *56th Native Infantry.*—1 wounded. *25th Native Infantry.*—1 killed ; 2 wounded.

61st Foot.—9 wounded. *36th Native Infantry.*—4 killed ; 9 wounded.

Sindh Horse.—2 killed ; 12 wounded.

Total 96 killed ; 706 wounded ; 5 missing.

INDEX